Interpreting
American Democracy
in France

ÉD. LABOULAYE.

Édouard Laboulaye, ca. 1860. Courtesy of François de Laboulaye.

Interpreting American Democracy in France

The Career of Édouard Laboulaye, 1811–1883

Walter D. Gray

DELAWARE

Newark: University of Delaware Press
London and Toronto: Associated University Presses

Associated University Presses
440 Forsgate Drive
Cranbury, NJ 08512

Associated University Presses
25 Sicilian Avenue
London WC1A 2QH, England

Associated University Presses
P.O. Box 338, Port Credit
Mississauga, Ontario
Canada L5G 4L8

The paper used in this publication meets the requirements of the American National Standard for Permanence of Paper for Printed Library Materials Z39.48-1984.

Library of Congress Cataloging-in-Publication Data

Gray, Walter D. (Walter Dennis)
    Interpreting American democracy in France : the career of Edouard Laboulaye, 1811–1883 / Walter D. Gray.
      p. cm.
    Includes bibliographical references (p.) and index.
    ISBN 0-87413-461-7 (alk. paper)
    1. Laboulaye, Edouard, 1811–1883. 2. Laboulaye, Edouard, 1811–1883—Contributions in American history. 3. Historians—France—Biography. 4. Legislators—France—Biography.
5. Americanists—France—Biography. 6. France—Politics and government—19th century. 7. United States—Foreign relations—France. 8. France—Foreign relations—United States. 9. Statue of Liberty (New York, N.Y.) I. Title.
DC342.8.L13G73   1994
973'.07202—dc20
[B]
                                       92-59957
                                          CIP

Contents

Foreword

FRANÇOIS DE LABOULAYE

The first biography of Laboulaye is published by an American scholar. Why should this be so?

As Professor Walter Dennis Gray of Loyola University of Chicago so ably demonstrates, Laboulaye, a Professor of Comparative Law, had found a model in the American Constitution. He was to refer to it frequently. His open and inquisitive mind had led him to seek, not only in France, but also abroad, the concepts and experiences that would shape and then shore up his convictions.

In Benjamin Constant, in the works of Channing, and then in Tocqueville's report and considerations on his voyage to America, he had found sources for his reflection on the organization of societies. American political mores had particularly struck him. Doubtless no more than Tocqueville, did he imagine that France would copy the American Constitution. He knew to what extent the circumstances were different on either side of the Atlantic. But he had deemed certain clauses in the United States Constitution, such as the bicameral system, to be essential and of a general value.

For him, this was one of the conditions for a harmonious cooperation between the executive and the legislative, whereas a conflict between these two powers might well lead to the return of a despot. Likewise, concerning the balance between the three powers, in the American Constitution, he rediscovered Montesquieu's recommendations translated in concrete and practical terms.

In following Laboulaye's train of thought, it is one of Professor Gray's merits that he has shown to what extent the former gratefully recognized in the American institutions those principles which were his own.

The American scholar recalls that one of Laboulaye's students at the Collège de France, at that time Laboulaye was the administrator of the institution, on seeing him get to his feet to speak, leaned towards the person next to him and whispered in his ear, "Here comes Laboulaye. He's going to tell us about the U.S.A. all the time."

In France, his reputation was that of a great connoisseur and admirer of the United States Constitution and also of the country's
history. Yet, he had never followed Tocqueville's example and crossed
the Atlantic. His health was a serious handicap to him. But his knowledge came from his studies of texts and also the tales and analyses of
travelers whom he trusted. As Walter Gray shows, he was also kept
informed by his various American friends with whom he was constantly in touch. His address was given by mutual friends to many
American intellectuals and politicians who came to France. Even if
they did not have it at the outset, the United States diplomatic representative in France, Mr. James Bigelow, one of his friends, did not
hesitate to provide them with Laboulaye's address.

As Professor Gray detects with great perspicacity, it was the Revolution of 1848 and the coup d'état of 1851 that were the decisive
turning points in the history of liberal thought in France and, especially, in that of Laboulaye. The latter's attachment to freedom and
in particular to individual freedom in all its forms (religious freedom,
freedom of expression) had quite naturally placed him in the opposition during the Second Empire.

There again, the American example nourished this opposition. At
the Collège de France, Laboulaye's lectures on the history of the
United States constituted in fact a series of criticisms of the Napoleonic régime—subtle criticisms, but ones that were understood by a
great number of people, to such a point that the lecture theater in
which he taught filled up and spilled over. As Professor Gray points
out, Laboulaye's success became a manifestation of opposition.

As Professor Gray has seen and so well demonstrated, it was thus
that the example of America inspired Laboulaye, not only in his teaching but also in his public life as a *député,* after the defeat in 1871,
then later as a senator and, finally, as a senator for life.

We know his influence on the laws of 1875 which, without being,
strictly speaking, a constitution, laid the foundations of the Third
Republic. That he was subsequently somewhat disappointed by the
republic he had helped create, perhaps! But he never varied in his
attitude to and opinion of the value of the United States Constitution
and the way the government of the country worked.

It was Laboulaye who paid homage—in truth, who instigated the
act of homage—on the part of France to the United States, through
the gift of the Statue of Liberty. It was in his mind that the idea was
born. It was by virtue of his efforts that the donations were collected
throughout the country.

Professor Gray is not mistaken. He has understood the relationship of reciprocal friendship that sprang up between Laboulaye and the United States and he pays tribute to him on this score.

Without doubt, Laboulaye, the professor and the statesman, faithful to his convictions and his friendships wished to pass these on to his colleagues, his students, and his decendants.

He would have been happy to know that over a hundred years after his death, his message is appreciated on the other side of the Atlantic.

As an American, as an American scholar, it is of a "friend" that Walter Gray has succeeded in speaking.

Acknowledgments

I wish to express my sincerest thanks to Ambassador François de Laboulaye for granting me access to the papers of his great-great-grandfather that are in his possession at Le Quesnay, near Saint-Saens, in Normandy. I also wish to thank the Ambassador and Mme de Laboulaye for their hospitality on numerous occasions at Le Quesnay and in Paris when I was doing research for this book. Both were sources of constant encouragement and Mme de Laboulaye spent many hours assisting me in sorting and arranging the papers so that my research could proceed. M. Stanislaus de Laboulaye, their son, provided useful information on the history of the family as well as continuing the organization of the papers.

I also wish to thank Professor John Lukacs of Chestnut Hill College who many years ago was the first to interest me in Édouard Laboulaye. I owe a special debt of gratitude to the late Professor Jean-Claude Lamberti of the University of Paris-Sorbonne who offered me much encouragement in the early states of my writing as well as much information on nineteenth-century liberalism. M. André Dauteribes of The University of Dijon, France, also furnished me with information on the Laboulaye family.

Loyola University of Chicago awarded me a leave of absence to work on the manuscript as well as a summer grant to finish the project. I am indebted to both the University and its Research Services for these awards. The staffs and the holdings of the Bibliothèque Nationale and the Archives Nationales in Paris, the Bibliothèque Spoelberch de Louvenjoul in Chantilly, the Newberry Library of Chicago, the Cudahy Library of Loyola University of Chicago, the University of Illinois Library at Champaign, the University of Rochester Library, the Houghton Library of Harvard University, the Massachusetts Historical Society in Boston, the Pennsylvania Historical Society in Philadelphia, the New York Historical Society, the New York Public Library, the Wisconsin Historical Society in Madison, and the University of Washington Library were all essential to the completion of this work. Also my colleagues in the Department of History at Loyola, especially, its current chairman, Joseph A. Gagliano, and its former chairman, the late Robert McCluggage, have been a constant source of encouragement.

Finally, my most special gratitude and thanks go to my wife, Anne Callahan, who was a steadfast source of encouragement, praise, criticism, and editorial excellence. I dedicate this book to her.

Interpreting
American Democracy
in France

1

Introduction

Il y a quelque temps, je présidais une réunion, et l'un des auditeurs dit à son voisin, qui me l'a rapporté: voici M. Laboulaye qui se lève, il va nous parler de l'Amérique tout le temps.

[Sometime ago, I chaired a meeting, and a member of the audience said to the person seated next to him who told me: that is M. Laboulaye who is standing up, he will speak to us of nothing but America.]

—Édouard Laboulaye

Édouard Laboulaye, whose life spanned seven decades of the nineteenth century, was a distinguished savant, legal scholar, conferencier, essayist, professor, and politician. The worldview or intellectual commitment that best characterizes him is that of a liberal, however, for the France of the decades of the 1850s and 1860s, and 1870s, he was also the leading interpreter of the United States of America for his fellow Frenchmen. This study of Laboulaye attempts to interpret his public career as a liberal and as an Americanist. First, however, it seeks to clarify the recent interest both in France and America in nineteenth-century liberalism.

Nineteenth-Century French Liberalism before Laboulaye

The decade of the 1970s and 1980s has witnessed a renewed interest in nineteenth-century French liberalism. As Alexandre Delamarre, writing in the *Figaro Magazine,* so aptly remarked, "Il est vrai qu'aujourd'hui on assiste à un renouveau libéral, que le libéralisme, en France, obtient depuis quelques années une influence qu'il n'avait peut-être jamais connu" [It is true that today we are witnessing a liberal renewal, that liberalism, in France, has been gaining over the past several years an influence that it has perhaps never known be-

fore].[1] In France contemporary interest in nineteenth-century liberalism has stemmed, in part, from the political climate of the Fifth
Republic, notably, from those who supported the presidencies of
Georges Pompidou and Valéry Giscard d'Estaing in the 1970s and in
the early 1980s those who opposed the presidency of François Mitter-
and. Both the economic progress and the political stability of France
under Pompidou and Giscard tended to cause political thinkers to
reassess the great tenets of liberalism; another significant development
was the decline of Marxism as a worldview for Frenchmen during
the Fifth Republic, especially, during the years 1975–85.[2] The so-
called "new liberals" coalesced around the government of Jacques
Chirac who bravely attempted to foster a policy of cohabitation with
President Mitterand, a state of affairs that not all Frenchmen were
able to understand. This new interest in liberalism is particularly ap-
parent in the writings of the regular contributors to the influential
quarterly, founded by Raymond Aron, *Commentaire;* in fact many of
these liberal thinkers and academics are also members of the Institut
Raymond Aron, and their activities have produced an impressive number of new books and articles on liberalism. For example, Jean-Claude
Casanova, the editor of *Commentaire* as well as a frequent contributor, is also a regular contributor to the influential weekly *L'Express.*
Casanova discusses the liberal revival and defines contemporary liberalism in terms that explain its current interest in France:

> I take contemporary liberalism to mean a combination of democracy, the
> welfare state, and a market economy with state intervention. This model
> of liberalism derives from the classical mould but differs from it to the
> point of having been characterized under the two-fold influence of democ-
> racy and social welfare ideas, either as a synthesis of liberalism and social-
> ism or as a sort of reformed liberalism.[3]

This renewed interest has also extended to America where there is
also a revival of scholarship.

Two major comprehensive studies of French liberalism in the nineteenth century have been published in recent years by André Jardin
and Louis Girard. Jardin's *Histoire du libéralisme politique*[4] is the most
complete of the two; he begins with the struggle of the eighteenth-
century thinkers against absolutism and continues to the constitutional laws of 1875. He views these as the triumph of liberalism. This
study by Jardin, who is the editor of Alexis de Tocqueville's complete
works as well as his biographer, contains a careful, well-reasoned, and
perceptive analysis of each major liberal thinker from Montesquieu to
Jules Simon and the Duc de Broglie. Jardin's work emphasizes the late

eighteenth century and the early nineteenth century and does not give a great deal of attention to liberals after 1850. The second study by Louis Girard, an emeritus professor at the Sorbonne, represents a summary yet encyclopedic work that begins in 1814 and, like Jardin's, ends in 1875, which, for Girard, is also the triumph of liberalism in nineteenth-century France. Girard's book, *Les Libéraux français*,[5] is more in the nature of *notes de cours* or classroom lecture notes; it contains much factual information that is usually associated with university lectures but does not contain the extended analyses contained in Jardin's work. Both Jardin and Girard discuss and acknowledge, however briefly, Laboulaye's contribution to nineteenth-century liberalism.

Pierre Manent, the young editor-in-chief of *Commentaire* and a *maître de conferences* at the Collège de France, is another contemporary major writer on liberalism whose interest in the subject is not limited to France. Manent has published a *Histoire intellectuelle du libéralisme, dix leçons*[6] and also a two-volume anthology entitled, *Les Libéraux*.[7] The former begins with, what he terms, the theological-political problem in the Middle Ages, proceeds to discuss Machiavelli, Hobbes, and moves on to examine the thought of eighteenth- and nineteenth-century liberals. The tenth and last lesson is an analysis of Tocqueville. The anthology in two volumes unites the basic texts, in his view, of liberalism from Milton to Raymond Aron. Many of the texts he draws from are the writings of economists, a group of liberal writers he omits in the *Histoire intellectuelle*. Manent in his two works does not discuss Laboulaye's thought.

Most publications on French liberalism published in recent years by French and American scholars focus on those liberal thinkers and political leaders who were active prior to the death of Tocqueville in 1859. The first group to draw the attention of contemporary scholars are the Idéologues, those writers during the Directory (1795–99), the Consulate (1799–1804), and the Empire (1804–14) who were disciples of Condillac and who had experienced the French Revolution first-hand. They sought to salvage what they considered admirable or worth preserving from those tempestuous years. Accordingly, they believed in the perfectibility of the human race and held a firm faith in psychology.

Cheryl B. Welch, in her book *Liberty and Utility, The French Ideologues and the Transformation of Liberty* describes the Ideologues as:

First, they moved in a particular social orbit. . . . Second, the Idéologues shared certain political conditions. Though they might disagree on specific policies, they were anti-Jacobin after 1793, but also antiroyalist and anticlerical. Most favored a republic with a considerable role for an educated secular élite. After 1801 they opposed Napoleon, though they made varying degrees of peace with his regime. . . . Finally, and most importantly, the Idéologues continued the eighteenth-century belief in the necessity of a preliminary "science of man" for the reconstruction of society . . . they acknowledged the intellectual leadership of Destutt de Tracy and Pierre Cabanis, although they did not always agree with them.[8]

Although the Idéologues were close to the circle of thinkers that gathered around Mme de Staël and Benjamin Constant, they did differ from them with regard to monarchy and religion. Since the Idéologues were strongly antiroyalist, they "increasingly looked to the United States as a model of successful representative government."[9] They began a current in nineteenth-century French liberalism that looked to the United States for inspiration whereas most French liberals in that century, if they looked abroad, looked toward England. Like the Idéologues, Alexis de Tocqueville and Édouard Laboulaye will be exceptions in seeking inspiration from America and its institutions.

Among recent works published on several Idéologues, Emmet Kennedy's, *A Philosophe in the Age of Revolution: Destutt de Tracy and the Origins of Ideology,* concentrates on possibly the most eminent of them. According to Kennedy, Destutt de Tracy set forth the philosophy of the Idéologues in his *Éléments d'idéologie,* which appeared between 1803–15,[10] and it is to Destutt de Tracy that we owe the term, Idéologue. Interestingly, a small off-shoot of his *Éléments d'idéologie,* a *Commentaire de l'Esprit des lois* of Montesquieu was written in 1806, and although it was impossible to publish it in the France of Napoleon, it was translated into English by Thomas Jefferson and published in Philadelphia in 1811. Martin S. Staum has written a penetrating work on the other major Idéologue, George Cabanis, entitled, *Cabanis: Enlightenment and Medical Philosophy in the French Revolution.*[11] Cabanis is said to have reduced the spiritual side of man to a function of the faculty of his physical needs.

Although contemporaneous with the Idéologues, Mme de Staël and Benjamin Constant are described by Philippe Raynaud as "Les premiers grands théoriciens du libéralisme français sont deux écrivains formés dans l'esprit des Lumières, dont le premier mérite fut de comprendre que l'expérience révolutionnaire appelait une réévaluation critique de l'héritage du xviiie siècle" [The first great theoreticians of French liberalism were two writers formed in the spirit of the Enlightenment, whose major contribution was to understand that the revolutionary experience called for a critical reevaluation of the eighteenth century's legacy].[12] Like the Idéologues, Mme de Staël and

Benjamin Constant lived through the French Revolution and in their writings they tried to reconcile the thought of the eighteenth century with that of the Revolution and to evolve a synthesis.

Germaine de Staël (1766–1817), the daughter of the famous financier and finance minister, Jacques Necker, had experienced the French Revolution. During the Terror she retired to her family estate, Coppet, in Switzerland. During the Consulate and the Empire she became part of the salon opposition to Napoleon and he exiled her from France. She is well known for having traveled extensively in the German States and for her *De L'Allemagne* of 1810, the most important source of information for the French reading public of contemporary German culture, especially, philosophical thought. Her most important political-historical work, which earned her the title of "Mère de la doctrine"[13] of liberalism, was her *Considérations sur les principaux événements de la Révolution Française,* published posthumously in 1818. Mme de Staël's work on the French Revolution has recently been reprinted, and Renee Winegarten has written a brief but useful biography.[14] Mme De Staël wrote in *Delphine,* published in 1802, that the end of the social order was liberty:

La liberté ... est le premier bonheur, la seule gloire de l'order social; l'histoire n'est décorée que par les vertus des peuples libres; les seuls noms qui retentissent de siècle en siècle à toutes les âmes généreuses, ce sont les noms de ceux qui ont aimé la liberté! Nous avons en nous-mêmes une conscience pour la liberté comme pour la morale; aucun homme n'ose avouer qu'il veut la servitude, aucun homme n'en peut être accusé sans rougir; et les coeurs les plus froids, si leur vie n'a point été souillée, tressaillent encore lorsqu'ils voient en Angleterre les touchants exemples du respect des lois pour l'homme, et des hommes pour la loi; lorsqu'ils entendent le noble langage qu'ont prêté Corneille et Voltaire aux ombres sublimes des Romains

[Liberty is the first happiness, the only glory of the social order; history is decorated only by the virtues of free peoples; the only names which resound from century to century in all noble souls are of those who have loved liberty! We have within ourselves a consciousness of liberty, as we have of morality; no man would dare admit that he desires servitude, no man can be accused of it without shame; and even the coldest hearts, if their life has not been sullied, still quiver when they see in England the touching examples of the respect that laws have for man, and that men have for the law; and when they hear the noble language that Corneille and Voltaire attributed to the sublime shades of the Romans].[15]

Jardin remarks that "Il se rattache aux doctrines du xviiie siècle, mais en revalorisant Montesquieu et en rajeunissant l'anglophilie éclipsée par l'admiration pour la jeune Amérique" [Her political system is linked to eighteenth-century doctrines, and it revalorizes Montesquieu and rejuvenates an anglophilia which had been eclipsed by admiration for the young America].[16] Her views on liberalism epitomized the foreign as well as indigenous French influences on early nineteenth-century French liberalism. Mme de Staël's legacy continued after her death in 1817 as her daughter, Albertine de Staël, married Duc Victor de Broglie who was active in liberal politics until his death in 1870. Their son Albert de Broglie took part in the liberal opposition to Napoleon III and served as a premier of France in the 1870s.

Benjamin Constant (1767–1830), friend and admirer of Mme de Staël, wrote many political tracts and pamphlets during his long career, which extended from the French Revolution until his death in 1830. In his excellent study of Constant's political thought and his contributions to the making of modern liberalism, Stephen Holmes shows that from the experience of Napoleon, Constant "turned to the only direction he could; toward the gradual extension of voting rights to more and more citizens."[17] During the Bourbon Restoration, Constant, who served as a deputy for nine of his last eleven years, was politically influential during the Restoration and his liberalism enabled him to present an alternative to the arch-conservatives such as the Ultras or the international conservative politics of Metternich. Since he played a dominant role in Laboulaye's intellectual formation, a discussion of Constant's political thought will be deferred until chapter 2 where his influence on Laboulaye is traced.

Liberalism after Napoleon had, according to Pierre Rosanvallon, a triple task: first, to end the revolution, second, to construct a stabler representative government, and finally, to establish a government guaranteeing liberties founded on reason.[18] This latter task fell to the liberals of the Bourbon Restoration, a group of political thinkers, usually called Doctrinaires, who opposed the extremist political views of the Ultras, those died-in-the-wool supporters of the Comte d'Artois, who wished to turn France back to the days before 1789. The Doctrinaires, on the contrary, desired a government under a constitution that guaranteed individual freedoms, notably, freedom of the press. Their model was the Charter of 1814. In recent years several books have appeared that have increased interest in this group of liberal politicians and scholars, the Doctrinaires. These intellectual descendants of Mme de Staël included parliamentarians active during the Restoration in France (1814–30) such as Pierre-Paul Royer-Collard, Étienne Denis Pasquier, Joseph Fiévée, and Pierre-François de Serre,[19] and teachers at the Sorbonne and the Collège de France such as François Guizot, Victor Cousin, and François Villemain who inspired generations of students with liberal ideas. The lectures of Guizot on the history of civilization from the fall of Rome to the French Revolution were attended by the young Alexis de Tocqueville from 1829 until 1830 along with his friend, Gustave de Beaumont. In these lectures Guizot held that the growth of the Third Estate "was the most active and decisive element in French Civilization."[20] Guizot's lectures also included a lengthy treatment of English history in the seventeenth century, a century that culminated in the Glorious Revolution. Guizot exerted an influence on the young Tocqueville, but it is doubtful if Tocqueville, the aristocrat and soon-to-be student of American democracy, fully accepted Guizot's views.

The critical importance of the period of the Bourbon Restoration to any examination of nineteenth-century liberalism is brought into focus by Alan Spitzer in *The French Generation of 1820*, which deals with the politics, the writings, and the history of the generation dominated by the Doctrinaires. Spitzer's work constitutes a major contribution to the understanding of this period.[21]

The July Monarchy (1830–48) is usually considered as the first truly liberal government in nineteenth-century France. At first, liberals accepted enthusiastically the 1830 revisions of the French constitution, The Charter. They agreed with King Louis-Philippe that the politics of the *juste milieu*, or the middle-of-the-road, best fitted their aims. Adolphe Thiers went so far as to declare that all liberals had "rallied to the government, which itself was the liberal party."[22] During the course of the July Monarchy, however, liberals tended to desire reform and joined the *parti du mouvement*, which gradually drifted into political opposition, especially after 1840. Liberals now entered a new phase as they advocated an extension of the suffrage, a move that would have brought France very close to political democracy. Interest in democracy was stimulated by the publication of Tocqueville's *Democracy in America*, the first half of which appeared in 1835, the second in 1840. The book's publication also stimulated renewed interest in republican government, the United States being an example of a successful one. Republican thought in France had come to signify the First French Republic (1792–95), whose chief memory was the Terror. Now republican thought had an alternative in America, and its greatest exponent after Tocqueville's death would be Édouard Laboulaye.

After 1840, many liberals became political opponents of the July Monarchy, disagreeing with Guizot's policy of immobilism that denied any further political reforms. Guizot, who was the chief force in the government between 1841 and 1848, firmly believed that the 1830 Revolution did for France what the 1688 Glorious Revolution had

done for England. Also he viewed with disdain the various concessions made during the French Revolution by Louis XVI's government,
which led to excesses such as the abolition of the monarchy. And so,
for Guizot, further reforms were unnecessary; hence, his immobilism,
or resistance to any projected reforms. On the other hand, his liberal
opponents, such as Tocqueville and Thiers, advocated an extension of
the suffrage, freedom of the press, and other liberties. Some opposition
groups, notably the republicans, advocated universal manhood suffrage and an end of the monarchy.

   French political life was further complicated during the July Monarchy by the growing impetus of the republicans to establish a republic. The model for most republicans was the First French Republic.
The republicans were predominantly bourgeois and often descendants
of notabilities of the First French Republic or the Empire. Hippolyte
Carnot, for example, a leading republican during the July Monarchy,
was the son of Lazare Carnot, a member of the Committee of Public
Safety. Also many doctors, lawyers, and intellectuals became republicans. In the view of their political opponents the thought of a republic
evoked the Reign of Terror, Robespierre, and the Committee of Public
Safety as well as the instability of a plural executive. For monarchists,
the very idea of the republicans coming to power was anathema; they,
after all, had tried and executed Louis XVI. Laboulaye did not look
favorably on the First French Republic either but he was nevertheless
in favor of a republic, but one fashioned on the American example.

   For the July Monarchy the years 1840–47, were, in David H. Pinkney's words, *"Decisive Years."*[23] According to Pinkney, the French
economy in the 1840s was in the Take-Off phase of industrialization
with the revolution in transportation, the mechanization of industry,
the immense growth of production, and the accumulation of capital.
As wealth and transportation became more rapid there was a vast
change in the way of life of the French.[24] Although these economic
changes began under the July Monarchy, they became most evident
during the Second Empire and account for the tremendous French
prosperity of those years.

   Recent scholarship has focused for the most part on the liberal
writers and statesmen, François Guizot, Adolphe Thiers, Jules Michelet, and the perennial favorite, Alexis de Tocqueville. Pierre Rosanvallon has written a study of Guizot that points out his
contribution to liberal thought and to history as well as his influence
on a generation of young French students during the later years of
the Restoration. J. P. T. Bury and R. R. Tombs coauthored in 1986 a
political biography of Adolphe Thiers, the first such study in fifty
years to appear in English. Also Pierre Guiral has published a major

French biography of Thiers, the first significant one to appear in France in fifty years.[25] The completed works of Jules Michelet are in the course of publication and numerous monographs on his intellectual activities have appeared. In fact, there is almost as much interest today in Michelet as in his contemporary, Tocqueville.[26]

Alexis de Tocqueville has continued to excite the interest of scholars. The gradual publication of his *Oeuvres complètes*, begun over thirty years ago by J. P. Mayer, is currently edited by André Jardin and some twenty-odd volumes have now been published. Recent studies on Tocqueville by the late Jean-Claude Lamberti, James T. Schleifer, Roger Boesche, and Françoise Mélonio evidence the continued interest in Tocqueville. André Jardin has also published an impressive biography of Tocqueville, which at this moment stands as the definitive study of his life and thoughts.[27] Tocqueville clearly belongs to a different group of liberals as he was able to envision a democratic form of government that would include universal suffrage (which in nineteenth century France did not include women). He did not share Guizot's policy of immobilism or resistance to reform, and shortly before the February 1848 revolution, stated publicly that France was sleeping on a volcano.

In recent years publishers have reprinted many of the classic works of early liberalism, works that have been long out of print, such as Mme de Staël's, *Considérations sur la Révolution Française*, Benjamin Constant's, *Cours de politique constitutionnelle, De la force du gouvernement actuel de la France et de la nécessité de s'y rallier*, and *Des réactions politiques des effets de la terreur*,[28] as well as François Guizot's *Histoire de la civilisation en Europe*, Lucien Prévost-Paradol's, *La France nouvelle*, Edgar Quinet's, *La Révolution*, and the numerous reprints of Tocqueville and Michelet, a task that has involved many French publishers and editors. Only Tocqueville has enjoyed extensive reprinting in English, notably, his *Democracy in America*, his *Recollections*, his *Ancient Régime and the French Revolution*, and selected letters.

Most French liberals before 1848 agreed on the following principles: they wanted government to be limited, that there be a written constitution, some form of parliamentary monarchy or conservative republic (although they divided on following the English, the American, or the French political traditions), and a bill of rights guaranteeing basic freedoms of religion, press, association, and individual liberty. Decentralization of government was also a recurring theme for many of these liberal writers. They disagreed on the extent of the suffrage and until 1840 usually wished it to be restricted to the upper strata of the male population, perhaps the upper 10 percent of those male citizens who owned property. Rarely did they advocate women's suffrage. In economic matters, these writers and politicians usually espoused laiss-ez-faire, or as it was termed by them, economic liberty, though many of them had little understanding of economics. Before the Revolution of 1848, practically all liberal thinkers were either monarchists or conservative republicans. As Jean Rivero writes:

> for the liberals, the form of government—monarchy or republic—mattered less than the actual practice. . . . The main thing was that the legislative function and the executive function remain independent, balanced organs, and that the judiciary maintain total autonomy with regard to both these functions.[29]

This view was echoed by George Armstrong Kelly who wrote: "Lib-erals are reluctant to choose between liberal monarchy and conserva-tive republic as long as their conditions for freedom are met." And Kelly quotes approvingly of Benjamin Constant who wrote: "We are no longer in an age when monarchy was declared an unnatural power, nor do I write in a country where one is compelled to state that the republic is an anti-social institution."[30]

One can conclude that writers and publishers on both sides of the Atlantic are currently involved in scholarly activities surrounding what is often referred to as "The Liberal School"; however, their chief interest is mainly limited to the period, 1800 to 1848. Very little has been done on the political writers during the Second Republic and the Second Empire, the generation of the 1850s and 1860s, who formed what is usually called the liberal opposition to Napoleon III. And, although Tocqueville, a leading liberal figure before 1848, lived until 1859, he had virtually abandoned his political writings in order to write his *Ancien Régime et la Révolution Française*. His only politi-cal writings after 1848 were his *Souvenirs*, which recounted the revo-lutionary year of 1848 and his brief tenure as foreign minister. Only three major figures in the liberal opposition during the Second Empire have been the subjects of monographs in the last thirty years: Prévost-Paradol, Émile Ollivier, and Jules Simon. In this regard one can cite Pierre Guiral's masterful and exhaustive study of Prévost-Paradol written over thirty years ago, the biography of Ollivier by Theodore Zeldin written over fifteen years ago, and the study of Jules Simon by Philip A. Bertocci written over a decade ago.[31] Although the political careers of Prévost-Paradol and Ollivier ended in 1870, Jules Simon was active into the Third Republic where he served in several minis-tries. We should also keep in mind that Thiers's lengthy political career began in the July Monarchy, when he served in numerous posts including that of first minister, and ended in the Third Republic, but that during the Second Empire he lived in political retirement until 1863 when he was elected a deputy and he remained a deputy until the Empire fell in 1870; and under the Third Republic he was, from 1870 until 1873, provisional president. Thiers's major political activities then, were not during the Second Empire. Also neglected in recent historical studies are Edgar Quinet and Agénor de Gasparin, both of whom were identified with liberal causes. No doubt the neglect of liberal thought during the Second Empire is due in large part to the prejudice of French scholars against the Second Empire and the early years of the Third Republic.[32] It is the purpose of this study of Édouard Laboulaye to fill this lacuna by treating one of the key liberal writers of the Second Empire and one who also became an intellectual and political leader of the Third Republic.[33]

Laboulaye and his Family

Édouard Laboulaye was born on 18 January 1811 and died on 25 May 1883. His full name was Édouard-René Lefebvre de Laboulaye,[34] and he was descended from Jean-Baptiste René-Lefebvre de La Boulaye, his grandfather, who held the office of Sécretaire du Roi de la Grande Chancellerie de France from 1778 to 1788. It was an office that conferred nobility on the Laboulaye family. Laboulaye's father, Auguste René Lefebvre de Laboulaye, married Aglaé Charlotte Juliette Martinon. His properties were confiscated during the Revolution and he later served as a toll collector and a bureaucrat in the French government. No doubt his experience in the Revolution caused him and his sons to drop the *particule de noblesse* from their name. He had two sons, Édouard and Charles.

Charles, who had served in the army, opened a printing shop with his brother, and the two of them operated it together for a time. Édouard frequently and proudly referred to his early career as a typesetter when in later life he addressed groups of workers. Charles became an engineer and a scientist and published several technical books.

Édouard's first wife was Virginie Augustine Paradis who died on 24 June 1841. As a testimony of his devotion to her memory he dedicated his book, *Recherches sur la condition civile et politique des femmes depuis les Romains jusqu'à nos jours*,[35] published in 1841, to her. His second marriage, probably in 1843 or 1844, was to Micheline Tronçon du Coudray, a descendant of one of the lawyers who defended Marie Antoinette. She published a *Vie de Jeanne d'Arc* in 1877, a book that went through several editions.[36] Édouard Laboulaye had three sons,

Paul, René, and Lucien, two from his first marriage and one from his second. Lucien predeceased his father.

Paul de Laboulaye, his most famous son, survived his father and served in a variety of diplomatic posts including minister to Portugal and ambassador to Spain. His most important appointment, however, was as French ambassador to Russia, 1886–93; he played a crucial role in negotiating the Franco-Russian Treaty of Alliance. René was first a judge and later an administrator of the Postes et Télégraphes.[37]

Laboulaye rarely referred to his family in his correspondence but when he was asked in 1863 by the Loyal Publication Society of New York to furnish some details about his life and family, this is what he wrote:

> You ask me for some details about my age and my family. I am fifty-three years old [he was writing in 1863]; I have passed all of my life working alone outside of any coterie; . . . I was married at twenty-one for the first time, and I married twenty years ago in a second marriage the grand daughter of Tronçon de Coudray, the defender of Marie Antoinette, and the grand niece of Colonel Tronçon de Coudray, whom Franklin had sent us and was eventually drowned in the Schuykill. . . . I have three sons. One is the secretary at one of our embassies, and you will see him some day in Washington; at heart he is a true American. He was educated at Heidelberg and London and speaks German and English well. He is my eldest son and he is thirty, is married, and has two children. My second son is a judge in Paris; he is twenty-eight. My third son (the son of my second marriage) is nineteen years old and is studying to be a lawyer.[38]

Little is really known of Laboulaye's private life as he revealed little in his letters and his correspondents did not comment on details of their or his private life. This can undoubtedly be attributed to the male-centered society of the mid-nineteenth century for which domestic details were not considered to be historically significant or important.

Laboulaye was unique in that he drew the principal inspiration for his political views on democracy and the republican form of government from the American political experience. Unlike many of his French contemporaries he did not look to the French Revolution and the First French Republic as the model for a democratic society, or to England for his political ideals. As René Rémond forcefully asserts, Laboulaye was:

> Un homme illustre de façon exemplaire par son oeuvre et le développement de sa pensée politique: l'union du libéralisme et de l'exemple américain et leur ambiguité profonde: Édouard Laboulaye, dont le nom domine entre

1850 et 1860 l'histoire des relations intellectuelles entre la France et les États-Unis, comme celui de Lafayette avant 1830 et celui de Tocqueville sous le Régime de Juillet. Toute sa vie il fit figure de defenseur attiré des États-Unis et de leurs institutions, publiant livre sur livre, multipliant les articles et les études

[A man renowned in an exemplary manner for his work and the development of his political thought that centered on (European) liberalism and the American experience and that brought out the profound ambiguities resulting from this union, Edouard Laboulaye, whose name dominated the history of the intellectual relations between France and the United States between 1850 and 1860 as did that of Lafayette before 1830 and that of Tocqueville during the July Monarchy. All his life he was the image of the ardent defender of the United States and its institutions, publishing book upon book and numerous articles and studies].[39]

Theodore Zeldin underscores Rémond's assertions by stating that Laboulaye was "regarded as France's greatest expert" on the United States.[40] Laboulaye's student, Édmond Scherer, referred to his interest in America as a "tic intellectuel," or as it was expressed by Laboulaye himself who overheard his listeners say, "voici M. Laboulaye qui se lève, il va nous parler de l'Amérique tout le temps" [Look M. Laboulaye rises to speak, he will talk all the time about America]."[41]

Laboulaye's Public Career

Laboulaye was a leading figure in the liberal opposition to Napoleon III until the end of the Empire in 1870 and during the Third Republic he served as a deputy; after 1875 he became a senator for life and served as one until his death. His student, Émile Boutmy, described him as "un homme de grand savoir, un homme d'esprit et un homme de bien" [a man of great knowledge, a man of great wit, and a man of good will]."[42] Laboulaye was admitted to the bar in 1842; he had received his licentiate in law three years earlier. On 17 January 1845 he was elected, at the age of thirty-four, to the Académie des Inscriptions et Belles-Lettres of the Institut de France, to the seat vacated by Flauriel. His election by a vote of 28 to 6 was one of the largest majorities ever seen at the Académie des Inscriptions et Belles-Lettres[43] and was attributable to his early publications, three of which were awarded prizes by the French Academy. These early works were: *Histoire du droit de propriété foncière en Occident* (Paris, 1839), *Essai sur la vie et les doctrines de Savigny* (Paris, 1842), *Recherches sur la condition civile et politique des femmes depuis les Romains jusqu'à nos jours* (Paris, 1843),[44] and *Essai sur les lois criminelles des Romains concernant la responsabilité des magistrats* (Paris, 1845). These early works all revealed a strong influence of the German historical school. In the 1840s he was a frequent contributor to the legal review, *Revue de législation et de jurisprudence,* edited by his friend and fellow legal scholar, Louis Wolowski.[45]

The Revolution of 1848 played a major role in Laboulaye's life. During the early months of the Revolution he served on two commissions, one dealing with education and one with constitutional questions. He resigned from the commission on education when it instituted changes in the Collège de France, a measure of which he disapproved. He became disillusioned by the turn of events after the June days and also with the drafting of the new constitution, which he considered unworkable. The reason for his resignation from this commission was his distress that the framers of the constitution had provided for only a single-chambered legislature. The events of 1848 turned his life from one of the reclusive scholar to one of a scholar actively interested in contemporary problems.

When the chair of comparative law at the Collège de France became vacant in 1849, Laboulaye, then only thirty-eight, received this coveted appointment and held it until his death in 1883. He succeeded the controversial Eugène Lerminier, who was forced to resign his chair. During the Second Empire Laboulaye contributed regularly to the opposition newspaper, *Le Journal des Débats.* Laboulaye also served on the editorial boards and contributed occasionally to three other reviews; the *Revue historique du droit français et étranger,* the *Revue Germanique,* and the *Revue nationale.* Until 1848 Laboulaye was a highly esteemed and erudite scholar who wrote only for other savants; the Revolutions of 1848, as he himself acknowledged, turned him into a political writer.[46] Henceforth, his writings would enjoy a wider appeal.

During the Second Republic (1848–51) he began his consideration of American history and finished the first volume of his *Histoire des États-Unis,* which was published in 1855. After the coup d'état of 2 December 1851 and the establishment of the Second Empire a year later, France endured a period of authoritarian rule complete with censorship of the press, the stifling of political life as it had been previously known in France, and the end of significant political opposition in the chambers. During the 1850s, sometimes called the period of Caesarism, it was often difficult to publish articles opposing the imperial government; a more devious approach was often necessary. Laboulaye's study of American history was interrupted by the political climate of the 1850s. The coup d'état of 2 December 1851, and the repressive measures that followed it, especially the censorship, led Laboulaye to lecture on less controversial subjects; he was especially cautious after three of his colleagues, Edgar Quinet, Jules Michelet, and Adam Mickiewicz, were dismissed from the Collège de France because of their political views.[47] Although Laboulaye sympathized with them, he did not wish to lose his academic position; consequently, from 1852 until 1857 he lectured on the noncontroversial subject of Roman legal institutions. Then between 1857 and 1862, Laboulaye lectured on the legal and political institutions of pre-Roman Gaul, Roman Gaul, the German tribes, the Merovingians, and on Salic Law. During these years he also translated William Ellery Channing's works, published a book of essays on religious liberty, as well as one on morals and politics. He became a regular contributor to the *Journal des Débats* in 1852.[48]

Only after the liberal reforms of Napoleon III in the early 1860s did Laboulaye resume his course on American history and resume his discussion of more controversial subjects. In the dreary years of the 1850s Laboulaye's position was best described by his student, Rodolphe Dareste, who pointed out, "Il y a des cas où le seul parti à prendre et de laisser passer l'orage ou de gagner du temps" [There are cases where the only position to take is to let the storm pass and to gain time].[49] His indirect approach to politically sensitive issues in his political writings can be seen in an 1858 collection of essays on the subject of religious liberty, which had been published previously in the *Journal des Débats*.[50] In this collection of essays Laboulaye raised not only the issue of religious liberty; under the pretense of discussing religious liberty he was able to raise the issue of political liberty, an issue that the leaders of the Second Empire did not wish raised. By raising the issue of religious liberty, Laboulaye managed to raise the issue of liberty in general, in such a sophisticated diversion that the censorship laws were not violated. Even the censors of the Second Empire could hardly quarrel with the idea of religious freedom.

Laboulaye's first decade as a professor at the Collège de France did not bring him large classes; in fact, he was terrified of lecturing, as he stated many years later to an audience of workers, when speaking "I became red in the face. For ten years my fear of the public gave me palpitations. If I had been made to speak when I was younger, I would have been spared these needless sufferings."[51] By the end of the decade of the 1850s, however, he himself said to his students in 1859,

Professeur depuis dix ans, c'est la première année qu'un auditoire un peu nombreux vient à mon cours. Jusqu'là j'ai vécu et parlé dans une honorable

solitude, et pour un petit cercle d'amis dévoués. . . . Aujourd'hui qu'on
sent en France le besoin de ces idées qui font la grandeur de l'homme,
vous êtes venus en plus grand nombre, et c'est pour moi une grande joie
de profiter de ce réveil général

[A professor for ten years, this is the first year that there is a fairly large
attendance at my courses. Until now I have lived and spoken in an honorable solitude, and for a small circle of devoted friends. . . . Today when in
France one feels a need for ideas that constitute the grandeur of man, you
have come in greater numbers, and it is a great joy for me to benefit from
this general awakening].[52]

By 1864 the *Revue Nationale* editorialized by publishing the first two
lectures of his course in comparative legislation and compared his
lectures to those of the great teachers during the Restoration:

Dans les départments, bien des personnes, nous en somme convaincus,
regrettant de ne pouvoir assister à ces savantes et utiles leçons. Du moins
nos abonnés auront la faculté d'en lire le texte soigneusement réproduit
comme sous la Restauration, les leçons de MM. Villemain, Cousin, et
Guizot étaient immédiatement publiées et se répondaient à plusieurs mil-
liers d'exemplaires. Nous estimons que celles de M. Laboulaye sont dignes
du même honneur

[In the departments, many, we are convinced, regret not being able to
attend, these learned and useful classes. At least our subscribers will be
able to read the text carefully reprinted as they were during the Restoration when the lectures of Villemain, Cousin, and Guizot were published
immediately in editions of several thousand copies. It is our opinion that
those of M. Laboulaye are worthy of the same honor].[53]

By 1869 *Appleton's Journal* carried an anonymous article on Laboulaye and commented:

Last winter M. Laboulaye lectured on Mondays and Thursdays, at one of
these rooms, and it was easy to see that he was the professor *"de prédilec-
tion"* with young France. So great was the demand of seats that many
would wait through the hour of the lecturer before him, that they might
thus make sure of a place for Laboulaye. When his hour came, there was
no spare room, for those who sat or stood, among men or women, a queer
mixture assembled there. Young and eager faces were seen beside those
who wore the shrewder expression of years. Rough, uncultured men min-
gled their hearty applause with the more cultivated and high-bred. Men
and women of all civilized nations gathered there. French, American,
English, and Germans; and among the women a few Russians in grand

toilettes, stood out in contrast to the sedate French blue-stockings, who came to hear and take notes.[54]

Another American commented in 1873 that Laboulaye lectured "with hundreds of pretty American girls at his feet."[55] John Bigelow remarked that "He spoke with unfaltering fluency, as if thoroughly imbued with his subject, while his humor, which was refined, frequently wreathed the features of his audience in smiles. He was occasionally interrupted with mild applause."[56] What especially pleased Laboulaye was the attendance of workers at his lectures.

Bigelow furnished us with one of the few physical descriptions we have of Laboulaye when he recounted a visit he made to Laboulaye's home in the Rue Taitbout in October 1861 shortly after Bigelow arrived in Paris to assume his duties as consul-general of the United States. He wrote:

When I called I was conducted into one of a suite of spacious rooms, crowded with books and numerous tables groaning under all the apparatus and teeming with the confusion of active and prolific authorship. The walls were decorated sparely with curious and rare engravings. I found Mr. Laboulaye, who presently entered, a gentleman of apparently middle age—he was then, in fact, in his fiftieth year—with a fine, compact figure, about five feet seven inches high, of pleasing address, and altogether an attractive-looking man. He wore no beard, nor had he much occasion for the razor; he had the rich olive complexion which prevails among the Latin race; his voice was gentle and low, though clear and admirably modulated; his hair, thin and brown, was brushed smoothly to the head, which, with his black frock coat buttoned close to the chin—I never saw him dressed otherwise except at dinner—gave him a slightly clerical appearance.[57]

In 1876 when Laboulaye spoke at the Opéra at a fund-raising concert for the Statue of Liberty, he was described in a Parisian newspaper as a figure "dressed in a kind of high-necked tunic buttoned to the top and revealing only the line of the white neck; clean shaven; the hair grey, worn long and brushed back."[58] He was compared in *Le Figaro* to a Quaker.[59] Laboulaye's necrology in *Le Petit Journal* said that when one looked at him one did not ask if he was a republican, a member of the left center, or the center right but "Est-il méthodiste, presbytérien ou quaker" [Is he a methodist, a presbyterian, or a quaker]?[60] In short, he did not change his mode of dress as the years passed.

Although Laboulaye did not attract large numbers of students until late in the decade of the 1850s, his writings and his public addresses established his reputation as a leading savant; a thinker of almost universal interests, who held a place at the center of French intellectual life during the Second Empire and corresponded with many of its leading figures such as Guizot, Tocqueville, Prévost-Paradol, Jules Simon, Montalembert, Ernest Renan, Augustin Cochin, to name only a few.

Laboulaye's bibliography comprising books, pamphlets, essays, children's stories, fairy tales, and articles on many diverse subjects totals over two hundred entries. On each Christmas or New Year's Day Laboulaye published a fairy tale for children in the *Débats*.[61] Many of his works were translated into English and some were translated into German and Italian. One of his short stories was even translated into Gaelic. Two themes dominated his writings during the Second Empire: liberty, religious and political, and America, her history and her institutions. For Laboulaye, who was disillusioned with the aftermath of 1848 in France, the study of American history and politics furnished a model of liberty and a stable political system that he hoped his fellow Frenchmen would emulate and establish American democracy in France. Furthermore, the course of American history in the 1850s and 1860s, the period of the American Civil War, illustrated for him the heroic efforts necessary to preserve liberty and to maintain a stable government.

Laboulaye took an active interest in the constitutional reforms and the drafting of constitutions for France in 1848, 1851, and in the 1870s. He played an active role in the latter as he was a major participant in drafting the Constitutional Laws of the Third Republic. He consistently cited the American Constitution as a model for France although the framers of the 1848 and 1851 constitutions disregarded the American paradigm. He considered it a personal triumph that France, in his view, incorporated a bicameral legislature with a president as chief executive in its Constitutional Laws of 1875. For Laboulaye, France, thereby, followed the American paradigm. As one of the founders of the Third Republic, his colleagues in the National Assembly in 1875 acknowledged his great service by electing him as one of the first senators for life.

In 1865, as the American Civil War was drawing to a close, Laboulaye held a dinner party at his home near Versailles. It was at this dinner, attended by the sculptor Frédéric-Auguste Bartholdi, that the idea of the Statue of Liberty was first conceived by Laboulaye; later he would serve as president of the Union Franco-Américaine, which raised funds for the statue between 1875 and 1880. The Statue of Liberty remains to this day a lasting and dramatic memorial to America's interpreter and friend, Édouard Laboulaye.

This study will discuss Laboulaye as a liberal and examine the genesis of his liberal ideas, which were inspired by American democracy. It will also examine his work on American history and his active polemical interests in such issues as the Civil War, slavery, religion, and education. Finally, an analysis of Laboulaye's influence in molding French liberal opinion in the 1860s and 1870s as well as his work as one of the founders and leading politicians of the Third Republic will complete the picture of his accomplishments and activities.

2

Laboulaye, the Liberal

Benjamin Constant sera longtemps encore l'expression la plus vive du libéralisme français.

[Benjamin Constant will be for a long time to come the embodiment of French liberalism.]

—Édouard Laboulaye

In his *Recollections* Alexis de Tocqueville captured the ferment of ideas that surfaced in the Revolution of 1848. Tocqueville with his uncanny insight into events wrote:

From the 25th of February [1848] onwards, a thousand strange systems came issuing pell-mell from the minds of innovators, and spread among the troubled minds of the crowd . . . it seemed as though the shock of the Revolution had reduced society itself to dust, and as though a competition had been opened for the new form that was to be given to the edifice about to be erected in its place. Everyone came forward with a plan of his own: this one printed it in the papers, that other on the placards with which the walls were soon covered, a third proclaimed his loud-mouthed in the open air. One aimed at destroying inequality of fortune, another inequality of education, a third undertook to do away with the oldest of inequalities, that between man and woman. Specifics were offered against poverty, and remedies for the disease of work which has tortured humanity since the first days of its existence.[1]

Thus did Tocqueville summarize the ideas of the men of 1848 and how these ideas, if put into practice, would have transformed France. Jean Rivero underscores Tocqueville by writing:

the February 1848 revolution was the work of the people of Paris, laborers and artisans largely worked up by confused socialist ideologies that were born as much of the misery of the proletarian condition in the early days

34

of industrialism as well as of the still uncertain theoretical reflections of Fourier, Proudhon, Cabet, Buchez, Louis Blanc or Blanqui.[2]

In recent years the seminal importance of the Revolutions of 1848 and the Second Republic has been reexamined by several social historians, notably Roger Price, John Merriman, Maurice Agulhon, Ted W. Margadant, and Thomas Robert Forstenzer who underscore the critical importance of 1848–51 in developing working-class consciousness as well as radical republican ideas. Price writes a social history of the Second Republic that draws on new source material, in particular electoral and economic statistics, to document the changing society and economy of the Second Republic.[3] Several recent historians, drawing from Charles Tilly's work in quantitative history, have published studies on the Second Republic. For example, John Merriman's work, also drawing on hitherto unused sources, discusses the repression of the revolutionary left during the period as well as a study of the red city of Limoges.[4] Maurice Agulhon's *La République au village* is devoted to a study of ordinary people in the Var Department of Southern France between 1789–1851.[5] He describes the period 1848–51 as a time of revelation when ordinary people in the Var voted for the first time; and they voted republican. Agulhon, whose work concentrates on Lower Provence, has done much to rehabilitate the republicans in the period 1848 to 1852 and thereby to rescuing them from the neglect of historians. Ted W. Margadant concentrates on the peasant uprisings against the coup d'état of Louis-Napoleon in 1851 and the manner in which Louis Napoleon's government repressed the republicans after the coup d'état.[6] Thomas R. Forstenzer discusses the role of the attorneys-general and the prefects in the fall of the Second Republic.[7] Forstenzer, as does Margadant, traces the government's measures to wipe out the democratic-socialist (démo-socs) political movement that had opposed the coup d'état.[8] All of these studies point out the rise of new ideas on how society should be constituted and the attempts to repress these ideas between 1848–52.

It is within the context of the traumatic nature of the threatened social upheaval in 1848 and its aftermath in France that we will situate Laboulaye's analysis of this politically and socially complex and turbulent time and to seek his analysis and his solutions to the problems facing his beloved France.

The Turning Point

The Revolutions of February and June 1848, which occurred in Laboulaye's thirty-seventh year, served as a major turning point in the evolution of his thought. He himself wrote some twenty-five years later that, "Ce sont les révolutions qui ont fait de moi un écrivain politique" [these were the revolutions that made a political writer of me].[9] He confessed that prior to 1848 "Mon goût me portait vers l'étude de l'antiquité et du moyen âge" [my taste carried me towards the study of antiquity and the middle ages], but that "La révolution de février 1848 détruisait tous mes projets et boulversa toutes mes idées" [the February Revolution of 1848 destroyed all my plans and overturned all of my ideas].[10] For him, this Revolution of 1848 broke with the liberal tradition, which had been established in France since 1814, and whose intellectual protagonists had been Benjamin Constant and Royer-Collard. He wrote *Considérations sur la constitution* to formulate his own vision of the constitution for the Second Republic.[11] It was this work that first directed his intellectual interest to America; much of the material for his *Considérations* was derived from what was at the time for him a hasty study of the American Constitution.

Even at this early stage in his political writings he compared and contrasted the *école révolutionnaire ou école française* with the *école américaine*. In his preface to his *Considérations sur la constitution* he drew up a table where in parallel columns he compared the two schools. For example in the *école révolutionnaire* the single-chambered Assembly was sovereign and derived its power from the people. The executive is subordinate to the Assembly and the judiciary is also subordinate to the Assembly. He contrasted this with the *école américaine,* which embodied the sovereignty of the people and where the will of the people is law; where a two-chambered legislature guarantees the rights of the nation and the sovereignty of the people; where the executive power is independent of the two chambers and the judicial power is entirely independent of the two houses. In the comparison he clearly favored the *école américaine*. He viewed the February Revolution as the triumph of the *école révolutionnaire* as it drew its ideological watershed from the period of the French Revolution of 1789–94, but more specifically, from the period of Jacobin rule in 1793–94. The *école révolutionnaire* was, of course, abhorrent to Laboulaye whereas for him the *école américaine* followed the course of true liberalism and democracy.[12]

Although his book was reasonably well received by the press, it was ignored by the framers of the Constitution of 1848. In fact, the Constitution's framers who created a unicameral legislature in the tradition of the *école révolutionnaire* placed the president or the executive and the legislature in conflict. Laboulaye declared, "La Constitution de 1848 donna bientôt les tristes résultats qu'on avait prévus.

Dès le premier jour il y eut conflit entre le président et l'Assemblée, et dès le premier jour le président, élu par le suffrage universel, fut plus populaire et plus puissant que l'Assemblée" [The Constitution of 1848 soon gave the sad results that one had forseen. From the first day there was a conflict between the President and the Assembly, and from the first day the President, elected by universal suffrage, was more popular and more powerful than the Assembly].[13] The Constitution of 1848, therefore, struck Laboulaye as an unstable and unworkable solution that was bound to fail. He wrote, "Les constituants de 1848 one dédaigné l'expérience américaine; ils ont rejeté la division du pouvoir législatif, ils ont organisé le pouvoir exécutif sur le plan qui tient à la fois de la monarchie constitutionnelle et de la république" [The drafters of the 1848 Constitution have scorned the American experience and they have rejected the separation of legislative power, they have organized the executive power in such a way that it adheres simultaneously to both a constitutional monarchy and a republic.][14] The president, elected by universal suffrage, and "more popular and more powerful than the Assembly,"[15] could serve only a single term of four years and was ineligible for reelection. Laboulaye commented that the Americans had understood these problems and that the American Constitution would be of help to France in the future.

In 1872 Laboulaye reviewed his study of the constitutional framers of 1848 and wrote that the true legacy of these constitutional framers was the bloody June days of 1848 and the Paris Commune of 1871, both of which he abhorred. He particularly disapproved of the process for revision provided in the Constitution of 1848 whereby a minority could deny the will of the majority.

By 1851, as Louis Napoleon's term was drawing to a close, and according to the Constitution was ineligible for immediate reelection in 1852, Laboulaye noted that the Prince-President was popular and if given the opportunity, would easily win reelection; he declared that he would not win Paris and certain other cities in France, but the countryside and small cities would vote for him in overwhelming numbers. In February 1851 Laboulaye wrote a pamphlet on the question, entitled, *La Révision de la constitution, lettres à un ami.*[16] Laboulaye argued that the logical procedure for France was to revise the Constitution. Since a three-fourths majority was necessary to pass such a bill, a minority having only one quarter of the seats in the Assembly could and did effectively block revision in 1851. If he wished to remain in power, Louis Napoleon had no other choice but to stage a coup d'état. Although Laboulaye detested coups d'état—he wrote "J'ai toujours eu en horreur ces coups de force dont le peuple est l'éternelle victime" [I have always had a horror of this use of

violence where the people are always the victims][17]—and argued that
the use of force was unconstitutional, he nevertheless viewed Louis
Napoleon's coup as precipitated by the misguided views of the Assembly's minority, a minority composed of republicans and royalists who
had left Louis Napoleon no other choice. From these two early writings the thrust of Laboulaye's liberalism became evident as did his
desire to draw upon the American experience in French constitution
making. His chief point was, that "si l'Assemblée n'avait pas voulu
fermer les yeux à l'évidence, son devoir selon moi eût d'amener une
transformation constitutionnelle. Avec la révision on aurait eu Louis
Napoléon pour président d'une République libérale" [If the Assembly
had not wanted to close its eyes to the evidence, its duty, in my
opinion, would have been to effect a constitutional transformation.
With this revision we would have had Louis Napoleon as president
of a liberal republic].[18] In the matter of constitutional revision Laboulaye's eyes had turned to America.

In 1849, when he gave his inaugural lecture at the Collége de
France, Laboulaye chose as his subject *De la Constitution américaine
et l'utilité de son étude,* which later would become the first chapter of
his masterpiece, *Histoire des États-Unis.* With his appointment to the
Collège de France, Laboulaye gained a forum to expound his views
and he soon became one of the most popular lecturers in that venerable
institution. His lecture hall, especially in the 1860s, was usually
crowded with an enthusiastic group of admiring students. In 1864 an
editor of the *Revue Nationale* prefaced one of Laboulaye's articles
with this comment, "une heure avant la leçon, la salle, les couloirs, la
cour du Collège de France sont envahis par une foule empressée au
moment où le professeur monte dans sa chaire, il est accuelli par une
véritable explosion d'enthousiasme" [an hour before the lesson, the
hall, the corridors, the courtyard of the Collège de France are invaded
by an eager crowd and the moment the professor goes up to the po-
dium, he is greeted by a veritable explosion of enthusiasm.[19] John
Bigelow described taking Richard Hay to one of Laboulaye's lectures
at the Collège de France on 26 January 1863:

> It chanced that the subject of his discourse was that period of our colonial
> history which embraced "the old French war." His room was full without
> being crowded. His manner at a lecture was dignified without being aus-
> tere or airy, which is more than can be said of some of the professors of
> note in the Latin Quarter. He spoke with unfaltering fluency, as if thor-
> oughly imbued with his subject, while his humor, which was refined,
> frequently wreathed his audience in smiles. He was occasionally inter-
> rupted with mild applause. I remember he gave us an opportunity of
> observing how differently the history of one's own country sounds when

expounded by a foreigner, especially if the national prejudices of the parties are involved.[20]

Laboulaye's duties at the Collège de France were to give two lec-tures a week during the academic terms (a schedule that would delight any contemporary American academic).[21] Since the Collège de France did not enroll students, he did not have to sit on examination commit-tees. The nature of his assignments at the Collège certainly left him a considerable amount of time for writing and research, and to prepare his lectures, which were usually published.

The events of 1848 and his appointment to the Collège de France in 1849 represent turning points in Laboulaye's thought, a moment that marks the origin and development of his liberalism; its genesis can be traced to three sources: the German Historical School of Juris-prudence; the French liberal tradition, particularly the writings of Benjamin Constant; and the American political tradition.

The Historical School

The historical school of law in Germany exercised a strong influence in France, especially among historians and legal scholars. The chief exponents of the historical school questioned the French natural law tradition emanating from the eighteenth century and also most of the laws made during the French Revolution and Napoleon, especially, the Code Napoléon. For the historical school "Law, to the Germans, was ultimately the product not of sovereign will but of custom."[22] For those Germans living under Napoleon's rule "Hardly better than the invading armies were the administrative reforms introduced by Napo-leon and especially the Code."[23] Friedrich Karl von Savigny emerged as the leading exponent and writer of the historical school. In 1814 Savigny, newly appointed to a professorship at the recently founded University of Berlin, published the manifesto of the historical school entitled, *On the Vocation of Our Age for Legislation and Jurispru-dence*.[24] Savigny once said of the Code Napoléon that it "broke into Germany, and ate in, further and further, like a cancer."[25] The eminent historian of Rome, Barthold Georg Neibuhr, also exercised a signifi-cant influence on the historical school.[26]

The major influence of German thought on France as we have estab-lished in chapter 1 originates with the landmark work of Mme de Staël, *De l'Allemagne*, which she had hoped to publish in France in 1810 but because of the problems we mentioned with Napoleon's censors it was published in London in 1813. Mme de Staël, however, conspicuously omitted any treatment of historians or legists from her study of Germany; it was her influence, moreover, on literature, the romantic movement, and philosophy that was immense. Beginning with the Bourbon Restoration (1814–30) German thought began to be fashionable in France and the French universities became the agency for its dissemination; consequently, German legal and historical thought had a marked influence on a young generation of French historians and legal writers. The lecture halls of François Guizot and Victor Cousin, both influenced by the historical school, were most effective in forming the world views of their students, Edgar Quinet and Jules Michelet. Saint-Marc Girardin, Guizot's successor at the Sorbonne, also came under the influence of the German school. Laboulaye, who attended Saint-Marc Girardin's lectures, dedicated his *Études contemporaines sur l'Allemagne et les pays slaves* to Saint-Marc Girardin and said, "I take this opportunity to express my thanks and my friendship."[27]

In fact, one might say that the entire generation educated in the 1830s in France was influenced by the historical school when what Donald R. Kelley terms "the German Impulse" came into prominence.[28] This "impulse" was so strong that a tour of Germany became an essential part of one's education. It was precisely during the first decade of the July Monarchy, the 1830s, that Édouard Laboulaye received his university education and was admitted to the bar. These years also saw his first publications that clearly reflected the historical school's influence, especially his book in praise of Savigny. As part of his education, Laboulaye followed in the path of his contemporaries, Quinet and Michelet, and made the obligatory pilgrimage to Germany. Here the young Frenchman retraced the steps Mme de Staël had made a generation earlier. In fact, Laboulaye was to make many trips to the German States during his lifetime.[29]

In 1841 Laboulaye returned from a mission to Germany where he studied German university education. He termed this trip a pilgrimage since it was then that he met von Savigny and wrote an essay analyzing his thought, which he published in 1842. His youthful enthusiasm, he was just thirty when he made the trip, is abundantly clear in the preface written in 1842, where he wrote that his aim was "de faire mieux connaître à la France les doctrines de l'école historique, j'ai cru faire un nouveau pas vers le but constant de mes travaux, je veux dire l'union scientifique de la France et de l'Allemagne, prélude d'une autre alliance que j'appelle de tous mes voeux" [to make better known in France the doctrines of the historical school, I thought that I made a new step towards the constant aim of my work, as I wish for the scientific union of France and Germany, a prelude to another alliance that would fulfill all my desires].[30] Thus Laboulaye sought not only the scientific and intellectual union of France and Germany, but he also hinted at "another alliance," possibly a political one, which would result in peace between the two nations.

On his visit to Germany, Laboulaye inspected the schools in Prussia, Baden, Wurttemberg, and Bavaria, as he was commissioned to do in 1840 by the minister of education, Victor Cousin.[31] In his report he concluded that French universities, especially the faculties of law, needed to give political and administrative training to their students so that France would have a corps of public servants trained in public administration, diplomacy, and financial administration.[32] His proposals were taken up in 1845 by Salvandy, then minister of education, but the matter was never debated in parliament before the outbreak of revolution in 1848, no doubt because of the fierce debates in parliament on Catholic education and the monopoly of the University.[33] Salvandy did, however, appoint Laboulaye to the Haute Commission des études de droit, which was to recommend reforms in legal studies.[34] Laboulaye was aided in his advocacy of reforms in legal education by his friend, and Polish refugee of 1830, Louis Wolowski (1810–76), editor of the influential *Revue de lègislation et de jurisprudence*.[35] Laboulaye wrote several articles for the *Revue* and served on its editorial board. In his articles for the *Revue* he advocated reforms in legal education that would train administrators, diplomats, and financial experts.[36]

Laboulaye's proposals did manage to touch off a controversy with the prominent lawyer, Alexandre Ledru-Rollin (1807–74), who vigorously defended the French educational system in the Faculties of Law. He accused Laboulaye and others of being unpatriotic by trying to introduce German educational methods. Ledru-Rollin wrote an open letter to Laboulaye and said "C'est vrai que j'ai attaqué l'école historique dont vous êtes admirateur" [It is true I attacked the historical school of which you are an admirer].[37] The *Revue de législation et de jurisprudence* editorialized that the vicious attack by Ledru-Rollin was one of the reasons that Laboulaye was elected to the Académie des Inscriptions et Belles-Lettres.[38]

Under the Second Republic Laboulaye was appointed to La Haute Commission des Études Scientifiques et Littéraires but he served only briefly as he resigned in protest in 1848 over the reorganization of the Collège de France and was succeeded by Drouyn de Lhuys. His resignation was triggered by the Second Republic's attempt to set up an École d'Administration within the Collège de France, an attempt that lasted only a year, until 1849.[39] Laboulaye did not forget his vision of a school to train public administrators but he would have to

wait until 1872 and the founding of the École libre des sciences politiques by his pupil and protégé, Émile Boutmy.[40]

Eugène Lerminier for whom, in 1831, the chair of comparative law
was created at the Collège de France, had published a thesis on von
Savigny in 1827.[41] In his days of active lecturing at the Collège de
France, Lerminier espoused the ideas of the historical school to his
students.[42] The next titular of Lerminier's chair would be Édouard
Laboulaye. When Laboulaye succeeded Lerminier and assumed the
chair of comparative law in 1849, the legal views of the historical
school were already well known at the Collège de France.

Thus the ideas of the historical school were au courant in the 1830s
and 1840s in France. It is not surprising then that Laboulaye was
attracted to them and that Donald R. Kelley could refer to Laboulaye
as "the Germanizing legal historian."[43] But we want to make the further point that Laboulaye chose to follow not such mainline German
philosophers as Kant, Fichte, or Hegel but rather two relatively minor
German philosophers, Heinrich Ahrens and K. F. C. Krause, both of
whom applied the philosophical principles of the German Idealists to
politics. The German legal scholar who exerted the strongest influence
on Laboulaye's intellectual formation was Friedrich Karl von Savigny.
On one occasion von Savigny acknowledged Laboulaye as his disciple,
and von Savigny's influence can be seen in Laboulaye's early scholarly
interests: property rights in the West, the condition of women in
Rome, and Roman criminal law, as well as a laudatory study of von
Savigny himself.[44]

The Swiss scholar, professor at the University of Heidelberg, and
proponent of the historical school, Johann Kaspar Bluntschli, explained von Savigny's precept that it is not the caprice of the legislator
(for example, Napoleon and his law Code) who makes the law, but
"it is produced above all by internal and silent forces,"[45] when he
defined the historical school in the following manner:

> the historical school . . . does not thoughtlessly and servilely honour actual
> facts, but recognizes, explains, and interprets the inner connection be-
> tween Past and Present, the organic development of national life, and the
> *moral idea* as revealed in its history. This method certainly starts from the
> actual phenomena, but regards them as living and not as dead.[46]

Laboulaye echoed the historical school when he wrote, "All science,
all of politics, are divided between the two schools of thought: the
school of the absolute, or philosophical school; and the school of experience, or historical school."[47] In succinct terms, according to Kelley,
the historical school "provided a modern, expert, and empirical alter-

native to the rationalist legacy of Jacobinism and Bonapartism."[48] The shift to the historical school echoed the celebrated report of M. de Salvandy, the Minister of Education, who said, "La France a passé l'âge des théories. Les idées générales, les principes abstraits ont fait leur temps" [France has passed beyond the age of theories. General ideas, abstract principles have had their day].[49] In a sense, Laboulaye agreed with Guizot's dictum that, "When history speaks, it is well of politics to listen."[50] In Laboulaye's lifetime, Lieber in New York, Laboulaye in Paris, and Bluntschli in Heidelberg formed what Lieber used to call a "scientific cloverleaf" of the historical school.[51] Lord Acton described the historical school as having "no masters in France and only one disciple, who was [Laboulaye]."[52] Throughout his life, Laboulaye was to have a distrust in abstract political ideas and also a fear of revolution.

The influence of the historical school on Laboulaye's scholarly works after the 1840s would be one of method rather than of content. More importantly, in this respect Laboulaye, unlike most exponents of the historical school in Europe, never became a conservative in politics; instead he drew his political ideas from such French liberal writers as Benjamin Constant, Royer-Collard, Alexis de Tocqueville, and Alexandre Vinet.

Constant's Influence

The major influence on Laboulaye's liberal ideas from within France came from Benjamin Constant (1767–1830); in fact it was Laboulaye who introduced the French reading public of the 1860s to Constant's writings when in 1861 he gathered Constant's chief political writings into a two-volume edition entitled, *Cours de politique constitutionnelle*.[53] During Laboulaye's lifetime a second edition was published in 1872. When Sainte-Beuve, the reigning literary critic, and soon-to-be-named senator by Napoleon III, reviewed these volumes in 1862 he referred to Laboulaye as the "savant professeur," and he noted that Laboulaye "was pleased to find in these texts [of Constant] his own principles and his own doctrine."[54] After having read what he termed Sainte-Beuve's "piquantes causeries," which were highly critical of Constant, Laboulaye wrote Sainte-Beuve and defended Constant by saying,

En ce qui me touche vous avez raison de me compter parmi les disciples d'une école qui croit à la liberté parce qu'elle croit à la bonté de la nature humaine. Cette école a ce grand avantage que partout où ses principes ont été appliqués, ils ont réussi; et j'ai peine à croire que la France puisse supporter en fait de liberté, ce qui a fait la prosprité et la paix de l'Angle- terre, et de l'Amérique, de la Hollande, de la Suisse et de la Belgique

[As regards myself you are right to number me among the disciples of a school which believes in liberty because it believes in the goodness of human nature. That school has the great advantage that wherever its principles have been applied, they have succeeded; and I have difficulty believing that as regards liberty France would not support what has brought prosperity and peace to England, America, Holland, and Belgium].[55]

In his lengthy Introduction Laboulaye clearly shows his indebted- ness and his admiration for Constant. Laboulaye quoted approvingly Guizot's speech receiving Père Lacordaire into the Académie Française wherein Guizot described Constant as "Un homme qui a joui d'un grand renom populaire, et que les libéraux appelaient leur publiciste" [A man who enjoyed great popular renown, and who the liberals called their publicist].[56] Laboulaye added his own verdict, "Benjamin Constant sera longtemps encore l'expression la plus vive du libéralisme français" [Benjamin Constant will be for yet a long time the liveliest expression of French liberalism].[57] He remarked that forty years ago Constant "set down the essential conditions for liberty."[58] and Con- stant's definition of liberalism doubled as his own political credo:

J'ai defendu quarante ans le même principe: liberté en tout: en religion, en philosophie, en littérature, en industrie, en politique; et par liberté j'entends le triomphe de l'individualité, tant sur l'autorité qui voudrait gouverner par le despotisme, que les masses qui réclament le droit d'as- servir la minorité à la majorité"

[I have defended the same principles for forty years: liberty in everything: in religion, in philosophy, in literature, in industry, in politics; and by liberty I mean the triumph of individualism, as much over that authority which would govern by despotism, as over the masses who call for the right to subject the minority to the majority].[59]

In his analysis of Constant, Laboulaye began by comparing the idea of liberty among the ancients with that of the moderns. Laboulaye also made this distinction in the essay, "La Liberté antique et la liberté moderne," which he published in January 1863.[60] For Constant, and also for Laboulaye, liberty for the ancients was the liberty of small communities that depended on slavery to allow the citizens to engage full time in fulfilling their civic responsibilities. This period of history was now over. Liberty for the moderns was a liberty suited to a commercial and manufacturing society that was based not on slavery but on independence and allowing time for the pursuit of private pleasures as well as civic duties. The period had now begun where, according to Laboulaye, "the individual has the right to be sovereign . . . the citizen does not ask for anything more other than to be free in all his private actions."[61] Jean-Claude Lamberti in his work on Tocqueville cited approvingly Laboulaye's description of ancient and modern liberty and asserted that "in many respects" Laboulaye was Tocqueville's disciple. Laboulaye wrote:

> Among the Ancients, the gods were attached to the walls of the city and existed only with the permission of the Senate or Caesar. To proclaim that God has rights was to destroy the unity of despotism. Therein lies the germ of the revolution which separates the ancient from the modern world. . . . The sovereignty of God forever broke the tyranny of the Caesars. Indeed, from the day that sovereignty is recognized, the immortal soul has duties and therefore rights—rights and duties which are independent of the state and over which the prince has no authority. Conscience is emancipated, the individual exists.[62]

He also argued that in antiquity political sovereignty was given first rank. He wrote, "it subordinated and sacrificed the individual to the state; the moderns put the individual first; the state was only the guarantor."[63] Crucial to the establishment of modern liberty was the role of Christianity. Laboulaye also pointed out that Constant desired neither centralization of the state nor the extension of administrative law and procedures into the arena of private life.

Constant was enthusiastic and optimistic concerning modern liberty, and although he did not approve of the excesses of the French Revolution, he approved of its principles. The revolutionaries were not mistaken about principles, but about means to effect them that were anachronistic, among which he would certainly include revolutionary justice and the Terror. If one were to eliminate the anachronism, modern liberty would thrive, be beneficial to humanity, and be as powerful as the Revolution itself.[64] Laboulaye also echoed Constant's view of the French revolutionaries and was to be an opponent of revolution all his life.

Constant claimed that the first liberty the state ought to respect was religious liberty;[65] to this end separation of church and state was essential; the state would be more Christian if it were not attached to any church. Constant concluded his discussion of religious liberty by saying, "il en est de la religion comme des grandes routes: j'aime que l'État les entretienne, pourvu qu'il laisse à chacun le droit de préférer les sentiers" [It is with religion as it is with national roads: I agree that the State should maintain them, provided that each citizen has the right to prefer taking paths].[66] Constant, according to H. Gou-hier wrote "Free peoples are religious peoples," and that "a free government needs religion, because it needs disinterestedness." Gouhier also remarks that "Constant was opposed to two widely held opinions: first, that religion is a natural ally of despotism, and second, that the absence of religious feeling is favorable to freedom."[67] Laboulaye observed that Constant's views allowed for toleration not only of all Christian sects but also of Jews; Laboulaye trusted that religious liberty would also eventually be extended to the Moslems of Algeria.[68]

After religious freedom Constant advocated freedom of education; he called for the complete neutrality of the government in regard to education. Only with government neutrality, he argued, could intellectual life flourish in a society. Closely tied to the idea of freedom of education was what Laboulaye termed the freedom of association, namely, that people could come together to form an association and that others could form parallel associations in education, public charity, and the like. For example, Catholics could have a theological faculty in Paris or an orphanage in Amiens while Protestants could have a theological faculty in Strasbourg or Montauban and an orphanage in Nîmes. Also, free thinkers could open parallel institutions, such as a university in some French city or other charitable institutions. All of this would be done without state interference or regulation. From these major freedoms of religion and education flow all of the other liberties that Constant labels individual liberties.

For Constant the chief individual liberty was freedom of the press, which must be placed beyond all governmental restraint by judicial guarantees and jury trials.[69] Further guarantees of individual liberty would be the responsibility of ministers to the parliament and, above all, to a parliament that comprised numerous representatives who were independent or could withstand governmental pressure. A larger representation in parliament, Constant argued, would allow opposition deputies to be elected and to sit in the Chamber of Deputies. He wrote, "Such are the boulevards upon which individual liberty is today surrounded." Constant managed to write most of these liberties into the *Acte additionel* of 1815, guarantees that were accepted by Napoleon during the Hundred Days.[70] Finally, Constant evoked the freedom of municipal powers. "It is necessary," he declared, "to introduce into our administration much federalism but a federalism different from that we have known up until now."[71] Constant clearly wished to end the administrative centralization emanating from Paris and to emulate the localism or federalism of the German states. After all, Constant, like so many others, had followed the "German impulse" and traveled to the German states.

Laboulaye summed up his views on Constant in a letter to Sainte-Beuve:

Pour moi j'ai foi dans les idées que défendait B. Constant, idées aujourd'hui répandues dans tous les pays libres et qui ont ce grand avantage qu'elles ne menacent aucun gouvernement, et qu'elles poussent à la liberté et ne pas aux révolutions. C'est pas d'un seul côté que je trouve ces idées très fraîches, et je suis convaincu que Benjamin Constant n'a jamais été un sceptique qu'en jouant un rôle, au fond de l'âme (des écrits en témoignent) il a toujours une foi dans la liberté

[For myself, I have faith in the ideas Constant defended, ideas that today are spread throughout all free countries and that have the great advantage that they threaten no government, and that they move towards liberty and not towards revolutions. It is on every side that I find his ideas very fresh, and I am convinced that Benjamin Constant has never been a sceptic except to play a role; in the depths of his soul (his writings are witness to this) he has always had faith in liberty].[72]

Le Parti Libéral

In the early 1860s Laboulaye's scholarly output of books dealing with liberalism was significant. Earlier, in 1858, he had published *La Liberté religieuse,* a collection of previously published essays on a variety of religious topics but whose major pieces dealt in a general manner with the theme of religious liberty.[73] This work was followed in the 1860s by the publication of his edition of Constant's *Cours de politique constitutionnelle* in 1861, his *Études morales et politiques* in 1862, his collection of essays entitled *L'État et ses limites* in 1863, and the summation of his views on liberalism in *Le Parti libéral, son programme et son avenir* also in 1863.

Le Parti libéral was published shortly after the campaign of 1863 to elect members to the Corps Législatif, the lower house of the French parliament for a term of six years. The book, as he intended, became a veritable manifesto of the liberal opposition during the remaining years of the Second Empire. Laboulaye wrote Francis Lieber that the book was "notre programme."[74] Lieber replied, "I find in it (*Le Parti libéral*) how much we agree on many, probably on most important points within the sphere of civil liberty, and besides there is so much in the book that interests and instructs me."[75]

Le Parti libéral had an immense success and sold over 10,000 copies in five years and required another edition in 1868;[76] the book was also reprinted in 1872. Significantly, the book was written at a time when French political life was beginning to revive after the first liberal reforms of Napoleon III and also the elections of 1863. It was in these elections that the members of the opposition had found it possible to publish cautiously worded dissenting opinions and many had hoped to be able to win some seats in the elections, which would increase the number of opposition deputies from the five republican deputies, called "les cinq," elected in 1857. In fact, the opposition did win some thirty-odd seats in a chamber of some two hundred and sixty seats. The victories of the opposition deputies were accomplished in spite of governmental pressure, official candidates, and control and intimidation of the press. Laboulaye, himself, originally stood as a candidate in the second district of Paris but withdrew in favor of Adolphe Thiers. Upon withdrawing he asserted that Thiers's liberalism was not the same as his, "as I do not have the same taste for centralization that he [Thiers] admires . . . but I think that all should rally behind the name which is the most eminent and well-known."[77] He clearly displayed his political realism and also saw the value of name recognition.

In *Le Parti libéral* Laboulaye argued that two types of freedom are advocated by the liberal party: individual liberties and political liberties. In the category of individual liberties he included what he termed social and municipal liberties, asserting that France's liberal governments between 1814 and 1848, although motivated by good intentions, had not succeeded in fully establishing these liberties.[78] To illustrate individual liberty he stated that the citizen, unless charged with a crime, should be able to act without fear of the police and he should be as much a master in his own home as a feudal baron was king in his castle. Individual liberties assume that one is innocent until proven guilty and that one has the right to a jury trial or a trial before an immovable impartial judge. These, he argued, "are the principles of '89, they are principles recognized by all modern constitutions."[79] According to Laboulaye, there were four chief modern constitutions; those of Belgium, Holland, Great Britain, and the United States, and he consistently cited these constitutions as models for the French.

Religious liberty was the most important of the social liberties and had, in fact, been a central preoccupation of Laboulaye in the 1850s. A devout Catholic himself, Laboulaye became interested in the works and the thought of William Ellery Channing. He translated many of Channing's works into French and wrote several commentaries on his thought; many of his ideas concerning religious liberty and against slavery were inspired by Channing, who for Laboulaye, was the

American Fénelon.[80] Laboulaye was also influenced by the Swiss Protestant theologian, Alexandre-Rodolphe Vinet (1767–1847), who advocated religious liberty and the separation of church and state.[81]

Another formative influence on Laboulaye was Alexis de Tocqueville. Tocqueville, like Laboulaye, departed from the mainstream of French liberals in that he drew inspiration from America rather than from England for his liberal ideas. In fact, Tocqueville and Laboulaye were unique in that both saw the origins of modern democracy in America.[82] Although Laboulaye corresponded with Tocqueville and wrote his official eulogy for the *Journal des Débats,* an essay he later included in his *L'État et ses limites,* he nevertheless had reservations concerning Tocqueville. Laboulaye suggested that Tocqueville had not read Constant's works as he never cited Constant on ancient and modern liberty, especially Constant's famous speech at the Paris Athénée in 1819.[83] Laboulaye wrote: "How much toil and fatigue that noble mind might have spared itself had he read the liberal publicist. In all his pamphlets, of which he *probably* knew nothing, would he not have found his own thoughts expressed with as much finesse as force?"[84] In a recent study on Tocqueville Jean-Claude Lamberti states that "Tocqueville left no direct evidence of having read Constant, whom he never cites."[85]

Francis Lieber, who knew Tocqueville and also corresponded with him, wrote Laboulaye:

Ah, what a delight it would be to talk with you on public affairs, as I did with Tocqueville. We always differed on one point. I was, with reference to France, an Orleanist. I thought that the greatest amount of liberty and the greatest chance of civil development was offered to France in that type of government. He did not seem to think so, as at least I feel so. But I loved him much. His was a rare nature.[86]

To this observation of Lieber Laboulaye replied:

Je suis de votre avis sur son compte, et je crois qu'il eut mieux fait de se rallier franchement au gouvernment des Orléans. Mais c'était une belle âme, et son livre sur l'Amérique a répandu beaucoup de bonnes idées en France. Selon moi il lui manquerait un peu de précision dans l'esprit, il aimait trop les idées générales, et il ne rendait pas un compte assez exact de la société américaine, mais à tout prendre son livre méritait le grand succès qu'il a eu

[I agree with you about him, and I believe that he would have done better to rally openly around the Orléans government. But he had a beautiful soul, and his book on America spread many good ideas throughout France.

In my view, he lacked some precision in his thinking and was too fond of general ideas, and his account of American society was not exact but nevertheless his book deserved its great success].[87]

Alexis de Tocqueville was also influential in forming Laboulaye's views on religious liberty.[88]

Laboulaye acknowledged his indebtedness to Channing, Vinet, and Tocqueville frequently in his writings, especially in his Introduction to Constant's *Cours de politique* and in his letter to Sainte-Beuve.[89] To underscore his interest in religious liberty in the 1850s he published a collection of essays in 1858 under the title, *La Liberté religieuse.*

The importance placed on religious liberty was also evident in Laboulaye's statement published in 1863 in *L'État et ses limites* where he wrote, "religious liberty is the spirit of modern societies, it is the root of all other liberties."[90] He advocated the principle of a free church in a free state in the very year that the same proposition uttered by Montalembert, a prominent liberal Catholic leader and correspondant of Laboulaye, at the Congress of Malines, Belgium, drew forth a condemnation from Pius IX and bitter denunciations from the French integral or ultra-conservative Catholics. Laboulaye was a strong advocate of the separation of church and state, although its chief advocates were usually Protestants or free thinkers.[91]

In the matter of religious liberty, Laboulaye was much concerned about the plethora of administrative regulations concerning the French churches, especially the Catholic Church, which was supported by the state and had the status of an official religion. For him, all such regulations would cease if there was a separation of church and state. He said, "the state does not know the faithful, it only knows the citizen."[92] All provisions in administrative codes that regulate religion should be eliminated. He recognized that his proposals were difficult for Catholics because for fifteen hundred years the church had been intimately linked to the French state in the so-called union of throne and altar. He observed that quarrels between church and state were peculiar to the Old World, and did not pertain to the New World of America where there was separation of church and state and where, with its thirty or forty churches the church-state conflicts, the "*odium theologicum,* the noxious weed of Christianity,"[93] had never been an issue. In addition to America he cited the examples of England, Holland, and Belgium as countries where religious liberty was embodied in their laws.

On the question of freedom of education Laboulaye also advocated the withdrawal of the state from educational matters. He saw no need for either administrative codes, or for regulations that hamper the

operation of schools. In the matter of state-supported schools he promoted decentralization, which would move authority away from Paris
to give local authorities the power to exercise control over the public
schools in their local areas. He noted that primary education in some
modern states was under the control of the local community and not
centralized in the capital.

As concerns higher education in France he asserted that historically
it had been first in the hands of the church and that now it was in
the hands of the state. He argued that for either the church or the
state to control education was an unacceptable solution and one not
congenial with his liberal views. In higher or university education
he was against the French system where the minister of education
determined policy in the name of the central government. He described and endorsed the autonomy of the German universities, especially the state-supported faculty that existed alongside the system of
the *Privatdozent*. He said, "the state can offer education, it does not
have to impose it."[94] He also agreed that French higher education
was stifled by centralization and, for him, state control epitomized
intellectual centralization, which was the least justifiable form of centralization.

Laboulaye advocated the establishment of public subscription libraries, citing as a model, the library founded by the Franklin Society.[95]
He congratulated the minister of the interior, M. Persigny, on his
support of this movement for public subscription libraries. These public libraries were to be accessible to the citizenry and he advocated
and indeed participated in lectures given to support subscription libraries for the working classes. His book, *L'État et ses limites*, grew
out of just such a series of lectures given in the early 1860s.[96] For
him, there should be no government regulation of these lectures and
neither should police permissions be required for them.

Linked to freedom of education in Laboulaye's network of individual liberties were: freedom of charity, freedom of association, and
municipal liberties. By freedom of charity he envisioned what we
would term today the private sector, namely, charitable institutions
would be established and supported by private donations and philan-
thropy without governmental interference or regulation. Freedom of
association implied the right to form an organization, for example, a
commercial or business organization. He lamented that the establishment of such organizations in France required governmental permission and he offered for consideration the English example, where no
governmental permission was needed to form an association and
claimed, that, in part, this accounted for England's economic strength.
In regard to municipal liberties the old enemy that obstructed their

establishment was centralization. What disturbed him most was that the citizens of Paris, including himself, were denied control of their own municipal government in violation of the principle of "no tax' ation without representation." Cities and towns must be able to gov' ern themselves without central direction from Paris and all municipal taxes should be voted by the municipalities themselves and not levied or decreed by the central government in Paris. For Laboulaye, as for Tocqueville, centralization was the legacy of the Ancien Régime. The chief source, however, for Laboulaye's views on centralization was Joseph Fiévée (1767–1839), who was a liberal deputy during the Res' toration. Laboulaye frequently cited Fiévée's *Histoire de la session de 1817* to support his own opinions on centralization that were so cru' cial to his liberalism.[97]

Laboulaye next turned to a discussion of political liberty and, for him, the essential condition was that basic freedoms ought not to restrict liberty but, on the contrary, they should guarantee it.[98] He noted that of all the regimes that France had had since 1789 "le plus insupportable sera toujours le despotisme bâtard d'une chambre unique" [the most unbearable will always be the bastard despotism of a single chamber] because it paralyzed the government, oppressed the people, and it favored anarchy and tyranny.[99] Laboulaye laid down four conditions essential to political liberty: first, there must be univer' sal suffrage (at this point in time he was speaking of universal suffrage for men, although he does express sympathy for women's suffrage); second, there must be a national representation, freely elected, which exercises influence and legitimate control on the government and which in fact frames legislation on finances, peace, and war; third, an independent and sovereign judiciary that has nothing to fear or to gain from power, it is to the irremovable judges and the juries that belong the protection of the laws and the defense of individual liber' ties; fourth, a press free from all administrative restrictions, which has the right to publish everything except what would cause personal injury or provoke a crime. He noted that these political liberties are already found in Britain, America, Belgium, Holland, and Switzer' land. He concluded his discussion by stating that these elements of political liberty did exist in the Constitution of 1852, but only "*en germe.*"[100]

Laboulaye proceeded to analyze the current state of politics in France by discussing the various organs of government and how they could become more liberal; popular education, national representation, ministerial responsibility, the Senate, initiative in legislation, justice, and the freedom of the press all came under consideration. Popular education, necessary for the worker, the citizen, and the Christian, would, he argued, best be served by free public libraries and free public lectures. Many shared his advocacy of popular education; his views of the system of free public education controlled by local school boards in the United States owed much to the thought and career of Horace Mann.[101]

In discussing national representation he observed that in the Constitution of 1852 the two chambers did not have the right to initiate legislation, amend legislation, receive petitions, or question (interpellate) ministers, four rights he deemed essential for any representative body. For him, ministers should be responsible to the chambers and he said, "ministerial responsibility in all monarchies is an essential condition of liberty."[102] He advocated the choosing of ministers from members sitting in the chambers as in the British monarchy, which would be the best model for France to follow. The Constitution of 1852 did not establish ministerial responsibility in fact although it appeared to do so in principle. "In France," he said, "we have scorned the wisdom of our neighbors."[103]

In considering the Senate he hoped that it would become like a chamber of peers rather than the appointive body it was, intended to contain the most talented minds in France; the desideratum would be when "the legislative power is exercised collectively by the Emperor, the Senate, and the Corps Législatif." Laboulaye would not approve of the imperial constitution until it was revised in 1870 and this only after many significant liberal concessions had been made by Napoleon III between 1860 and 1870.[104] He also advocated that the right of initiating legislation be shared by the Emperor, the Senate, and the Corps Législatif.[105] In a lengthy analysis he also reiterated his view that an impartial system of justice and an independent and sovereign magistracy were essential components of liberty.

Finally, he considered freedom of the press. The press was the forum of modern peoples since the morning newspaper was read each morning by millions who after this daily ritual often had the same opinions and the same thoughts. He stated that, "If one suppressed the press, it would at the same time suppress liberty."[106] Indeed, for him, the press was another guarantor of liberty, but the first guarantor of justice was publicity, which would only come from the freedom of the press.[107] "Not only is freedom of the press the guarantor of all individual and social liberties but it is also the guarantor of public liberty."[108] Universal suffrage means nothing without freedom of the press, both the chambers and the judiciary need a free press. He noted that criticism of the judiciary by the press was not accepted easily in France as the judiciary claimed it was above criticism, a claim that Laboulaye denied. For Laboulaye, criticism of any organ of government was proper and a guardian of liberty; and he evoked Tocqueville's description of freedom of the press in the United States to bolster his claim.[109] He advocated putting an end to all censorship in any form in France, all permits for printers (which he claimed were only a disguised form of censorship), official warnings, tax stamps, and suppressions and fines; and he advocated tolerant or reduced postal laws for the press.[110] Laboulaye noted that the government favored those publications devoted to literature and science but that it raised taxes and otherwise tried to harrass those devoted to politics.[111] All of these restrictions on freedom of the press were part and parcel of the press laws in France until 1867 when certain liberal reforms were granted by the Emperor. He concluded his analysis by pointing out that the "press is not only a weapon of the opposition but also a powerful force in education, progress, and government,"[112] and he added, "The press is the keystone of true liberalism."[113] And he drew here again comparisons with Britain, the United States, Holland, Belgium, and Switzerland. In reviewing *Le Parti libéral* the distinguished Orientalist, Silvestre de Sacy, wrote in rather discordant terms, "pour mon compte, je le déclare, je n'ai pas le moindre envie d'échanger ma qualité de Français contre celle d'Amérique ou de Hollandais" [For my part, I here declare, I have not the least desire to exchange my identity as a Frenchman for that of an American or a Dutchman].[114]

During the first half of the decade of the 1860s, Laboulaye pursued his vision of liberalism in books, in numerous articles in the *Journal des Débats* and other journals, in numerous public lectures, and from his lecturn at the Collège de France. He developed close ties with other liberals in France such as Augustin Cochin, Agénor de Gasparin, Charles de Rémusat, Prévost-Paradol, Jules Simon, Henri Martin, to name but a few; most of them also wrote pamphlets, articles, and books on the liberties Laboulaye espoused. But it was his influence especially that became paramount in the 1860s, an influence disseminated through prolific writings and his popularity as a professor and public lecturer. It was at this crucial time in his intellectual development that he began an extensive correspondence with influential Americans, many of whom became his friends.

3

Laboulaye, the Americanist

Nommé professeur, mon devoir était écrit. C'était de faire connaître l'Amérique à la France.

[Once named professor, my duty was clear. It was to make America
known to France.]

—Édouard Laboulaye

Laboulaye's writings on America fall into three groups each of which
provides a distinct access to his interpretation of America: the *Histoire
des États-Unis,* the lectures and articles on American life and history,
and the writings on the Civil War. His scholarly activity for almost
two decades was devoted to America; the major theme was that the
United States furnished France the best example of a people who
enjoyed liberty, both political and religious. He earnestly desired that
the France of his day reflect on America and draw on the American
experience to reform its own political institutions. Edmond Scherer,
a pupil of Laboulaye, wrote that "L'Américanisme était devenu une
espèce de tic intellectuel chez Laboulaye" [Americanism became a sort
of intellectual tic for Laboulaye].[1]

Although Laboulaye was the Second Empire's chief Americanist,
his views on American society and customs were often naive, largely
because he never visited the United States. He was, however, invited
to do so on numerous occasions; John Amory Lowell invited him to
lecture at the Lowell Institute in Boston; Henry Villard, of the American Social Science Association (Laboulaye was a corresponding member), invited him to do a lecture tour under the auspices of the
association; the presidents of two new universities, Daniel Coit Gilman of Johns Hopkins and Andrew D. White of Cornell, also invited
him to lecture at their institutions; and Francis Lieber repeatedly offered to arrange a lecture tour. Laboulaye declined all invitations
claiming that his health would not stand the trip.[2] During the later

decades of his life he was held in such high esteem by Americans that American intellectuals, politicians, grandes dames, and diplomats visiting Paris tried to attend his lectures or visit him at his home.

Histoire des États-Unis

Laboulaye's masterpiece, the *Histoire des États-Unis*, assumes considerable importance when one realizes that it was originally a course of lectures at the Collége de France, in fact, the first course on American history offered in a French institution of higher education. In the first half of the nineteenth century American history was not taught in French schools because until 1848 the chronological limit for all historical instruction ended in 1789. In 1848 the limit was extended but only to 1814. American history, therefore, was absent from the curriculum of French schools not because of prejudice but because of its modernity. Laboulaye inaugurated his pioneer course in American history in December 1849.[3] Although French public opinion was aware of America, it was thanks exclusively to the Marquis de Lafayette who, after his reappearance in French political life in 1830, made American history an integral part of French political life.[4] Apparently, Laboulaye was urged to study America by his professor at the Sorbonne, Victor Cousin, an eclectic philosopher and for a brief time in 1840 a minister of education under Louis Philippe. Similarly, Tocqueville's work, also on America, created an interest in American institutions, customs, and history during the generation of the July Monarchy. The historian and statesman of the July Monarchy, François Guizot, also added to the interest in America when he published an essay on the life of Washington in 1839 that introduced the French edition of Jared Spark's collection of Washington's correspondence.[5]

The dramatic increase of interest in America in the 1850s, which resulted in the publication of more books on the subject in that decade than in the preceding thirty-five years, can be partially accounted for by France's unsuccessful experiment with a republican system of government with a president (1848–51) that was roughly modeled on the American Constitution. This interest was also fostered by the American Compromise of 1850, a series of congressional acts designed to deal with slavery in Texas, California, and New Mexico as well as to legislate on the return of fugitive slaves. This compromise signaled that slavery was a major issue and one that might cause a split in the Union. After 1850 slavery came to overshadow all other political issues in America for the French; preoccupation with slavery was heightened by the publication of *Uncle Tom's Cabin (La Case de l'on-*

cle Tom) in 1852. In fact, in the 1850s the French reading public became acquainted with two new American authors, Harriet Beecher Stowe and Edgar Allan Poe. Stowe's book enjoyed an immense success in France and established its author's reputation; it also aroused sympathy in France for the blacks. The French reading public had now found a new American author to replace the ever-popular James Fenimore Cooper who died in 1850. In 1852 Charles Baudelaire published his translation of Edgar Allan Poe's works in the *Revue de Paris,* and Poe's works as well as Stowe's excited the French reading public.

Several other factors sparked French interest in America: the California Gold Rush, the possibility of secession, and the beginnings of America's major industrial development. These factors, combined with both the speed and relative safety of transatlantic travel and the publication of numerous books and pamphlets that informed the French public on contemporary America, created a context for Laboulaye's lectures on American history at the Collège de France that were eventually published as his *Histoire des États-Unis.*[6]

Laboulaye published the first volume of his *Histoire* in 1855 and it comprised lectures he gave in 1849 and 1850. In it he traced the founding of the thirteen colonies down to the middle of the eighteenth century. The second volume, published in 1866, began with what he considered the origins of the Revolution and concluded with the Peace of Paris in 1783. The final volume, also published in 1866, contained a detailed analysis of the Articles of Confederation, essays on individual founding fathers, and concluded with the ratification of the Constitution. The final two volumes were a published version of the lectures between 1862 and 1864.[7]

Laboulaye's introductory lecture, entitled, "De la constitution américaine et de l'utilité de son étude," was delivered in December 1849.[8] He did not continue immediately with lectures on American history but, instead, remaining true to the historical school, he prefaced his study of America with a series of seven lectures on the theory of law, which he gave in the spring of 1850; the lectures proper on American history began in the fall of 1850. In preparing these lectures Laboulaye was aided by Robert Walsh, the United States consul-general in Paris from 1844 to 1851 who resided in Paris until his death in 1859. Walsh, who was also a well-known journalist and bibliophile, opened his extensive library on American history to Laboulaye and supplied him with numerous books including works on American history, religion, and social institutions by such authors as George Bancroft, Edward Everett, William Ellery Channing, Richard Hildreth, and Joseph Tuckerman.[9] In the Preface to the first volume Laboulaye took special care to acknowledge his great indebtedness to

George Bancroft[10] and at this time he also began a correspondance with Bancroft that lasted until the Franco-Prussian War in 1870.[11]

In his introductory lecture Laboulaye stated clearly his procedure for studying American history as well as his view of France and America:

> Ainsi, importance historique et scientifique, utilité prochaine, telles sont les deux principales raisons d'étudier la constitution américaine sérieuse-ment, en détail, pour en apprécier le véritable caractère, pour en pénétrer l'esprit, et ne pas dans un intérêt purement spéculatif, mais pour en tirer une instruction efficace, une règle de conduite, un profit immédiat et certain.

> [Thus, historical and scientific importance, immediate usefulness, such are the two principal reasons for seriously studying the American Constitu-tion, in detail, so as to penetrate its true character, to appreciate its spirit not only for purely speculative purposes, but in order to draw from it useful lessons, a rule of conduct, an immediate and certain benefit].[12]

He argued that Americans forged a lasting government because they were practical men, not theoreticians. Laboulaye repudiated theoreti-cians and stigmatized them as "la plus dangereuse espèce d'hommes d'État" [the most dangerous species of statesmen].[13] Frenchmen, he noted, were prone to become theoreticians, especially when they drew up constitutions and law codes. The Americans, he countered, were men of experience, and they evolved a workable constitution that safeguarded their liberties. Laboulaye did not wish his countrymen to copy the American Constitution uncritically, but to extract what he called "the spirit" of the Constitution. He told his listeners it was important to distinguish "ce qui est de l'essence du gouvernment libre de ce qui est purement américain; en deux mots, ne copions pas la Constitution des États-Unis, mais profitons des leçons qu'elle ren-ferme, et, tout en restant Français, ne rougissons pas de suivre les exemples et d'écouter les conseils qu'a laissés un Washington" [what is of the essence of a free government from what is purely American; in a word, let us not copy the Constitution of the United States, but let us profit from the lessons it contains, and, while remaining French, let us not be embarrassed to follow the example or listen to the advice given by a Washington].[14]

America, he argued, did not demand of a constitution what it could not give, whereas France was continually demanding the impossible from her constitutions. Laboulaye never ceased to remind his listeners that since 1789 America had had but one constitution, while France had had fourteen. Also, the Americans had only undergone one revolution (he was speaking in 1849), while the French had experienced ten. Laboulaye's major aim as a scholar was to aid his countrymen in establishing a stable and liberal constitution. He deplored the Consti-tution of 1848 whose framers had disdained the American experience by having a unicameral legislature and an executive who combined some of the prerogatives of a constitutional monarch with those of the chief executive of a republic. Laboulaye told his students his plan and aim for lectures on American history: "en étudiant la Constitution des États-Unis, nous ferons un cours comparé de politique constitu-tionnelle, nous aborderons franchement ces problèmes, qui renferment notre avenir et devant lesquels un citoyen ne peut rester indifférent" [in studying the Constitution of the United States, we will take a course in comparative constitutional politics, we will openly confront its (the United States Constitution's) problems, in which we can see our own future and to which a citizen cannot remain indifferent].[15] Thus he was examining the American Constitution with the view of arguing that some of its provisions would be useful in a future French constitution.

In tracing American history down to the Constitution, Laboulaye developed several leitmotifs that explained, for him, American history. He first examined the origin of liberty in America and he distinguished between liberty in the abstract and liberty in practice, and secondly, between religious and political liberty. For Laboulaye, the American concept of liberty originated in the Magna Carta. In this view he was faithful to the historical school in asserting that America was part of a long historical evolution. He said, "Les États-Unis sont un empire nouveau mais c'est un peuple ancien; c'est une nation européenne, dont la civilisation compte non par années, mais par siècles. Ce que nous nommons la jeunesse de la nation en est au contraire la virilité" [The United States is a new empire, but it is an ancient people; it is a European nation, whose civilization is counted not in years but in centuries. What we name the nation's youth, is on the contrary, its virility].[16] The American Revolution did not establish liberty for the colonists, since they already enjoyed it, but it did give them self-government. He wrote, "La cause véritable de la Révolution fut que le peuple américain, maître de ses destinées en fait, voulut l'être en droit" [The true course of the revolution was that the American people, master of its destiny in fact, wished to be so in law].[17]

A second leitmotif, and one that is a counterpart to the liberty motif which runs through Laboulaye's thought, is that religious ideas form the basis of society. For him, the faith of a people molded and determined its political institutions. He discussed religious liberty, and consistent with his liberal views, he considered it an essential counterpart to political liberty. America enjoyed both religious and political liberty and although she furnished Europe with an example of the ways in which the two liberties related, her tradition was Puritan and republican. The problem for Laboulaye was whether France, with her Catholic tradition, could ever enjoy these same liberties. He would resolve this problem a decade later in *Le parti libéral*. In part, America herself furnished the answer, for Laboulaye was amazed that Catholicism flourished in America and that it flourished in a republic rather than in a monarchy. He condemned the anti-republican attitude of most French Catholics, arguing that a republican government and Catholicism were not incompatible. On this point, Laboulaye was far in advance of his contemporary Catholics who were mostly monarchists and partisans of the political right. He strongly believed that in the future the Catholic church would have to make changes to come into harmony with the century, especially, as concerned the church's reliance on the state, often embodied in the concept of the so-called union of throne and altar. Laboulaye also deplored the church's support of conservative governments. One of his contemporaries, Al-kan Ainé and the author of a brief biography, described Laboulaye as "un chrétien sincère et ferme dans la foi de ses pères" [a sincere Christian, steadfast in the faith of his fathers].[18]

Laboulaye saw in Puritanism the origins of democracy. For him, the first document of American history was the Mayflower Compact of the Puritans, which had established an absolute equality among the pilgrims. A precondition for democracy was political liberty and political liberty had begun in America with the Puritans, who had inherited and transmitted to America the traditions of English liberty that had begun with Magna Carta.[19] The Puritans had also established self-government in the form of the New England town meeting, which contained "qualité admirable qui contient à la fois l'esprit d'ordre et l'esprit de liberté, l'indépendance et le respect" [an admirable quality that contains at the same time the spirit of order and the spirit of liberty, independence and respect].[20]

Although the New England town meeting had been important in developing American institutions, Laboulaye considered the Carolinas of almost equal importance because of their lawgiver, John Locke.[21] In discussing the Carolinas, Laboulaye was early drawn into a discussion of what he considered the one odious institution in America that was the antithesis of liberty, slavery. His views on slavery were strongly influenced by William Ellery Channing, and he urged his students to read Channing's work on slavery, which Laboulaye personally translated into French in 1855.[22] From this time onward Laboulaye became active in anti-slavery movements, to which he devoted much of his time in the 1860s. Laboulaye concluded the first volume of his *Histoire* with a general discussion of colonial America.

Laboulaye sent a copy of the first volume of his *Histoire* to Edward Everett, an American statesman, who had been senator and secretary of state. Everett wrote Laboulaye:

> I have read it with profit and satisfaction. It is, at all times, a source of pleasure to Americans to find the history of their country well understood and candidly developed by foreigners; who have not always had recourse to good authorities, nor treated the theme with impartiality. I anticipate from the continuance of your History still greater gratification, as you will descend to a period more intimately connected, in its characters and interests, with the times in which we live.[23]

Unfortunately for Everett, Laboulaye stopped with the signing of the Constitution and did not include "the times in which we live" in his *Histoire*.

Laboulaye's study of American history was interrupted by the French political climate of the 1850s. After the coup d'état of December 1851 and the proclamation of the Empire a year later, France entered into a period of political repression that characterized the first decade of the Second Empire. The political climate of the authoritarian empire only began to be relaxed with the granting of the first liberal reforms in 1860 by Emperor Napoleon III. Consequently, Laboulaye did not resume his lectures on American History until 1862. The series of lectures delivered between 1862 and 1864 forms the last two volumes of his *Histoire*. These lectures earned him added distinction as they were given during the American Civil War and were extremely popular. Also, between the 1860s and the 1880s, according to Christophe Charle, the reputation of the Collège de France reached one of the peaks in its history, and he cited approvingly Ernest Renan's comment, "il a compté en son sein les chefs du mouvement intellectuel," [it counted in its bosom the chief figures in the intellectual movement].[24]

In the last two volumes of his *Histoire* Laboulaye returned to leitmotifs established in the first volume. His lectures on the American Revolution are not a detailed chronological history but are concentrated rather on the political and diplomatic events leading to the Revolution. The main events of the Revolution are merely sketched; there are five lectures on events up to 1778 and only two on events after 1778. George Washington captivated Laboulaye's imagination; he described America's first chief executive as one who "ressemble aux héros de la Grèce et de Rome par sa parfaite intelligence de la liberté, c'est le premier homme des temps modernes. Il a compris que la liberté était la loi de l'avenir" [resembles the heroes of Greece and Rome; in his perfect understanding of liberty, he is the first man of modern times. He understood that liberty was the law of the future]. In ana-lyzing the work of Washington, Franklin, Hamilton, and the other Founding Fathers he said, "Ce n'est pas seulement à l'Amérique, c'est au monde qu'ils ont donné la liberté" [They gave liberty not only to America but to the world].[25]

His final lectures began with an analysis of the Articles of Confeder-ation and the reasons for their failure, and he continued with a series of biographical sketches of the Founding Fathers—Alexander Hamil-ton, James Madison, Edmund Randolph, James Wilson, and Gouver-neur Morris.

Laboulaye concluded his masterpiece with an analysis of the Consti-tution. In this analysis, Laboulaye drew heavily from eighteenth-cen-tury writers and statesmen such as Montesquieu, Rousseau, Turgot, Louis XVI, and Napoleon. He was especially interested in Montes-quieu, whose views on the separation of powers and the restraints on authority greatly interested him. In fact, one of Laboulaye's last major scholarly projects was to edit a seven-volume edition of Montesquieu's works.[26] In his analysis of the Constitution he stated, echoing Montes-quieu, "Partout on proclame que la première condition de la liberté, c'est que le pouvoir exécutif, le pouvoir législatif, et le pouvoir judi-ciaire soient séparés" [Everywhere one proclaims that the first condi-tion of liberty is that the executive power, the legislative power, and the judicial power be separated]. He continued by saying that if this rule is not followed "suivant l'expression de Montesquieu, tout est perdu" [following the expression of Montesquieu, all is lost].[27]

In writing his analysis of the Constitution, Laboulaye frequently cited the works of William Alexander Duer, Judge Joseph Story, James Kent, George Tricknor Curtis, James A. Bayard, and Furman Shep-pard on the American Constitution.[28] The one source on the Ameri-can Constitution that Laboulaye had surely read was the analysis of the American Constitution in Tocqueville's *Democracy in America,* but in his *Histoire* Laboulaye made no mention of Tocqueville.

Laboulaye lectured twice a week. Once on American history and his other series of lectures alternated between a course on France in the eighteenth century and one on the French Revolution. Preparation for this series of lectures that was published in the *Revue des cours littéraires de la France et de l'étranger*[29] made Laboulaye familiar with events, ideas, and personalities in France that were contemporaneous with the American Revolution and the Constitutional Convention. Also, Laboulaye first discussed the similarities and dissimilarities between the two revolutions in a lecture he gave at the Collège de France on 8 December 1850 opening his course on comparative legislation, it was entitled, "L'Amérique et le Révolution Française."[30] Surely, he was one of the first, if not the first, to see the Atlantic character of the Revolution or, to say the least, the interconnection between France and America during the revolutionary epoch. He proudly pointed out, for example, that Washington's library included a carefully marked copy of Montesquieu.[31]

During the academic year, 1863–64, Laboulaye lectured on the Constitution of the United States. Here more than anywhere else he influenced a generation of students at the Collège de France where the halls were always filled for his lectures. The *Revue Nationale* commented, "Every Monday, a great number of persons, who come to hear M. Laboulaye, find themselves unable to enter as the lecture hall is already filled."[32] In the course of treating various aspects of the United States Constitution, Laboulaye would draw comparisons to the political situation in France of the Second Empire. For example, in his lecture on *le droit électoral* (electoral law) he cited John Stuart Mill approvingly for his advocacy of women's suffrage and he pointed out that it did not not exist in the American, English, or French Constitutions.[33] To buttress his case for his French audience, he even noted that Condorcet advocated the political equality of women. In 1843, Laboulaye himself had published a work on the history of women, which he intended to revise.[34] It was these remarks, usually made in the course of an analysis of one aspect or another of the American Constitution, that won the respect of what his contemporaries in the United States termed the "women's movement." Susan B. Anthony described Laboulaye as "the friend of the United States and of the women's movement."[35] Laboulaye regularly lectured to women. He wrote, "I lecture to ladies and young women and I take for my subject the history of women. I hope that these lectures will result in an interesting and inquiring book, but it will not be written this year."[36] Alkan Aîné remarked admiringly that "Ses cours eurent le plus grand succès et furent constamment suivis par un public d'élite, et nous y vîmes même des femmes prendre des notes." [His courses enjoyed a very great success and were attended regularly by an educated public, and one even saw women taking notes].[37]

In discussing *le droit électoral*, Laboulaye pointed out that in the French Constitution the representation in the lower house, the Corps Législatif, failed to reflect the political beliefs of French society. In the course of his lectures he made frequent reference to the elections of 1863 citing the example of Adolphe Thiers (Laboulaye had withdrawn in favor of Thiers's candidacy). Laboulaye became an early advocate of proportional representation when he argued that, if the liberals of what he termed the *école constitutionnelle* are 20 percent of the people they ought to have 20 percent of the seats in the chamber. He pro-ceeded to make an all-out attack on the electoral system then in prac-tice in France and asserted that it was the tyranny of a majority over a minority. He found the system of official candidates and governmental pressure in support of these candidates intolerable. No doubt he was influenced by the results of the off-year election of 1864 in Paris when he stood for election and received only 914 votes out of 15,000 cast. For him, this tyranny of the majority was particularly odious because the minority was not properly represented in the chambers. For exam-ple, in the period between 1857 and 1863 there were only five opposi-tion deputies in the chamber and they were all republicans. Even after the elections of 1863 there were only thirty-four opposition deputies and this in a chamber of 283 seats. To buttress his arguments he cited the English Reform Bill of 1832, which extended suffrage to the Brit-ish middle class, as being more representative and more liberal than the current French system of universal suffrage.

In short, Laboulaye used his lectures on the United States Constitu-tion to criticize Second Empire France, no doubt moving his students to political opposition. Also, his students were certainly aware that Laboulaye, himself, stood briefly for an opposition seat in the 1863 elections; he stepped aside in favor of Adolphe Thiers. He also ran unsuccessfully as an opposition candidate in Paris in a by-election in 1864, in Strasbourg in 1866, and in the Seine-et-Oise in 1869. His repeated candidacies certainly betokened a keen interest in contempo-rary politics but as one writer said, "He was too liberal for some, too moderate for others."[38] Laboulaye was fortunate in that the heavy censorship of the régime did not fall on his work as it did on Étienne Vacherot's book, *La Démocratie*, published in 1860, which drew a three-month jail sentence for its author who advocated democracy for France.[39]

Laboulaye's analysis of the American Constitution differs markedly from Tocqueville's *Democracy in America*, written some twenty-five years earlier. Where Tocqueville closely analyzes the text of the Con-stitution, Laboulaye tends to write a series of essays on various aspects of the Constitution; his concluding remarks, however, are cast in the model of an *explication de texte* of the provisions of the Constitution. Consistent with his general view of American history, he described the Constitution as the capstone of the long historical development that granted religious and political liberty to Americans. It expressed his own most cherished dream to write, "We understand that liberty is the law of his [man's] nature, that he is not permitted to renounce

it . . . despotism cannot give him happiness; man is, so to speak, condemned by God himself to be happy."[40]

In his concluding remarks, Laboulaye told the French that he did
not want them to copy the American Constitution or, for that matter,
the English Constitution exactly, since it would be unwise to introduce American or English customs into France. Instead he told his
students and readers:

> It is the spirit which must be seized. Once that spirit is yours, you will
> find the forms which will adopt it naturally. Must one be American or
> English to practice religious freedom, freedom of the press, individual free-
> dom? No, all of these liberties can be guaranteed by very simple institu-
> tions of which we already possess the germs, and which our fathers left
> us.[41]

Laboulaye thus ended his lengthy discussion of American history
and his words echoed a sympathetic understanding and love of
America. His message had been heard and was to be read by countless
Frenchmen, inspiring them to form an image of America as a land of
liberty and equality. The reader must keep in mind that Laboulaye's
views on American history must always be interpreted in the light of
his role as a member of the liberal opposition to Napoleon III.

Paris in America

Laboulaye's most widely read writing on America, judging from
publication statistics, was *Paris in America,* a fictional account of a
voyage to Paris, a community somewhere in New England. Laboulaye
published this work in 1863 under the pseudonym of Dr. René Lefebvre, the middle parts of his real name, the part of his name that he
never used. In this fictional account Dr. René Lefebvre received from
a spirit a pill that transported him to America; a fantasy trip that he
was never to be able to make in reality. The opium pill supposedly
enabled Dr. Lefebvre to know America well before he arrived in
New England. In this dream American customs were revealed to him;
everything surrounding the doctor had become American; his family,
a Yankee family of Methodists, his servant, a negro. He himself, under
a new name, finds himself successively in all the positions of American
life, retaining only his Parisian prejudices.[42] All changes when he
awakens. He has become an American in the midst of his family, who
are astonished at his madness. Eventually the doctor comes to realize
that he is in a utopia where the citizen has nothing to fear from its

laws. The church has gained its evangelical spirit and the Gospel has become the charter of liberty. Education opens all hearts to truth. The press is free and everyone can say what they think and think what they say. The state is a blessing. Such is the fictional account of Paris that exists somewhere in New England!

The work enjoyed an immense success, going through thirty-four French editions and eight English ones. Secretary of State Seward wrote to James Bigelow, American consul-general in Paris, that he was "infinitely pleased with its humor as well as its spirit."[43] Bigelow remarked in his eulogy on Laboulaye, given before the Union League Club of New York, that *Paris in America* "betrayed about as much ignorance as knowledge of social life in the United States," but that "of all the publications emanating from European sources during our war, none had more effect than this, in weakening the prejudice against the 'yankee,' which prevailed among what it was the fashion to call 'the better classes of Europe.'"[44] Edward Everett wrote Laboulaye after having read the book and declared, "No foreigner describes American topics, with superior *connaissance de cause*, very few with equal intelligence of the subject. . . . Your *Paris en Amérique* discloses an astonishing familiarity with the state of things in this country. . . . We feel that we have no more enlightened friend in Europe than yourself."[45] In a letter to Francis Lieber, Laboulaye expressed his appreciation for the English translation of what he termed his "extravaganza."[46] Lieber wrote Laboulaye that the work had "almost drawn tears of laughter from me."[47]

Laboulaye was immensely satisfied with his work as it brought him fame. He remarked:

> I have had only true popularity since last year. *Paris in America* which today has sold over 12,000 copies and whose success has done more for my name than twenty-five years of serious study. Today I am *popular*, artisans read my books in a loud voice at their working places, and it is not impossible that *Paris in America* soon will make me a deputy from Paris. What causes me to rejoice in this success, is that America profits more than I do. It is today the ideal of all of our good workers. Give us time and we will become a democracy.

He commented further, "Youth crowds into my courses and *Paris in America* is selling more copies every day, I have today in France and elsewhere a school much more numerous than I would have commonly thought."[48]

The *New York Tribune* summed up an American view of *Paris in America* when it wrote, Laboulaye's "*Paris in America*, a peculiar and fantastical, but most successive and instructive work, a French philosopher's dream, of Yankee land, is one of the most original and entertaining books of our day."[49] The *Revue des Cours* made the extravagant statement that "If anything, *Paris en Amérique* would be superior rather than inferior to the *Lettres Persanes.*"[50] Courcelle-Seneuil in the *Journal des Économistes* declared, "Under the guise of this odd title and under the cover of a common pseudonym, a man of great wit, talent and knowledge has just published one of the most amusing books of our time."[51]

An American Trinity: Channing, Franklin, and Mann

Three Americans of different backgrounds exercised a profound influence on Laboulaye in the decades of the 1850s and 1860s, namely, William Ellery Channing (1780–1842), Horace Mann (1796–1859), and Benjamin Franklin (1706–90). His views on slavery, education, religion, politics, and American life are directly traceable to the influence of these three Americans. Abundant evidence of their importance in Laboulaye's thought are the numerous essays, translations, books, and articles of Channing's and Franklin's works into French as well as several essays on Mann that he published over the years.

A major influence on Laboulaye's thought came from the savant and Unitarian minister, William Ellery Channing, whose writings, especially those on slavery, Laboulaye translated into French in the 1850s. James McKay of the Loyal National Society recounts in his preface to the English translation of *Separation: War Without End,* published in 1864, Laboulaye's discovery of Channing:

> Laboulaye was walking along the Quai Voltaire looking at the bookstalls. His eye caught the title of a book in English; [it was a volume of Channing's sermons] he took it up, opened it, read a few moments, demanded its price, paid it . . . and with his eyes still fixed upon its pages, resumed his walk towards the Champs Elysées. Arrived there, he seated himself . . . and continued to read on until the last page of his new acquisition was finished; and then, . . . instead of returning home, he went in a state of great excitement to M. Armand Bertin, at that time editor-in-chief of the *Journal des Débats,* and on meeting explained: "Congratulate me, I have to-day put my hand on a great man." And such was the enthusiasm with which he spoke of his new discovery, that M. Bertin begged him to make his great man at once known to France.[52]

Laboulaye shortly thereafter published an essay on Channing in the *Journal des Débats.*[53]

In 1854 Laboulaye published his translation of the social writings of William Ellery Channing, which was preceeded by a brief essay on Channing's life and doctrines.[54] A year later he published a transla-tion of Channing's works as well as his works on slavery, which he preceeded with a preface and his own study on "Slavery in the United States."[55] A brief sketch of Channing's life as well as an essay analyz-ing his writings was also contained in his work, *La Liberté religieuse.*[56] But to cite only these works on Channing, parts of which were trans-lations, would be to miss the importance of Channing in Laboulaye's thought. After 1854 he makes numerous references to Channing in almost all of his major works dealing with slavery, religion, or educa-tion. Edward Everett, a disciple of Channing, furnished him with information and sent him books as did the American consul-general, Robert Walsh. Walsh was sent a copy of *Oeuvres sociales de Channing* and wrote Laboulaye to thank him and told him that he had known Channing and his disciple, Joseph Tuckerman.[57] Tuckerman, the son of the leading Unitarian divine and friend of Channing, also provided Laboulaye with information about his father and Channing.

Slavery became a major preoccupation for Laboulaye. Like many of his fellow French liberals, he condemned slavery on moral and humanitarian grounds while often neglecting the economic and social factors that characterized slavery. His great interest in antislavery movements in the late 1850s and 1860s can also be viewed as one aspect of his liberal opposition to Napoleon III. Antislavery writings coming from France always had a double entendre since French lib-erals identified themselves as slaves under the authoritarian rule of the Second Empire: their demands for more and more liberal reforms can only be viewed in this context. Initially, Laboulaye, who advo-cated a gradual ending of slavery, differed from Channing who wished slavery abolished immediately, he wrote; "Channing is not clear enough in the means he proposes to guard against the dangers of a sudden emancipation; this is the only reproach I have for him, the only blemish I find on his work." Laboulaye, on the other hand, favored a gradual or progressive abolition of slaves and he said in 1862; "to demand immediate abolition, is to walk, in my opinion, into the abyss; one compromises the holiest of causes."[58] Slavery, according to Labou-laye, "is a poison that enervates the master; it has corrupted even re-ligion."[59]

Channing's ideas and views on education also attracted Laboulaye. Channing supported the idea that one of the keys to a good educa-tional system was the training of teachers. He enthusiastically sup-ported the initial efforts of Horace Mann in his reforms of the Massachusetts schools as well as his espousal of public education. Like Channing, Laboulaye placed great value on education as a preparation for citizenship and he warmly endorsed Channing's cry of "Liberty and Religion."

In the 1860s Laboulaye began lecturing to the public at various halls in Paris as well as in provincial cities; his book, *L'État et ses limites,* published in 1863, was first given as a series of popular lectures in the nature of what we would call today adult education. They were directed to workers, to the public at large, and often they were associated with a movement to establish public subscription libraries. Laboulaye developed into a talented *conférencier* and was in great demand. Many of his lectures were sponsored by the Société Franklin or the Société du Travail. The Société Franklin, founded in 1862 in memory of Benjamin Franklin, had as its aim the establishing of public subscription libraries. Franklin had founded a public subscription library in Philadelphia that later would be known as the Library Company of Philadelphia. Laboulaye gave the first public lecture sponsored by the Société Franklin on 27 April 1865 with a lecture entitled, "La Jeunesse de Franklin."[60] His lecture, which was also a genteel fundraising one, began:

> En tenant sa première séance publique, la Société Franklin a pensé qu'il était convenable et juste de rendre hommage à l'homme sous le nom duquel elle s'est placée, à Benjamin Franklin, premier inventeur, premier fondateur des bibliothèques de souscription. La Société m'a fait l'honneur de me choisir pour remplir cette mission; j'ai accepté sans fausse modestie et avec plaisir

> [In holding its first public meeting, the Société Franklin thought it suitable and right to pay homage to the man under whose name it was founded, to Benjamin Franklin, the first inventor, the first founder of subscription libraries. The Société has paid me the honor of choosing me to fulfill this mission. I accepted without false modesty and with pleasure.][61]

The home of the society was in Paris on the Rue Christine and eventually the former cabinet minister, Chasseloup-Laubat, became its president.

Laboulaye was fascinated by Franklin; and as with Channing he translated, edited, and annotated several volumes on Franklin. He introduced each of these volumes with a brief but helpful essay on Franklin for his French reading public. In 1865 he completed his editions of Franklin by publishing an edition of Franklin's *Autobiography.*[62] Although it was based on the American edition of 1840 edited by Jared Sparks, who had bowdlerized Franklin's work whenever he thought the original text was vulgar or in bad taste, Laboulaye also drew much material for his annotations from James Parton's *The Life and Times of Benjamin Franklin.*[63] Unfortunately, Laboulaye did not have access to the complete text of the *Autobiography,* which was not discovered until 1867 in Paris. Laboulaye was instrumental in discovering it and in arranging for its purchase by James Bigelow, who later published the complete text of the *Autobiography.*[64]

In 1869 Laboulaye published a French edition of Franklin's essays, which he entitled, *Essais de morale et d'économie politique.*[65] These selections, totaling seventy-eight texts on diverse subjects, were also based on Jared Spark's edition of Franklin's works and include his epitaph, his will, and an essay on swimming, all of which are intended to illustrate the religious, moral, economic, and political thought of Franklin as interpreted by Laboulaye. In his summation he said:

> En nous faisant aimer le travail, l'ordre, l'économie, en nous montrant le prix de la liberté et de l'égalité, Franklin nous réconcilie avec la vie, et nous apprend à nous trouver heureux ici-bas. Connaît-on beaucoup de philosophes qui aient rendu un plus grand service à l'humanité?

> [By making us love work, order, economy, by showing us the price of liberty and equality, Franklin reconciles us with life, and teaches us to be happy here below. Do we know many philosophers who have rendered a greater service to humanity?][66]

In 1872, Laboulaye published an abridgement of *Poor Richard's Almanach* along with several letters and notes.[67] Franklin's text was preceeded by Laboulaye's, "La Jeunesse de Franklin," which served as his introduction to this small volume published in the series, *Bibliothèque Franklin.* In the days after the Commune of 1871, the editors of the *Bibliothèque Franklin* wished to publish editions of classics for factory workers and peasants. The editions were designed to be cheap—they usually sold for three or four sous and were small enough to put in one's pocket. By lending his name to this publishing venture, Laboulaye once again demonstrated his concern for popular education of the workers as an integral part of his liberalism. One of Laboulaye's contemporaries, Alfred Sirven, described him as "the Franklin of our century," which was a fitting summation of Laboulaye's adulation of Franklin and appropriately encompassed the scope of Laboulaye's own varied interests.[68] Laboulaye ended his essay on Franklin by affirming his faith in education: "Voilà l'exemple qu'il nous faut suivre. Il faut réunir dans une sainte croisade; mais une double servitude à abolir en France, celle de l'ignorance et celle de la misère. Nous ne pouvons les combattre que par l'instruction" [Franklin is the example we must follow. We must unite in a holy crusade; we have a two fold servitude to abolish in France: that of ignorance and that of poverty. We can only combat them by education].[69]

Laboulaye's earliest formulation of his views on American educa-tion were in an article he published in October 1853 in the *Journal des Débats*. It was ostensibly a review of a two-volume edition of the *Orations and Speeches* of Edward Everett, however, it was an essay on education in America as seen by Laboulaye and based loosely on Everett but more substantially on Channing. It was also in this essay where he first mentioned and praised the work of Horace Mann.[70]

The Massachusetts educator, Horace Mann, would become a major influence in the formation of Laboulaye's views on education. Begin-ning in the 1860s, Mann often served as the subject of Laboulaye's popular lectures and was usually cited when Laboulaye discussed edu-cation.[71] Mann's views on and accomplishments in education were a source of endless wonder for Laboulaye as was his life, the life of a self-made man from New England. Mann, whose father died when he was thirteen, grew up in extreme poverty and had to struggle for his education but he was able to enter Brown University and to graduate within three years. After graduation he taught at Brown and then went to law school. A distinguished political career opened for him with election to the Massachusetts legislature. In 1837, Governor Edward Everett appointed Mann the first secretary of education of the Commonwealth of Massachusetts, a position he held until 1849. Mann was encouraged during the early stages of his work as secretary of education by William Ellery Channing who was very concerned with the training of teachers.[72]

In 1853, Mann toured Europe at his own expense to study educa-tional systems and was particularly impressed by the German system. He was influenced on this trip to Germany by the former French minister of education, Victor Cousin, who had also traveled to the German States and wrote a report praising the educational system of Prussia.[73] When the young Charles Sumner was in Paris in 1836, he visited Cousin who "asked particularly about Mr. Mann."[74] Mann's report on his travels, according to Laboulaye, was "a masterpiece."[75]

Mann's solution to the problems of education was to build both elementary and secondary public schools. Laboulaye commented, "Établissez les écoles, et vous chasserez l'ignorance, la crime et la misère, vous diminuerez les haines et vous ferez la fortune et la gran-deur du pays par l'aisance, la moralité et le bonheur de chacun" [When you establish schools, you get rid of ignorance, crime, and poverty, you diminish hatred, and you make the fortune and the gran-deur of a country by the well-being, the morality, and the happiness of each].[76] For Mann, education should be available to all and he took special care to see that schools were properly constructed with adequate ventilation. Also, what particularly struck Laboulaye, was that each student was to have his own desk. Mann advocated coeducation, which was a major innovation in education. He was also suspicious of religious instruction in the schools and resisted the more zealous Protestant divines who envisioned the public school as a vehicle to propagate their conservative religious views. For Mann education was to be a pleasurable experience and was characterized by Laboulaye as, "le temps de l'école, c'est le bon temps" [school days, that's the good time].[77] It was to Mann, according to Laboulaye, that Americans owed the system of normal schools to train teachers.

In his unstinting and uncritical praise for Mann, Laboulaye frequently got carried away to such an extent that the factual material becomes distorted. A few examples will suffice. After the death of John Quincy Adams in 1848, a former president and long-time member of the House of Representatives, Mann ran for his seat in the House and won. Laboulaye, inaccurately stated that he was elected to the Senate and sat alongside Daniel Webster, the distinguished senator from Massachusetts. A second example, in 1858 Mann was nominated to run for governor on the ticket of the Free Soil Party. He was defeated. Laboulaye has him winning the election but refusing the governorship so he could become president of Antioch College in Ohio.[78] Laboulaye was correct in reporting that Mann finished his days as president of Antioch College.

Although Laboulaye's publications on Mann were not as extensive as those on Channing and Franklin, he did include an essay on Mann in his *Discours populaires* published in 1869.[79] He also published a translation of Mann's *The Republic and the School* in 1873, which also contained an essay by Laboulaye on Mann's life. This work was published when Laboulaye was deeply involved in the reform of French higher education under the Third Republic.[80] Like Channing and Franklin, Laboulaye cited also Mann frequently in his writings and affirmed his ideas. The greatest test, however, of Laboulaye's work as the interpreter of American democracy and which drew forth his greatest energies was the American Civil War.

4

Defender of the North

On the high ground of moral progress and culture, the two ablest defenders of this country, in the time of its death-struggle with the domineering and barbarizing slave-power, have been the two Frenchmen, De Gasparin and Laboulaye.
—Anonymous, "Laboulaye on the United States of America"

The Setting

Abraham Lincoln's election to the presidency in 1861, replacing the pro-Southern Pennsylvanian, James Buchanan, marked a crucial turning point in America's passage towards the Civil War. After Lincoln's inauguration on 4 March 1861, it was only a few weeks until the attack on Fort Sumter in the harbor of Charleston, South Carolina, occurred on 12 April 1861 and signaled the formal start of hostilities. The mere fact of Lincoln's election in November 1860 had set off a sequence of events the first of which was the secession of the state of South Carolina when, as early as 20 December 1860 when it passed an ordinance dissolving "the Union now subsisting between South Carolina and the other States."[1] South Carolina's action was followed within six weeks by Mississippi on 9 January, Florida on 10 January, Alabama on 11 January, Georgia on 19 January, Louisiana on 16 January, and Texas on 1 February 1861. The other states that would make up the eleven states of the Confederacy—Virginia, Arkansas, North Carolina, and Tennessee—seceded after the fall of Fort Sumter, which surrendered on 14 April 1861. Henceforth, the objective of Lincoln's foreign policy and that of his new secretary of state, William H. Seward of New York, was to prevent the English and the French governments from recognizing the Confederacy or in any way giving diplomatic, economic, or other encouragement to the rebellion of the South. What concerns us here are the diplomatic policies of the French government.

73

Lincoln's election necessarily resulted in a change in United States representation abroad as the American representatives appointed by the Buchanan administration were usually Southerners and sympa- thetic to secession. John Bigelow wrote: "The diplomatic agents of the United States under the administration of President Buchanan, were mostly pronounced secessionists, and of those who were not, none, I believe were in sympathy with the new [Lincoln's] administra- tion."[2] In France, Charles James Faulkner, a Virginia lawyer and judge, resigned as minister and was replaced on 29 April 1861 by William Lewis Dayton, then serving as attorney-general of New Jer- sey. In 1856 Dayton had run unsuccessfully on the republican ticket as vice-presidential candidate with the presidential candidate, John C. Frémont. Lincoln had met Dayton on a train and was so impressed with him that he named him minister to France although Dayton knew no French.[3] Dayton arrived in Paris in May and formally pre- sented his credentials in an audience with the Emperor Napoleon III on 17 May 1861. He speedily assessed the situation and wrote to Secretary of State William Seward saying:

> If a gentleman accustomed to the use of the pen, and especially if he had some acquaintance with the leading men connected with the European press, could be sent over here in the possession, nominally, of a *good* consulate (the duties of which could be performed by clerks) while his attention could be readily directed to the press, it might be of great use in giving a right direction to public sentiment. It is a duty which a public Minister could not, *with propriety,* perform, if he would.[4]

Dayton's letter led Seward to approach a young journalist of talent and a former editor of the *New York Evening Post,* John Bigelow, to accept the post of consul-general in Paris.[5] It was Seward's plan that Bigelow would "devote himself more to Union public relations than to commercial affairs."[6] Dayton made no effort to learn French and had to rely upon an interpreter when dealing with French officials. On the other hand Bigelow, who had studied French, made a conscien- tious effort to become fluent in the language, which greatly assisted America's Paris mission. Seward also desired to strengthen the posi- tion of his diplomats in Paris by sending a high-level emissary to visit Napoleon III and his foreign minister, Édouard Thouvenel. Arch- bishop John Hughes of New York accepted this task but on the condi- tion that Thurlow Weed, a leading New York politician, accompany him in an unofficial capacity. Their mission was to attempt to sway the French government away from any act favoring the Confederacy and also to exercise pressure on French public opinion by encouraging those intellectuals, journalists, and writers who were favorable to the North. Also, Hughes would obviously have access to French prelates whom, it was hoped, would be influenced to support the North.

With the arrival of Dayton in Paris in May and Bigelow in September, America's new diplomatic representation was complete. As the third member of this mission, "the colored porter" (as Bigelow termed him) remained a holdover from previous missions. Considering the present-day size of the American diplomatic and consular mission in Paris, it is hard to believe that three people could carry on its functions in the 1860s. Matters of communication with Washington were hampered by the fifteen to twenty days it took to cross the Atlantic; consequently, news of the Trent Affair reached France in November at the same time as Archbishop Hughes and Weed arrived in Paris. The Trent Affair, an affair when a Union man-of-war stopped a British ship leaving Cuba and took off and arrested two Confederate agents, James M. Mason and John Slidell. This action was certainly a violation of neutral rights. Elements of public opinion in France, and especially England, were inflamed against the North. In Paris, Bigelow acted quickly and resolutely to calm matters by drafting a statement on the Affair that placed the blame on the Union ship's captain and exculpated the government of the United States. Thurlow Weed secured the signature of the most eminent American then visiting in Paris, retired General Winfield Scott, former general in chief of the United States Army and hero of the Mexican War, to a document drafted by Bigelow and which Bigelow succeeded in placing in the leading Paris dailies of 3 December 1861.[7] Bigelow scored a major diplomatic and propaganda victory with this statement exonerating the American government. Bigelow also gave ample evidence that he was well suited for his job as consul-general.

Laboulaye's Initial Response

Laboulaye's response to the great test of the Federal Union, the American Civil War, revealed his unmistakeable interest in America. He reacted immediately, and, as was usual with Laboulaye, his reaction was protracted and followed the contours of his biases. That he should side with the North, contrary to the official French governmental position, was predictable due to his commitment to liberty and his firm disapproval of slavery. To examine Laboulaye's ideas on the Civil War brings one to the center of the intellectual milieu opposing the Second Empire.

At a time when Napoleon III's government seriously considered recognizing the Confederacy, Laboulaye was devoted to the Union cause and viewed American constitutional government as one that had to be preserved for the sake of humanity. His lectures contained numerous references to the Civil War wherein his sympathy for the North was evident. Certainly, his students were conversant with his articles in the *Journal des Débats* and in other journals defending the North as the citadel of liberty and condemning the South as the protector of slavery. As Serge Gavronsky points out, "Laboulaye's authority as an expert on American affairs went uncontested after the death of Alexis de Tocqueville."[8] Mary L. Booth, the translator of many French works into English, termed Laboulaye "le plus américain de tous les Français" [the most American of all the French].[9]

The French attitude towards the Civil War was of crucial importance to the Union and the Confederacy. In the early years of the Civil War the government of Napoleon III, as well as the British government at the time, favored the Confederacy to the extent of giving serious consideration to recognizing it. There was, however, widespread sympathy for the North among intellectuals and some of the common people.[10] The attitude of the common people suffered some changes as the cotton famine began to develop and caused serious unemployment in the textile industries. Also, French export industries suffered greatly from the Union blockade of the South as well as from the decline in imports in the North because of the war effort. The silk export industry in Lyon suffered the greatest hardship as one-quarter of its foreign exports went to the United States. Also badly hurt by the disruption of shipping were the porcelain manufactures of Limoges, the glove makers of the Upper Marne, the lace makers in the Upper Loire, watchmakers from Besançon, velvet manufacturers from Amiens—even the exports of armagnac fell off dramatically! With distress in many export industries as well as the shortage of cotton for the mills of Rouen, Alsace, and the Nord, it is no exaggeration to state that the American Civil War had major consequences in France. It is not surprising, therefore, that certain segments of French public opinion favored recognition of the Confederacy, although it must be said that Napoleon III never made a public statement praising the South. He did, however, offer his good offices to mediate between the contending parties.

Through its administrators and the official press the government made certain that the Confederate cause achieved a hearing in France. On the other hand, the nongovernmental press gradually came to support the North due in large part to the writings of Count Agénor de Gasparin, Lucien Prévost-Paradol, Augustin Cochin, Henri Martin, Count Charles de Montalembert, Duvergier de Hauranne—to name only a few—who joined with Laboulaye to bring about a change in French governmental policy. But it was in the writings and public activities of Édouard Laboulaye where one heard the expression of the most powerful voice supporting the Union cause, a voice that spared no means to rouse French public opinion, as well as American, to support that cause. Andrew Dickson White, the future president of Cornell University, visited France in late 1863 and early 1864 and commented that Laboulaye's "lecture room was a center of good influences in favor of the American cause; in the midst of that frivolous Napoleonic France he seemed by far the 'noblest Roman of them all.'"[11]

Laboulaye's first major article on the Civil War, entitled "La guerre civile aux États-Unis," was ostensibly a review article of two books on America by Count Agénor de Gasparin and Xavier Eyma. This article was published in the *Journal des Débats* on 2–3 October 1861.[12] Count Agénor de Gasparin completed *Un grand peuple se relève* in March 1861 at the very time of the inauguration of President Lincoln. An American edition, translated in a week by Mary L. Booth,[13] was published in mid-June 1861 under the title, *The Uprising of a Great People, The United States in 1861*. De Gasparin, a devout Protestant, who had served in the Chamber of Deputies during the July Monarchy and the Second Republic, retired from politics during the Second Empire, spending much of his time in Switzerland and devoting himself to the campaign to abolish slavery in those parts of the world where it still existed such as Brazil, Cuba, Haiti, and the United States. In 1862 the second part of his *Un grand peuple* was translated into English, again by Mary L. Booth, under the title *America before Europe. Principles and Interests*.[14] Xavier Eyma's two-volume study, *La République américaine: ses institutions, ses hommes* was the second book under review that drew little attention from Laboulaye, although Eyma had traveled extensively in the United States and had written some eleven books on America.[15]

In "La guerre civile aux États-Unis," Laboulaye extravagantly praised de Gasparin for his pro-Northern sympathies while devoting only a few well-chosen sentences of praise to Eyma's book. Laboulaye then gave an extensive exposition of his own views of the Civil War. He asked, "What is at the heart of this fratricidal struggle? On this point, at least in Europe, everyone is in agreement. Everyone believes it is the execrable institution; however, after establishing this general cause they hasten to consider the interests of commerce and industry; then it is not of slavery that one speaks but of free trade and of cotton."[16]

To support his position Laboulaye quoted extensively from Senator

Charles Sumner of Massachusetts, his friend and correspondent, who addressed the United States Senate for four hours on 4 June 1860 on "The Barbarism of Slavery."[17] In this address Sumner stated: "the transcendent issue was between slavery and freedom; and whether settled in debate or civil war, it was not to be put aside by any considerations of fear or policy always, until the slave became a free-man, he insisted that this issue should be supreme and constantly present in the public mind."[18] The *Sermons* and *The Trial of Theodore Parker,* Parker was a disciple of Channing and a fervent abolitionist, also were used by Laboulaye. He cited approvingly Parker's work on behalf of fugitive slaves and applauded Parker's statement, "À Boston, je suis le ministre de tous les esclaves fugitives" [At Boston I am the minister of all the fugitive slaves].[19] Laboulaye made further references to the writings of the American economist, Henry C. Carey, a North-erner and Republican who held that there existed no real conflict of interests between different social classes. Carey wrote, "The interests of the capitalist and the laborer are . . . in perfect harmony with each other, as each derives advantage from every measure that tends to facilitate the growth of capital."[20] Laboulaye declared that "Carey's name was known to all of our economists."[21] Laboulaye had received Carey in Paris in 1856.[22]

For Laboulaye the best summation of the Northern position as well as its defense was a sermon preached by the Unitarian minister, Henry Whitney Bellows, on 21 April 1861. Bellows concluded a long perora-tion by putting forth the following argument: "L'Amérique est une nation, comme l'Angleterre, comme la France, comme la Russie; elle a sa vie, sa destinée, son orgueil, son caractère, son âme; elle les dé-fendra aussi longtemps qu'elle aura une once d'argent dans sa caisse, une goutte de sang dans les veines" [America is a nation, like England, like France, like Russia; she has her life, her destiny, her pride, her character, her soul; she will defend them as long as there is an ounce of silver in her coffers, a drop of blood in her veins].[23] Laboulaye summed up his view by writing: "To encourage the States of the South, to push ourselves into a premature recognition, to intervene in this struggle on the side of slavery, would be to deny our past. In America as everywhere else, France can only be allied to liberty."[24]

In "La Guerre Civile aux États-Unis," Laboulaye displayed his acute interest in America's problems and based his analysis on leading anti-slavery and pro-Northern writers. In fact, he displayed an in-depth knowledge of recent publications in the United States, an admirable understanding that reflected his training as a scholar. John Bigelow, who had only recently arrived in Paris, read Laboulaye's acticles with keen interest writing:

On last Sunday and Monday of September [actually 2–3 October 1861], and very shortly after I reached Paris, I read, in the *Journal des Débats,* two elaborate papers, written in a spirit of cordial sympathy with the North, and, what surprised me more, with a singularly correct appreciation of the matters at issue between the two antagonized sections of our Union: they were signed E. Laboulaye, de l'Institut.[25]

Laboulaye's articles on the Civil War brought him into a direct confrontation with Michel Chevalier. Chevalier, who sympathized with the South, had been the chief commentator on American affairs for the *Journal des Débats.* With the publication of Laboulaye's articles the *Débats* changed its editorial policy and thereafter remained unwavering in its support for the North. Laboulaye was responsible for this change in editorial policy. Henceforth, Chevalier confined himself to writing on economic affairs.[26]

Laboulaye published two articles on the Civil War, entitled, "Les États-Unis et la France," in the *Journal des Débats,* 26–27 August 1862. In these lengthy articles he clarified his views on the Civil War. He began by expressing his concern over the numerous individuals and newspapers in France supporting the South, he observed, "although the South has many friends in France, and slavery has found more favor than we would have imagined," but reassured his readers that "the North has gathered, however, a host of defenders who have not abandoned the old and glorious traditions of France."[27] In short, Laboulaye linked France's historic role as a defender of liberty with the Northern cause; the South, tied as it was to slavery, was unworthy of France's support. Senator Charles Sumner termed the pamphlet "a masterpiece," adding "Nothing better has been produced in Europe or America by the discussion of the war."[28]

Laboulaye's arguments centered on three propositions concerning the Civil War. First, slavery was the true cause of the Rebellion as the desire to perpetuate and propagate slavery became the cornerstone of a new public policy.[29] Second, the Southern states had no right to separate from the Union as to separate was to revolt. He said further that the South could not demonstrate, in justification of this extreme measure, that any of its rights had been violated or menaced. Third, the commercial interests of France demanded neutrality for ending a devastating and fratricidal war. The political interests of France required her to remain faithful to the grand traditions of Louis XVI and Napoleon. The unity of the United States—that is, of the only maritime power that could balance that of Great Britain—was for Europe the only guarantee of the freedom of the seas. In writing this treatise Laboulaye relied heavily on de Gasparin's *L'Amérique devant l'Eu* rope,[30] Senator Sumner's, *The Rebellion, Its Origins and Main Spring*,[31] and George Fisch's, *Les États-Unis en 1861*.[32] Also he drew extensively from his own previously published works on slavery and other American questions.

In arriving at his conclusions he traced American history step by step down to the outbreak of the Civil War from the Wilmot Proviso of 1847, the Compromise of 1850 and the Fugitive Slave Law that was passed as part of this Compromise, the Kansas-Nebraska Act of 1854, to the Morrill Tariff passed in 1861 in the last days of the Buchanan administration. Here again he exhibited a thorough knowledge of recent American history, no doubt a reflection of the excellent works sent to him by his American admirers as well as those books provided by the two American consuls-general, Thomas Walsh and John Bigelow. In the pamphlet version of this work, he added two notes, the first, on the foreign policy of Louis XVI and his foreign minister, Count Charles Gravier de Vergennes, towards the American colonies during the War of Independence, and the second, a note on Napoleon's attitude towards the United States at the time of the Louisiana Purchase in 1803. These notes were intended to buttress his arguments that France's historical role would be to aid the preservation of the Union.

Laboulaye stated his view of the conflict in "Les États-Unis et la France" so convincingly that the American consul-general in Paris, John Bigelow, wrote Laboulaye requesting his permission to reprint the articles at his own expense. He wrote to Laboulaye, "If I do not miscalculate their importance they will place Europe as well as the United States under permanent obligation to their author."[33] He also told Laboulaye that he would send a copy to each "member of the legislature of France, all the diplomatists and the principal journals of Europe and the prominent manufacturing centers of France."[34] Bigelow also wrote to Secretary of State William Seward, and informed him of Laboulaye's articles and described them as "most timely and effective."[35] An abridged version of the pamphlet was translated and published in the *Boston Daily Advertiser* on 15 and 18 October 1862, and this translation in abridged and unabridged versions was also printed in numerous American newspapers.

In "Les États-Unis et la France" Laboulaye praised France's historic role as the supporter of the United States, which began in 1778 with the signing of a treaty of alliance between the two nations during the American Revolution. He also cited Napoleon's statement at the time of the Louisiana Purchase:

Pour affranchir les peuples de la tyrannie commerciale de l'Angleterre, il faut la contre-poiser par une puissance maritime qui devienne un jour sa rivale: ce sont les États-Unis. Les Anglais aspirent à disposer de toutes les richesses du monde. Je serai utile à l'univers entier si je puis les empêcher de dominer l'Amérique comme ils dominent l'Asie

[To deliver the nations of the world from the commercial tyranny of England, she must be counterbalanced by a maritime power that one day may become her rival, and this power is the United States. The English aspire to dispose of all the riches of the world. I shall do a service to the whole world if I can prevent them from becoming the masters of America as they have become the masters of Asia].[36]

If France recognized the Confederacy, it would be violating a long-established historical precedent. In this respect, Laboulaye was also criticizing Napoleon III's sympathy for the South as a violation of the Napoleonic tradition, a tradition Napoleon III was always praising and using as a basis for his acts. Many Americans tended to explain Napoleon III's favoritism to the South as reflecting the bad treatment he received when visiting the United States in 1836–37. The Duc d'Aumale, the son of King Louis-Philippe, certainly not an unprejudiced observer, wrote to Cuvillier-Fleury on 15 January 1862, "Quelqu'un lui faisant, récemment, quelques observations courtoises sur la malveillance pour la grande République 'Ils m'ont mal reçu en 1836,' fut-il répondu sèchement. Violà les souvenirs qui influent aujourd'hui sur la destinée et la politique de la France" [Recently someone was making a few courteous observations about his [Napoleon III's] ill-will towards the great republic: "They received me poorly in 1836," he answered dryly. Here then are the memories that today influence the destiny, and the affairs of state of France].[37] Napoleon III never made a public statement praising the Confederacy but did on several occasions express admiration for the United States.

With Laboulaye, as with most other liberal writers, attacks against slavery must not be interpreted as being solely motivated by their Northern sympathies. Their criticism served a dual purpose: to attack Napoleon III's political system, which the political opposition often equated with "slavery," and to support the cause of liberty in the North. As Donaldson Jordan and Edwin J. Pratt remarked in *Europe and the American Civil War,* "so Laboulaye . . . in defending the Union, [was] attacking Napoleon III and Imperialism."[38] Also, in writing of American affairs the scissors of the censor were avoided where a too direct attack on French political practices could bring a host of problems for an editor running from official warnings, to fines, imprisonment, or suppression.

Slavery, however, occupied a central position in Laboulaye's view of the Civil War. He wrote, "there is one fact which dominates every-thing: that is slavery. The victory of the South means the perpetuation and extension of slavery along with all its miseries and all its infa-mies."[39] His article was timely as it was published at the moment when the imperial government was considering recognizing the Con-federacy. Some governmental officials seriously even argued for some form of French intervention. Laboulaye held that the Confederacy and the institution of slavery could only be saved by foreign interven-tion. He argued, "If England and France do not come to the aid of the South, the cause of slavery is lost."[40] He continued his argument against slavery by citing the writings of Channing and Parker to show that slavery was killing the Union. In a great oversimplification of the issues he told his readers, "All efforts of public opinion, in the South as in the North, had not had any other purpose than to prepare the triumph of a policy of liberty or the politics of slavery."[41] Slavery, according to Laboulaye, "was a poison which inebriated the master and it corrupted everything including religion."[42] In one of his sharper comments, he referred to the Southern churches and said, "In all the passages of the Bible they read a justification of slavery. It is not the crucified Lord they worship, it is slavery."[43] The American minister William L. Dayton wrote Laboulaye in the warmest words to thank him and also informed Laboulaye that he was sending copies to Presi-dent Lincoln and Secretary Seward. Laboulaye wrote to thank Dayton and also to acknowledge the thanks Dayton conveyed from Lincoln and Seward. Laboulaye informed Dayton "toutes mes sympathies sont pour l'Amérique, son peuple, et ses institutions" [all my sympathies are for America, its people and its institutions]."[44] In another letter he told Dayton that if there was anything his pen could do for America he was "tout à votre disposition" [entirely at your disposition].[45]

In November 1862, Laboulaye published in the *Revue Nationale* another article, "Pourquoi le Nord ne peut accepter la séparation," which was translated and reprinted in New York by the Loyal Publica-tion Society under the title: *Separation: War without End*. The histo-rian, Frank Freidel, considered this pamphlet "possibly the most brilliant paper to be published"[46] by the Loyal Publication Society, which published about a hundred pamphlets. In this pamphlet he addressed the entire legal question of secession or separation and, as was predictable, he found that the Confederate States had no right to secede. In this brief work his legal training as well as his expertise in American political institutions and history became evident once

more. Laboulaye continued his argument that the North was the innocent party in the Civil War. "We cannot repeat it too often: the North
is not the aggressor. It only defends, as every true citizen should, the
national compact, the integrity of the country. It is sad that it has
found so little support in Europe, and especially in France."[47] Writing
as he did in 1862, Laboulaye was not overly optimistic about the
outcome of the war, but he said the only recourse for a liberal was
"to sustain and encourage the North to the last—to condemn those
whose ambition threatens to destroy the most perfect and the most
patriotic work of humanity—to remain faithful to the end of the war,
and even after defeat, to those, who will have fought to the last
moment for RIGHT and LIBERTY."[48] Laboulaye also stressed the disastrous economic consequences that would fall upon Europe from the
intervention of any European country in the American Civil War.[49]
In a note added in July 1863 to a new French edition of the pamphlet,
Laboulaye was more optimistic about a Union victory as he had just
received news of the capture of Vicksburg.[50] He wrote, "ce n'est pas
à Richmond, c'est sur le Mississipi [sic] que se décidera le sort de
l'Union" [It is not at Richmond but on the Mississippi that the fate
of the Union will be decided]. He also added a brief but poignant
note for his American readers:

Qu'il me soit permi en finissant de remercier les américains de l'acceuil
fait à mes articles. Traduits et publiés dans une foule de journaux, portés
jusqu'aux sources du Mississipi [sic], répandus jusqu'au fond des solitudes
de l'Ouest, ils one été reçus partout comme la voix d'un ami, comme un
souvenir de la France, la première et la plus sûre amie de l'Amérique.
Puisse au moins cette voix trouver des échos dans le pays de La Fayette,
et prouver aux États-Unis que la France est toujours restée fidèle à l'Amérique et à la liberté. (Juillet 1863)

[Permit me in concluding to thank the Americans for their reception of
my articles. Translated and published in numerous newspapers, carried as
far as the source of the Mississippi, spread deep into the Western plains,
they were received everywhere as the voice of a friend. May that voice
at least find echoes in the country of Lafayette, and prove to the United
States that France has always remained faithful to America and to Liberty.
(July 1863)].[51]

One can only guess at Laboulaye's jubilation a few days after he
penned these words and heard of the Union victory at Gettsyburg on
1–3 July 1863, news of which reached France on 20 July 1863. Francis
Lieber wrote Laboulaye, "I hope the very decided victory we gained
last week over our enemy will bring some good fruits even to Europe,

and stay, if possible, the unfortunate desire of the Emperor [Napoleon III] to interfere as mediator in our complications. It can only lead to great suffering all around."[52]

For Laboulaye, the Civil War posed a moral problem, a political problem, and an economic problem for France. The moral problem was the most important for him as the simple truth was that the North was right and the South was wrong. Just as France could not support a government based upon slavery, in politics she could not abandon her old ally and friend of almost a century. The economic problem was more difficult because of the cotton shortage in France but here Laboulaye said the cotton shortage was a device of the South to force the European powers, especially France and Great Britain, to intervene in aid of the South.[53] Laboulaye tended to ignore the fact that French export industries were also seriously disrupted by the Civil War and this was possibly as great a factor as the cotton famine.

The Emancipation Issue

In the first two years of the Civil War, the French defenders of the North could draw little comfort from the military situation. News from the battlefronts in America largely consisted of Union defeats such as Bull Run (21 July 1861), the disastrous Peninsular Campaign of General McClellan in April and May 1862 that failed to take Richmond, the Second Battle of Bull Run (29–30 August 1862), and Fredericksburg (13 December 1862), to name only the most famous defeats. These could only be balanced against the Union victory at Pittsburg Landing/Shiloh of 6–7 April 1862, and the fall of New Orleans in May 1862.

The Battle of Antietam/Sharpsburg on 17 September 1862 (or Antietam as it is known in the North) was "a strategic Union success. . . . It frustrated Confederate hopes for British recognition and precipitated the Emancipation Proclamation. The slaughter at Sharpsburg [Antietam] therefore proved to have been one of the war's great turning points."[54] Since Laboulaye and other French liberals placed such great emphasis upon slavery as a cause of the rebellion, they welcomed and certainly desired that President Lincoln emancipate the slaves. Five days after the Battle of Antietam Lincoln told his cabinet "I think the time has come" to issue an Emancipation Proclamation.[55] On 23 September 1862 the famous Emancipation Proclamation was published and one of its key paragraphs, "that on the 1st day of January A. D., 1863, all persons held as slaves within any state or designated part of a State the people whereof shall then be in rebellion against the United States shall be then, thenceforward, and forever free."[56]

Many Frenchmen were bewildered by the proclamation as it did not free the slaves in the border states, who remained loyal to the Union, or in those areas occupied by Union troops but it only freed those slaves in States in rebellion and not occupied by Union troops. Many Frenchmen misunderstood the constitutional prerogatives of the American president. "Lincoln acted under his war powers to seize enemy resources; he had no constitutional power to act against slavery in areas loyal to the United States."[57]

News of the Emancipation Proclamation reached Paris on 5 October 1862 and was given prominent space in all of the Parisian papers. The initial Parisian reaction was most favorable.[58] Eventually, governmental papers became critical noting that where the Union troops were in control, slavery remained whereas in areas they did not control—and who knew if they ever would control them—slavery was abolished. This criticism ignored or misunderstood the constitutional issues involved. Laboulaye, however, understood the constitutional question and he defended and praised Lincoln's act, which he termed courageous. Some French liberals tended to condemn Lincoln's action as half-hearted for not freeing the slaves in states and parts of states controlled by the Union armies—here they clearly misunderstood the American Constitution.

The Loyal National League of New York, a society whose membership was for all practical purposes identical with that of the Loyal Publication Society, was made up largely of radical Republicans, Republicans to the left of Lincoln, who were strong in their views on the total abolition of slavery.[59] The president of the league, Francis Lieber, had emigrated from Germany thirty-five years earlier. Lieber, a distinguished legal scholar, corresponded with many European intellectuals and sought to secure their support for the Union cause. Thirty-seven letters from Lieber to Laboulaye exist as do twenty of Laboulaye's replies. Their correspondence began in 1863 and ended with Lieber's death. Lieber urged a more moderate approach to political matters and, above all, he urged the league to support Lincoln, especially in the forthcoming election in 1864. The league addressed an open letter to de Gasparin, Laboulaye, Henri Martin, and Augustin Cochin that was adopted at a mass meeting, known as the Sumter Meeting, in Union Square in New York City on 11 April 1863.[60]

The letter began by thanking all four for their messages and articles supporting the North. The league then addressed the question of slavery and said:

To destroy slavery, the acknowledged cause of the war, and at the same time to preserve intact the wise inhibitions of the constitution, according to the settled construction of that instrument, has been from the beginning a question of no little practical difficulty to the national administration. . . . The President's recent proclamation of emancipation is a proof; for while it by no means completes the work, even in idea, it is at last a great step in the right direction. Issued under his constitutional powers as commander-in-chief of the army and navy of the United States, and as a measure of war, its direct operation must of necessity be restricted to such districts of the country as still remain in unsubdued rebellion; but indirectly, and as a ground of *right* to freedom for the slaves, its scope is much wider and more important.[61]

The authors of the *Letter* went further and praised Laboulaye: "We are glad to perceive, from a quite recent letter of your great historian and publicist, a name honored equally by the enlightened men of this country as of yours, that this act of our Chief Magistrate is clearly understood and appreciated in France."[62] In a personal letter Lieber referred to the "noble zeal" of the four French savants.[63] In a letter to Francis Lieber Laboulaye expressed his gratitude:

J'ai reçu dans ma vie beaucoup de brevêts et de diplômes d'académies et d'universités, mais aucun témoignage d'estime pouvait m'être plus agréable et plus honorable que celui que la Ligue de l'Union a bien voulu m'adresser. Je le garderai pour la laisser à mes enfants, afin qu'ils sachent bien que si le premier article de foi d'un Français et d'aimer la France, le second est d'aimer l'Amérique

[I have received many diplomas and degrees from academies and universities in my life but no testimony of esteem pleases or honors me more than the one that the Union League has just addressed to me. I will keep it as a legacy for my children, so that they may know that the first article of faith for a Frenchman is to love France and the second is to love America].[64]

On 31 October de Gasparin, Laboulaye, Martin, and Cochin replied to the address of the Union National League. Their reply was delayed as they awaited de Gasparin's return from a trip to the Orient. Drafts were sent to him but the main text was written by Laboulaye and edited by Cochin with consultations by letter with de Gasparin, who had returned to Switzerland, and Martin, who was away from Paris.[65] From the private correspondence over this "Reply," it is obvious that the four took the matter most seriously and drafted it with all the care that one would devote to a major state paper. The fact that they took almost six months to draft a reply attests to the seriousness with which they viewed their task and also their desire for unanimity of views. Lieber told Laboulaye: "As to the *noble Réponse,* which you have sent to the Loyal National League, all who have read it feel, I may say, an almost enthusiastic delight. Thank you and your co-signers a thousand times." Lieber also informed him that an initial printing of ten thousand would be made of the English translation and also that three thousand copies would be printed in French.[66]

Their reply to the league's letter began with an assertion that they were not addressed as individuals but in reality the letter: "speaks to France, who cherishes, as a national tradition, the friendship of the United States. It speaks to European opinion, which will rise up and declare itself more clearly as it recognizes that the struggle is between Slavery and Liberty."[67]

The Loyal Publication Society obtained funds from the Union League Club of New York to send fifty copies of Frank Moore's *Rebellion Record* (of which only the first six volumes had been published in early 1864) and the first forty-four pamphlets published by the Loyal Publication Society.[68] The membership of the Loyal Publication Society and that of the Union League were practically identical.[69] These fifty sets were sent to monarchs, important libraries, organizations, editors, and pro-Northern leaders. Laboulaye, Cochin, Henri Martin, and de Gasparin were among the fifty to receive such sets. Certainly, this is a testimony to the esteem in which Laboulaye and his circle were held in the North; they were the only ones in France to receive them. Although Queen Victoria and the tsar of Russia were sent sets, none were sent to Napoleon III.

Laboulaye acknowledged receipt of this gift by writing:

> I have received the magnificent volumes of the "Rebellion Record" which some honorable citizens of New York have been pleased to send me. I do not know how to thank them for the especial honor which they have done me on this occasion. If I have been fortunate enough to defend the cause of the North, I have been a thousand times recompensed by the good wishes of your compatriots, and I can say that at the bottom of my heart I am one of you—a true American. It only remains for me to express the desire that the "Rebellion Record" will terminate soon by the triumph of a cause which is that of justice, of liberty, and of humanity.[70]

Union Victories: The Tide Turns

Until the twin victories of Vicksburg and Gettysburg in July 1863, there was always the possibility of French and English recognition of

the Confederacy. These victories in the Civil War gave every indication of an eventual Union victory as the Confederate States were
split into two parts as the Union forces held the Mississippi Valley.
Also, with the reopening of the Port of New Orleans and the Mississippi to transport, the North could return to somewhat normal conditions in those former areas of combat. The defeat at Gettysburg
marked a major military confrontation as well as a stunning defeat of
the Confederacy and ended once and for all the prospect of French
or English recognition or intervention.

Parisian newspapers devoted a considerable amount of space to the
draft riots in New York City that followed the news of the Battle of
Gettysburg on 11–17 July 1863. According to McPherson, it was "the
worst riot in American history."[71] Laboulaye told Lieber that this
stress on the riots was "exploitées dans nos journaux, par les partisans
du Sud" [exploited in our papers by the partisans of the South].[72]

A complicating issue in Franco-American relations had begun to
develop contemporaneously with the Civil War, namely, the French
intervention in Mexico. Originally, in 1861 this was a joint English-
Spanish-French expedition to force Mexico to pay the debts it owed
to these three nations. In 1862, however, the English and the Spanish
withdrew and left the French alone in Mexico. This touched off
Napoleon III's dreams of a great Latin Empire, "la grande pensée" of
the reign, a dream to poise as a counterbalance to the power of the
United States in the Carribean.[73] Eventually, a French expeditionary
force took Mexico City in June 1863 and Napoleon III offered the
Archduke Maximilian, the brother of Emperor Franz Joseph of Aus-
tria, the crown of the new Mexican Empire.[74]

The French intervention in Mexico added a new dimension to the
Civil War as the Confederate States looked favorably on Napoleon's
Mexican venture with the added hope that it would lead to French
recognition of the Confederacy. On the other hand, Lincoln and his
government were hostile to the French intervention and to Maximilian. The United States refused to recognize either Maximilian or the
French conquest of Mexico. Napoleon III, on his part, did not want
a head-on clash with the North. Until the Civil War ended with a
Union victory, the United States was powerless to intervene in Mexico. Laboulaye wrote Lieber that France was hurt by the Mexican
expedition but that the new parliamentary session in November would
raise difficult questions about it as the opposition now had some
thirty-odd seats.[75] It was, however, only a question of time until the
American Civil War was over and the Union would be in a position
to take positive action to force the withdrawal of the French troops

from Mexico. The Mexicans, themselves, however, would execute Maximilian in 1867.

The Mexican intervention, usually known in French history as the Mexican fiasco, caused serious concern to Laboulaye and his circle. They viewed the Mexican intervention as a hostile act to the North and an act favoring the Confederacy. Because of censorship public condemnations of Napoleon III's Mexican policy in the press were impossible; however, in private correspondence, in public lectures, and in the classroom, opposition could be expressed. Also after the elections of 1863 there was a small but vocal minority in the Corps Législatif that could and did speak freely since they enjoyed parliamentary immunity and these debates were published. Laboulaye received many letters from his friends and colleagues in America expressing their disapproval of the Mexican intervention. Lieber wrote Laboulaye that he and Senator Sumner disapproved of Napoleon III's Mexican policy. Laboulaye assured Lieber that the "l'impopularité de l'expédition du Mexique est pour l'Empereur une leçon difficile. Vous n'avez rien à craindre de notre côté" [The unpopularity of the Mexican expedition is a difficult lesson for the emperor. You have nothing to fear from our side][76]

Honors and Sadness

By 1864 Laboulaye had achieved eminence as an interpreter of America in France and in America. His lectures on American history at the Collège de France, which formed the last two volumes of his *Histoire des États-Unis,* were drawing to a close. He had only recently published *Paris in America,* which brought him fame, and also a volume of essays, *L'État et ses limites,* a statement of his liberalism in *Le Parti libéral,* and numerous pamphlets on the war as well as occasional public lectures. Edward Everett, himself a former senator and secretary of state, summed up the view of many when he wrote Laboulaye:

> We are all ever grateful to your for your unwearied efforts, in the cause of the Government of Loyal People of the United States. We feel that we have no more enlightened or influential friend in Europe than Yourself. We are satisfied that, if the Truth is gradually forcing its way, in reference to our great contest, in spite of the frauds and falsehoods, by which our misguided opponents seek to resist its progress in Europe, it is owing, in no small degree, to your strenuous exertions.[77]

Everett also informed Laboulaye that he had been elected unanimously an honorary member of the Massachusetts Historical Society. News of other honors reached Laboulaye as he was awarded an honorary doctorate from Harvard University on 20 July 1864; the Union League Club of New York ordered his portrait to be painted by Fragnani and hung in the club; the Union League Club of Philadelphia enthroned a bronze bust of Laboulaye in its lobby.[78]

Laboulaye's humanitarian interests became evident in the concern he had for the care of the wounded in battle, an interest shared by Francis Lieber. The activities of the United States Sanitary Commission, a nongovernmental agency devoted to the care of the wounded and supported by private donations, were followed by Laboulaye. The Sanitary Commission became the predecessor of the Red Cross in America.[79] Lieber asked him to send autographed manuscripts to be auctioned off at one of the fairs held to raise money for the Sanitary Commission. Lieber urged Laboulaye to secure manuscripts from his friends to be sold at the fairs. Laboulaye, to judge from Lieber's letter, secured a great number of items to be sold at these fund-raising fairs.[80] Laboulaye referred to the work of the Sanitary Commission as "les miracles de charité qui fait le Sanitary Commission" [the miracles of charity accomplished by the Sanitary Commission].[81]

Laboulaye was in regular correspondence with George A. Matile who worked for the commission and was also a friend of Secretary of State Seward. Matile, a noted Swiss jurist and legal scholar, fled Switzerland after the Wars of the Sonderbund and the Revolutions of 1848 and came to live in the United States. Matile, who corresponded occasionally with Laboulaye from 1856 until 1876, drew on their common interest in legal studies. It was Matile who gave Laboulaye's works to Seward and relayed Seward's messages to Laboulaye. Later, Laboulaye would correspond directly with Seward.

The approaching American elections in November 1864 caused Laboulaye grave concern. Lieber wrote him that "All enthusiasm for Mr. Lincoln had melted away." Lieber continued by describing Lincoln's opponent in the election, General McClellan as "a *flunky* of the South, and, therefore thinks slavery a very nice thing."[82] Lieber concluded his letter by asking Laboulaye to write a letter favoring Lincoln's reelection, which he would have published in the United States.

Laboulaye wrote a pamphlet and published it in the *Revue Nationale* on 10 October 1864 in which he urged Lincoln's reelection. He sent the copy to John Bigelow who forwarded it to the State Department in Washington where it was translated and printed by the Union Congressional Committee.[83] In the title of the pamphlet Laboulaye was referred to as "The Great Friend of America." Laboulaye had also sent a copy of the pamphlet to Francis Lieber and another to Mary L. Booth for translation. Laboulaye's central thesis was stated at the beginning of the pamphlet: "In the life of Nations, there are supreme moments in which the choice made is decisive of the future; the greatness and the freedom of the People are at stake; an instant of weakness, all is lost; an instant of energy, a last effort, and all is saved."[84] For Laboulaye, the crucial moment was at hand. He argued, "The election of President Lincoln may assure the triumph or the ruin of the North, it will decide the question of Union or Separation."[85] He argued passionately that the reelection of President Lincoln would mean "the maintenance of the Union" and "the abolition of slavery," whereas the election of General McClellan would mean "re-establish-ment of Union such as may be" with "slavery continuing [as] a domes-tic question."[86] In a letter to Francis Lieber he wrote: "Pour moi je me considère comme un citoyen américain, et je m'interesse autant à la prochain élection, que s'il s'agissait de la France, et de notre avenir" [For my part, I think of myself as an American citizen, and I am just as interested in the up-coming elections as if it were a question of France and our future].[87] He concluded his tract with a plea for Lin-coln's reelection:

> Therefore we wait with impatience the result of the presidential election, praying God that the name which shall stand first on the ballot shall be that of honest and upright Abraham Lincoln; for the name will be a pres-age of victory, the triumph of Justice and Law. To vote for McClellan is to vote for the humiliation of the North, the perpetual upholding of slav-ery, the severance of the great republic. To vote for Lincoln, is to vote for Union and Liberty.[88]

Just when Laboulaye and his circle were enjoying the electoral vic-tory of Abraham Lincoln, they learned of the sudden death of William L. Dayton, the American minister in Paris, on 1 December 1864. Dayton's death at the Hotel du Louvre in the room of an acknowl-edged courtesan provided some gossip and embarrassment to the American community in Paris, but it did not exceed the limits of French tolerance.[89] John Bigelow arranged a funeral service in the American Church in Paris. The French foreign minister, M. Drouyn de Lhuys, attended the ceremony, although Laboulaye was the only Frenchman asked to speak. Laboulaye praised Dayton: "Il sut main-tenir les relations des deux pays sur le meilleur pied, à des conditions égales, c'est à dire également honorables pour les deux pays" [He knew how to keep relations between our two countries on the best footing, under equal conditions, that is to say, equally honorable].[90] Laboulaye was no doubt gratified to learn that Dayton's successor was to be the

American consul-general in Paris and his friend, John Bigelow. Bigelow was to remain as American minister to Paris until 1866.

Laboulaye closely followed the events leading to the end of the Civil War, and when he heard of Lee's surrender to Grant at Appamattox on 9 April 1865, he was overjoyed. His joy turned to sadness one evening a few days later when he was delivering a speech on Benjamin Franklin. During the speech he learned of the assassination of Lincoln. Later, he wrote a moving tribute to Lincoln's memory that was translated and published in a volume, entitled *Lincolniana*.[91] In his stirring tribute to Lincoln, he concluded with the following words:

> America will not be the only one which will honor Mr. Lincoln. It is not to his country alone that Mr. Lincoln has rendered a service: it is to all humanity. History, it must be admitted, is too often only a school of immorality. It shows us the victory of force or stratagem, much more than the success of justice, moderation, and probity. It is too often only the apotheosis of triumphant selfishness. There are noble and great exceptions: happy are those who can increase the number, and thus bequeath a noble and beneficient example to posterity! Mr. Lincoln is among these. He would have willingly repeated, after Franklin, that 'falsehood and artifice are the practice of fools, who have not wit enough to be honest:' all his private life, all his political life, was inspired and directed by this profound faith in the omnipotence of virtue. It is through this again that he deserves to be compared to Washington: it is through this that he will remain in history with the most glorious name that can be merited by the head of a free people,—a name given him by posterity,—that of **Honest Abraham** Lincoln.

With the ending of the Civil War the problems of Reconstruction would arise in the United States. Laboulaye continued to maintain his keen interest in American affairs, especially the welfare of the freed slaves, but he also became increasingly interested as well as a participant in French political life; and he never abandoned his cherished goal of seeing France adopt American ideas and institutions of liberty.

5

Last Years of the Empire

J'y contribue pour mon part autant que je peux, et j'admis avec
plaisir que les notions de la vraie liberté font un progrès sensible.

[I contribute what I can, and note with pleasure that the notions
of true liberty are making noticeable progress.]

—Édouard Laboulaye

In September 1865 Lieber asked the following question of Laboulaye:
"what do *you* mean by democracy when you speak of its hoped for
victory in Europe?" adding, "Real democracy has nothing to do, of
necessity, with liberty; absolute democracy is essential to liberty. Do
you mean, merely, hostility to privileges, or anti-toryism, or anti-'con-
servatism.'"[1] Laboulaye replied:

En France aujourd'hui ce mot est la traduction du *self government*. Ce ne
pas le pouvoir du nombre qu'il indique mais leur libre gouvernement.
Cette democratie là fait des progrès chez nous, surtout chez les ouvriers
des villes qui s'elèvent avec une rapidité singulière. C'est là qui est en ce
moment la vie dans la nation. Les bourgeois, les petits marchands, petit
propriétaires ne sont pas revenus de l'échec de 1848, mais les ouvriers
s'instruisent, s'associent, fondent des bibliothèques populaires, établissent
des cours publics et si la guerre ou les fautes du gouvernment ne viennent
pas troubler ce mouvement, on l'apercevra d'ici à peu de temps, du change-
ment considérable et heureux dans les idées du peuple. J'y contribue pour
mon part autant que je peux, et j'admis avec plaisir que les notions de la
vraie liberté font un progrès sensible

[In France today this word is a translation of *self-government*. It is not the
power of the numbers that it means, but their free government. This kind
of democracy is making progres in France especially among urban workers.
This is where the life of the nation is at this time. The bourgeois, small
merchants, minor property owners have never recovered from the failure

93

of 1848 but the workers are educating themselves, forming associations, founding public libraries, establishing public classes, and if war or govern-ment errors do not interrupt this progress we will very soon notice a considerable and happy change in the ideas of the people. I contribute what I can, and note with pleasure that the notions of true liberty are making noticeable progress].[2]

Thus Laboulaye defined what was, for him, democracy in the second half of the 1860s and in this statement he also revealed what was to be the direction of his activites for the remainder of his lifetime, to do what he could to educate the workers. For, as he stated in his letter to Lieber, it was the working classes that had to be educated for democracy and to become responsible citizens. For Laboulaye, the life of the nation resided in the workers. Furthermore, Laboulaye had great faith in the desire of the working class to teach themselves to participate wisely in the political process. Tied to this aim was his support of the movement for popular subscription libraries, one of the chief activities of the Société Franklin and of worker's education, a chief concern of the Société du Travail. Laboulaye was *président d'honneur* of both societies. Some of his speeches to workers and on behalf of the public subscription libraries were collected and published in his *Discours populaires* in 1869 and in his *Derniers discours popu-laires* published in 1881.[3]

Laboulaye persisted in his fight against slavery and inequality by continuing to play an active part in the French anti-slavery society. He made use of every opportunity to combat any assault on liberty with his pen or the spoken word. In his public addresses, his classroom lectures, his newspaper articles, and in his essays, he endeavored to propagate and explain his liberal ideas as expressed in *Le Parti libéral*. One of his major intellectual occupations in the late 1860s was his critical edition of Montesquieu's works, which were, as we have indi-cated elsewhere in this study, a remote source of Laboulaye's own liberalism; he worked unceasingly for what he called self-government and for the progress of true liberty.

Advice to Americans

Laboulaye's interest in America never waned. In August 1865, Senator Sumner wrote Laboulaye and told him that "the war has ended but not our strifes. I always foreseen that our military difficult-ies would be less than those which arise when the excitement of battle is over."[4] Laboulaye undoubtedly reflected on this letter when he

wrote later in the month to Secretary of State William Seward. Seward, who was seriously wounded in an attempt on his life that occurred on the same night as Lincoln's assassination, had a lengthy
convalescence during which George A. Matile, a friend of Seward's
as well as a correspondant of Laboulaye's, relayed greetings from Laboulaye to Seward and also from Seward to Laboulaye.[5] On 31 May
1865 Matile sent Seward an extract from a letter he had received
from Laboulaye:

> J'espère que Mr. Seward est depuis longtemps hors de danger. Dites-lui
> bien, je vous prie, tout l'intérêt que j'ai pris à ses malheurs, et combien
> je serai heureux d'apprendre son parfait rétablissement. Plus que jamais,
> l'Amérique a besoin de lui

> [I hope that Mr. Seward is well out of danger. Please tell him of my great
> concern for his misfortune and how happy I will be to hear news of his
> complete recovery. More than ever, America needs him].[6]

A few weeks later on 11 June 1865, Secretary Seward wrote to Matile, "This executed not without pain is among the very first fruits of
my convalescence. Please carry it to the glorious Laboulaye as my
acknowledgement for his kind words as you have brought it [sic] to
my knowledge." Matile sent it to Laboulaye, who wrote in his own
hand at the top of this letter, "Une des premières écrites par M.
Seward après les blessures que lui fit Booth [sic], l'assassin de Lincoln"
[One of the first [letters] written by Mr. Seward after being wounded
by Booth [sic], Lincoln's assassin]."[7]

During the Civil War Seward had corresponded occasionally with
Laboulaye and also had sent messages to him through John Bigelow.
Bigelow, Francis Lieber, George A. Matile, and Senator Sumner,
among others, had regularly sent copies of Laboulaye's articles and
books to Seward. It was no doubt on the basis of this epistolary friendship that Laboulaye wrote Seward on 31 August 1865 to offer him
political advice. This important letter, giving advice to Seward, was
a most extensive letter written by Laboulaye; it revealed his thoughts
on Reconstruction, the freed slaves, and American foreign policy towards Mexico and France. Laboulaye began by expressing his concern
for Seward's recovery and then addressed the question of Reconstruction and of the freed slaves, a subject of extreme interest to him.

> Il y a une question, sur laquelle à distance, je ne puisse avoir qu'une
> opinion arrêtée. . . . C'est celle du suffrage des Nègres. D'une part, il est
> fort délicat de donner un vote à des gens qui n'ont reçu aucune éducation;
> de l'autre il me semble dangereux de créer une inégalité de la peau, et de

rentrer ainsi dans la fausse position dont on n'est sorti que par une guerre terrible. Exclure des Nègres parce qu'ils ne sont pas des blancs, et cependant les compter dans la population électorale, c'est, ce me semble, recréer une aristocratie qui sera jusqu'aussi insolente et aussi dangereuse que celle que vous avez détruite. Pour une démocratie telle que la vôtre, pour un peuple à qui l'avenir du monde appartient, il me paraît peu sage de laisser subsister de pareil ferment d'inégalité et de discorde. L'incapacité personnelle du Noir passera en une génération, son incapacité légale et politique durera peut être aussi longtemps qu'a duré l'esclavage, et finira aussi violemment

[There is a question about which, from a distance, I can have only a limited opinion. . . . It is the negro vote. On the one hand it is a delicate matter to give the vote to people with no education; on the other hand, it seems to me dangerous to create an inequality of the skin and so return again to that false position from which you were extricated only by a terrible war. To exclude negroes because they are not white, and however, count them in the electoral population is, it seems to me, to recreate an aristocracy as insolent and dangerous as the one you have just destroyed. For a democracy such as yours, for a people on whom the future of the world depends, it seems unwise to permit such inequality and discord to ferment. The personal inequality of the individual negro will pass in a generation, his legal and political incapacity will last perhaps as long as slavery did, and will finish as violently].[8]

Thus did Laboulaye inform Seward of his views on how to handle the question of the freed slaves. It was not a position entirely consistent with his previously stated opinions on slavery, but it did acknowledge that freedom of the former slaves was a fait accompli and that a gradual emancipation of slaves would now be impossible. In this respect his previous criticism of Channing's advocacy in the 1850s of immediate freedom for all slaves in favor of a more gradual emancipation was adjusted to the realities of the situation and Laboulaye gracefully endeavored to adjust to the freedom of the slaves in a manner that he did not think possible or advisable a decade earlier. On 10 November 1865 Laboulaye addressed and presided at a *Meeting en faveur des esclaves affranchis aux États-Unis* (Meeting in favor of the freed slaves in the United States) held in Paris at the Salle Herz, where he gave a fuller statement of his views on the freed slaves.[9]

Laboulaye continued his letter by giving Secretary Seward advice on American foreign policy in regard to Mexico and also giving his own view on what the United States should do when faced with the French invasion of Mexico and the setting up of an empire there with the Hapsburg Archduke Maximilian as emperor. He informed Seward:

l'expédition du Mexique a toujours été impopulaire en France; la Chambre a manifesté son désir de la voir finir le plus tôt possible ... si on laissa la France à elle même, il n'est pas douteux pour moi; que l'expédition cessera d'ici en un an ou deux, et ne pourra jamais inquiéter sérieusement les États-Unis; mais si l'opinion populaire aux États-Unis d'emporter contre l'ancienne alliée, si l'on menace la France, ou si l'on lui fait une sommation impérieuse, je connais assez mon pays pour vous affirmer que la France entière prendra faute et cause pour l'Empereur et qu'elle ne cédera pas. ... On verra donc dans l'insistance des États-Unis une menace et peut être une injure addressée au peuple français; et cette prétendu menace sera exploitée par les ennemis nombreux que vous avez dans la presse française. ... Évitez-vous ces terribles extremités ce sera un nouveau service rendu à la paix du monde et à la liberté

[The Mexican expedition has always been unpopular in France; the Chamber has expressed its desire to see it ended as soon as possible ... if one leaves France on her own, I have no doubts but that the expedition will end in a year or two, and will never seriously trouble the United States; but if popular opinion in the United States is brought to bear against a former ally, if France is threatened or if she is issued an imperious ultimatum, I know my country well enough to tell you that all of France will rise up in support of the Emperor and she will not give up. ... American insistence will be seen as a threat and an insult to the French people: and that supposed threat will be exploited by your numerous enemies in the French press. ... Avoid these terrible extremes and it will be a new service to world peace and to freedom.

Laboulaye concluded his letter by begging Seward's pardon for his frankness.

On 19 September 1865, Secretary Seward replied to Laboulaye's letter by stating:

I appreciate your frankness and your benevolence in discussing the affairs which now necessarily engage the attention of the American people. Our present urgency is the restoration of the state, and with it the restoration of internal peace and harmony without which a nation consisting of many members held by only voluntary bonds without military or despotic forces could not long exist. ... For obvious reasons I cannot discuss in my private correspondence policies which divide the country into parties. I must therefore be content with saying this—we like every other nation must be content with nothing less and cannot reasonably ask more than the highest practical good.[10]

Seward thus did not discuss with Laboulaye in any detail his reaction to his letter, however, he did add in reference to Mexico, "Your suggestions concerning the Mexican question are very interesting and I shall beg your excuse for laying them together with your whole letter before the President." He closed by stating that Laboulaye would have to gather his views from "official revelations which are authorized by the government." Thus Seward gracefully acknowledged receipt of Laboulaye's letter but did not enter into a political discussion with him, who after all, was only a private citizen of France. Henceforth, Laboulaye would have to read the newspapers and official statements of the United States government. Some years later, in September 1871, Seward paid a visit to Paris and met Laboulaye and Seward declared it was "an especial pleasure to make the personal acquaintance of M. Laboulaye . . . a prominent republican member of the National Assembly."[11] Seward did not record their conversation nor did Laboulaye, although Seward did observe that Laboulaye was depressed over the recent defeat of France in the Franco-Prussian War.

Laboulaye was to engage directly in American politics twice in 1868. He became extremely interested in the impeachment process against President Johnson and wrote a letter supporting the movement to impeach, which was published in a Washington newspaper, *The Washington Daily Chronicle,* a paper edited by Colonel J. W. Forney.[12] Richard H. Crittenden, a prominent New York lawyer, wrote Laboulaye that his references to the "pending impeachment of the President evinces such a thorough appreciation of our national crisis which is to remove a president who has usurped unconstitutional powers."[13]

During the presidential campaign of 1868, Laboulaye offered advice to the American people and urged the election of General Ulysses Grant over Horatio Seymour. This article was first published in the New York French newspaper, *Le Messager Franco-Américain,*[14] and also in English translations in various other newspapers. The letter was solicited by the editor of *The Press,* a Philadelphia newspaper also edited by Colonel J. W. Forney, a friend and correspondent of Laboulaye and a staunch republican.[15] In addition to being the publisher of newspapers, Forney was also the secretary of the United States Senate. In this article, which is a reasoned yet passionate advocacy of the candidacy of General Ulysses M. Grant over the candidacy of his opponent, Horatio Seymour, Laboulaye claimed that Grant was Lincoln's logical successor and the one who would carry out his work. Laboulaye compared Grant favorably to Washington who, he said, was also a general. He continued by stating that he "had confidence in the common sense of the American people" and that he "did not doubt the election of General Grant." Laboulaye said that, although he was well known in America, he was not an American but that "what influenced him in this election was the interests of democracy in the entire world." He concluded by stating, "The defeat of Grant will be the joy of all oligarchies, his victory will be that of liberty, not only in the United States but throughout Europe. . . . The cry of republicans of the old world is Hurrah for Grant and for liberty!"[16] Forney wrote Laboulaye to thank him and said "I am gratified to be able to state that your letter has already caused an immense sensation and will exert a vast influence in favor of General Grant."[17]

On 16 October 1868 *The Press* editorialized on Laboulaye's article:

> The letter of Edouard Lefebvre Laboulaye, the eminent French philoso-
> pher, to the editor of *The Press*, in favor of the election of Gen. Grant, is
> copied far and wide. Its lofty spirit and Christian humanity, and its amaz-
> ing knowledge of the issues in the present struggle, have made it one of
> our best Republican campaign documents.

The editorial continued by stating that Laboulaye:

> had been an especial object of Louis Napoleon's vengeance. His quiet
> character and exalted eloquence have made him the idol of the working
> people, to whom for many years he has lectured once a week on morals,
> history, and politics. To these intellectual feasts they gather large crowds,
> and it is interesting to note how they hang upon his words.

The editorial noted that Laboulaye liked to lecture on the American Constitution but that several Imperial Senators objected "to this strong American tone to his lectures, and now at last he is silenced." Laboulaye, in fact, ceased lecturing on the American Constitution at the Collège de France because of governmental objections. The edito-rial concluded: "The sympathies of the whole liberal world will be awakened for a man who so sternly maintains his convictions in the face of the blandishments and threats of a powerful and corrupt gov-ernment."[18] Thus Laboulaye became involved in the presidential elec-tion of 1868. The recently retired United States minister to France, John Bigelow, wrote him, "You enjoy here a more endurable fame than any of your country's people now living, permit me to add that I think it well deserved."[19]

The Fight against Slavery Continues

In the years immediately after the American Civil War Laboulaye served as president of the *Comité française pour l'émancipation des esclaves*, which was founded in 1865. The Duc de Broglie and François Guizot served as *présidents d'honneur*, Augustin Cochin and Eugène Yung were secretaries while Henri Martin, Prince Albert de Broglie,

Agénor de Gasparin, and Edmond de Pressensé, among others, served as an advisory council.[20] Their original aim was to raise funds to reduce the poverty of the freed slaves by purchasing clothes and food for them. A parallel organization of women, in which Mme Laboulaye played an active part, was founded at the same time to make clothes for the freed slaves.[21] The proceedings of many of the committee's public meetings were published in the *Revue des cours littéraires de la France et de l'étranger,* as the editor of the review, Eugène Yung, was also secretary of the committee.

On 11 November 1865 at the Salle Herz in Paris the committee held its first public meeting and Laboulaye presided, although his eye disease made it difficult for him to see.[22] The topic of the discussion, which lasted for almost three hours, was the recently freed slaves in the United States. The subject was timely as the United States was in the process of ratifying the Thirteenth Amendment to the Constitution, which freed the slaves throughout the country. The Amendment passed the Senate in late 1864 and the House of Representatives on 31 January 1865. The process of ratification by two-thirds of the states was completed in December 1865. Laboulaye began with an address that praised the work of several French writers, notably Agénor de Gasparin, against slavery. He called attention to the French women who were the first to take on the task of raising money for the freed slaves and remarked, "J'ai toujours eu bonne opinion des causes auxquelles s'intéressaient les femmes" [I always have a good opinion of the causes that attract the interest of women].[23] Edmond de Pressensé, a prominent Protestant pastor, who also addressed the meeting, spoke of the four and a half million freed slaves and their great misery. He, too, spoke of the role of women, "Les dames françaises ont compris cela. . . . Dans ce noble travail, les femmes ne font que resserrer les liens qui uniront un jour le genre humain tout entier . . . je les remercie" [French women understood this. . . . In their noble work, the women only strengthen the bonds that unite all of humanity . . . I thank them].[24] As of 11 September 1865 the French women had collected in cash and clothing 45,000 francs and had pledges of 2,500 francs![25] It is interesting to note that in acknowledging the work of the French women no names were given; they were only referred to, by all speakers, as *les dames françaises* or the *comité des dames* or if an individual was referred to, it would be by title, such as *Mme la présidente,* not by name.[26] Laboulaye concluded his address by citing the example of Lafayette who came to aid the American colonies in their revolution, and he urged his listeners to support the American freed slaves in the same spirit. For the generation of the 1860s, obviously, giving funds would be evidence of fulfilling the spirit of Lafayette.[27]

Several Frenchmen who had just returned from the United States spoke, as did Mr. Leigh who was a representative of an American antislavery society in New York, and an American pastor in Paris, Dr. Sunderland, also spoke on the plight of the freed slaves.

A little over two months later another meeting was held in late January 1866. The scope of the meeting was enlarged to include the abolition of slavery not only in the United States but also in Cuba. This meeting, also lasting three hours, included speeches by Laboulaye, Augustin Cochin, Albert de Broglie, and Mr. L. A. Chamerovzow, the secretary of the British Emancipation Society.[28] The principal reason for this meeting was a request by the women's antislavery society, which wished to use the occasion to raise additional funds to purchase food and clothing for the freed slaves. Laboulaye noted approvingly their interest in public affairs and said that it "was their debut into political life." Laboulaye gave a report of their contributions in money and in clothing, which he noted fell behind what was raised in England and America. He regretted that the French did not have the same philanthropic traditions as other nations, asserting that French women wanted a fifth column in every family budget, a column where one would enter charitable contributions; they wanted to break the French habit of not giving to charity. French women hoped, too, that France's contributions would eventually match those of other countries.[29]

The French Committee on Emancipation began to widen its interests and to include slavery in other parts of the world. Laboulaye's son, Paul de Laboulaye, a French diplomat, was charged with writing a report on slavery in Brazil, and Augustin Cochin drafted a statement on slavery in the Spanish colonies.[30] The Committee was instrumental in founding an abolitionist society in Spain with Don Salustrand de Olozaga as president.[31]

A golden opportunity to further the antislavery cause presented itself in 1867 when the Universal Exposition was held in Paris and the French Emancipation Society hosted an international conference that was attended by representatives of abolitionist societies from the United States, England, and Spain. The United States was represented by William Lloyd Garrison and John Gorham Palfrey,[32] Great Britain by a committee headed by Joseph Cooper, William Allen, and L. A. Chamerovzow, and Spain by Don Salustrand de Olozaga.[33] The official French delegate was Prince Albert de Broglie, who was considered the "doyen" of the abolitionist cause in Europe. Other countries that were represented were Haiti, Brazil, and Venezuela, and M. Rainy represented what was termed "Africa." The sessions were presided over by Édouard Laboulaye, who in his brief opening remarks gave the purpose of the meeting: "C'est pour hâter ce moment que nous sommes réunis. Si nous pouvons hâter l'émancipation d'un jour, si nous pouvons épargner à ses pauvres gens qui sont encore esclaves quelques larmes, quelques souffrances, nous croirons avoir atteint no-tre but" [It is to hasten this moment that we have met. If we can hasten emancipation by one day, if we can spare the poor souls who are still slaves a few tears, some suffering, we will have achieved our goal].[34]

The conference voted upon a series of resolutions that aimed first to congratulate those countries which had already abolished slavery (England, France, Sweden, Denmark, Holland, the United States, Mexico, the Central American Republics, and Tunisia), and second, to urge the abolition of slavery in those countries where it was still practiced, the so-called civilized countries of Spain, Brazil, Portugal, Turkey, and Egypt. Although it recognized that slavery also existed in the noncivilized world, the conference wished to address itself first to what it considered the civilized world. The conference concluded with a series of resolutions passed unanimously urging all to work for the abolition of slavery and to exert all possible pressure on sovereigns who still permitted slavery.[35]

In the second part of the international conference, once again La-boulaye presided and this time gave a major address at the beginning of the session. He chose to give a thumbnail sketch of the antislavery movement's history starting with William Penn, and continuing by citing Montesquieu's views on slavery as well as those of the French Quaker writer, Antoine Bénézet. He continued by discussing the anti-slavery views of Benjamin Franklin, John Jay, Thomas Clarkson, Bishop Wilberforce, Thomas Fowler Buxton, Elizabeth Fry, Joseph Sturge, William Ellery Channing, Horace Mann, William Lloyd Gar-rison, and Senator Charles Sumner, all of whose work, he argued, had helped to end slavery in the United States and hopefully in a short period of time throughout the entire world.[36]

Laboulaye's speech was followed by one by William Lloyd Garrison who paid tribute to the French for abolishing slavery during the Re-public of 1848; he singled out Édouard Laboulaye, Augustin Cochin, Agénor de Gasparin, Victor Hugo, and their associates for being such a powerful force in aiding the United States during its Civil War, and "la cause de la liberté dans tout le monde" [the cause of liberty throughout the world].[37] Laboulaye ended the conference on slavery by saying:

On saura que dans une réunion composée d'hommes appartenant aux pre-mières nations du monde, il y a eu un accord unanime en faveur de la liberté, un ardent désir d'en finir avec cette abomination qu'on appelle l'esclavage; et c'est une grande chose qu'une assemblée comme celle-ci ait jeté dans la balance le poids de son autorité

[One will know that at a meeting of men from the first nations of the world, there was unanimous agreement in favor of freedom, an ardent desire to put an end to that abomination called slavery; and it is a great thing that such an assembly has thrown the weight of its authority into the balance].[38]

Thus ended the international congress held in conjunction with the Universal Exposition of 1867. It was a personal triumph for Laboulaye, who as chairman functioned as the spokesman and principal participant at the congress. Laboulaye's continued interest in the plight of the freed slaves and the eradication of slavery throughout the civilized world was evidenced in his correspondence and speeches.[39]

Political Frustrations

Laboulaye continued his active career in public life; he continued his teaching at the Collège de France, gave public lectures to workers and on behalf of public subscription libraries, made speeches against slavery, wrote columns in the *Journal des Débats,* and now he also envisioned a political career. His first venture into politics was during the elections of 1863 when he decided to run for a Parisian seat in the Corps Législatif. Thiers also indicated interest in the seat and Laboulaye graciously withdrew, claiming that Thiers, a former premier during the July Monarchy and a cabinet minister in various governments, was the better-known candidate and would probably win.[40] Laboulaye wrote a letter to the editor of *Le Siècle* that was published in the *Journal des Débats.*[41] He said:

Le libéralisme de M. Thiers n'est pas le mien, j'ai peu de goût pour la centralisation qu'il admire. En d'autres temps, j'aurais accepté la lutte sur ce terrain; mais aujourd'hui je crois que l'intérêt commun de la liberté exige que toutes les nuances s'effacent et que toutes les voix se réunissent autour du nom le plus considérable et le plus connu

[Thiers liberalism is not mine, I have no taste for the centralization he admires. In other times I would have taken up the challenge on these grounds; but today I believe that our common interest in liberty requires that all nuances be erased and that all voices unite around the strongest and best known name].

In similar circumstances his friend and fellow liberal, Prévost-Paradol, withdrew in favor of the more popular candidate, Adolphe Guéroult.[42]

In 1864 there was a by-election in Paris; Laboulaye decided to run and this time he did not withdraw. His opponents in the first electoral *circonscription* were the governmental or official candidate, M. Pinart, and Lazare-Hippolyte Carnot, the son of the great Carnot. Laboulaye campaigned on the platform of "Democracy and Liberty." His electoral poster was also one of the clearest statements of his political beliefs. He defined democracy as "un état social où grâce à l'entière liberté du travail, du crédit, de l'association, de la presse, grâce à l'enseignement largement et gratuitement distribué, les meilleures chances possibles sont offertes à tout homme honnête, économe et laborieux" [A social state where, thanks to complete freedom of work, credit, association, press, thanks to the widespread and free dissemination of education, the best possible opportunities are available to every honest, frugal, and hard-working man], and he continued by defining liberty as that which makes

> chaque citoyen maître et responsable de ses actions et de sa vie; c'est le règne de la loi substitué au règne de l'administration. Je demande la liberté pour tous, liberté de l'individu, de l'Église, de l'école, de la commune, du départment, et au premier rang je place la liberté de la presse, organe de la conscience publique, incomparable moyen d'éducation populaire, contrôle de tous les pouvoirs, suprême garantie de tous les droits

> [each citizen master of and responsible for his actions and his life; it is the reign of law in place of the reign of administration. I ask for liberty for all, liberty of the individual, of the church, of the school, of the commune, of the department, and above all else I place liberty of the press, the organ of the public conscience, incomparable medium for public education, which controls all power and is the supreme garantor of all rights].[43]

As a native Parisian he also advocated self-government for Paris. Understandably, he received the endorsement of the *Journal des Débats,* which said he was in the liberal tradition of Royer-Collard, Constant, and Tocqueville and urged Parisians to vote for him "il est un qui a toutes nos préférences comme il a toutes les sympathies des jeunes générations libérales" [as he fulfills all of our preferences and has all the sympathies of the young generation of liberals].[44] As the election drew closer, the *Journal* ran several articles urging Laboulaye's election.[45] Unfortunately for Laboulaye, he only received 913 votes in the election; Pinard received 4,979, and Carnot, the winner, received 13,554.[46] Laboulaye had to contend with both the official pressure in favor of the government's candidate and Carnot's real popularity.

This defeat did not daunt Laboulaye; he stood in 1866 for a seat in the Department of the Bas-Rhin, which included the city of Strasbourg. In this race he was pitted against an official governmental candidate, M. de Bussierre. He was more hopeful this time but once more he became the victim of official pressure and went down to defeat, but he received three-quarters of the vote in the city of Strasbourg, and declared, "I was defeated by the votes of the countryside."[47] During the campaign Émile Ollivier sent 3,700 francs to aid Laboulaye's campaign, which he raised among the opposition deputies in the Corps Législatif.[48] The *Revue des Deux Mondes* editorialized on the election, "La population d'une des plus grandes cités de France saura demain si à son gré la mesure des libertés publiques est comble, et si le pays est indifférent aux réformes libérales" [The population of one of France's largest cities will know tomorrow if by its wish the measure of public freedom is overflowing, or if the country is indifferent to liberal reforms].[49] Several thousand of his Strasbourg supporters, however, took up a collection of ten centimes a person to give him a gift as a token of their affection. They gave him an engraved silver inkstand in gratitude for his campaign in the Bas-Rhin. An inkstand, "that I keep today as the most precious of souvenirs."[50] A few years later in 1870, he would be taunted to return *l'encrier de Strasbourg*. After his defeat at Strasbourg he wrote to John Bigelow, "Quant aux campagnes elles sont toujours dans le main de l'administration; le paysan a peur et votera pour le gouvernment presque en tout pays" [As for the countryside, it will always be ruled by the administration; the peasant is afraid and will vote for the government in almost every district]. He continued, "Quant à moi je ne crois qu'on songe à moi pour les élections. Ma situation est singulière. Les idées que je defends font leur chemin parmi les jeunes gens et les ouvriers, mais n'appartenant pas à aucun parti je ne suis pas enrégimenté" [As for me I do not believe that one thinks of me for the elections. My situation is unique. The ideas I defend are making their way among the youth, and the workers, but they do not belong to any party, I am not enrolled].[51] In explaining his defeat he pointed out that democrats had a horror of all religious belief; that they adored Robespierre and Danton for whom he had a profound contempt because they were demagogues whose only legacy was the guillotine. For him, "without religion man could not be free." He concluded by stating "Les libéraux de la vielle école mettent toute la politique dans l'omnipotence des chambres, je suis de l'école américaine et j'enseigne que les chambres n'ont que des pouvoir délégués, et que le citoyen a les droits auxquels un parlement ne peut

pas toucher" [Liberals of the old school place politics in the omnipotence of the chambers. I am of the American school and I teach that
the chambers hold only delegated power, and that a citizen has rights
that parliament cannot touch].[52] He also reiterated to Bigelow that
he did not belong to any political party.

After his second electoral defeat Laboulaye turned to the writing
of a political satire on the bureaucracy of the Second Empire. This
300-page book, entitled *Le Prince Caniche*,[53] was a huge success and
went through seventeen editions. One can envision the humor when
one realizes that the French word, *caniche* means poodle! The book
was timely and was not very subtle in its criticism of the machinations
of the imperial bureaucracy. Frédéric Passy referred to *Le Prince Caniche* as "Quelle amusant caricature de la centralisation . . . et quelle
sanglante satire de l'éloquence officielle" [what an amusing satire of
centralization and what a biting satire of official eloquence].[54] By
means of his pen Laboulaye was able to poke fun at a regime whose
official pressure had denied him a seat in parliament.

Laboulaye, although representing "le libéralisme pur,"[55] was also to
run unsuccessfully in the general elections of 1869 for a seat near
Paris in the Seine-et-Oise Department.[56] This time he was defeated
by Barthélemy de Saint-Hilaire, who was also a distinguished savant
and a member of the liberal opposition. Only with the advent of the
Third Republic was Laboulaye's candidacy to be successful.

As the years of the Empire drew to a close, many opponents of
Napoleon III rallied to the support of the Empire. A critical turning
point was the election of 1869 which, in Theodore Zeldin's view,
showed the collapse of the old imperial system.[57] In large part this
was due to the gradual evolution of the political life of the Empire
towards what is termed the Liberal Empire. In addition, reforms in
the early 1860s permitted the publication of debates in the chambers,
the voting of the budget item by item, and an address to the emperor.
On 19 January 1867 Napoleon III allowed ministers to defend themselves in person before parliament, although they could not be members. Members of parliament could question or interpellate ministers
but the right to vote an annual address to the throne was abolished.
Also promised was a relaxing of the laws on meetings and the press.
Although Napoleon III promised further reforms in 1867 they only
became law in 1868, The Law of 25 March 1868 permitting public
meetings, usually termed the right of reunion, without the previously
required police permissions was passed. The matter for discussion at
these reunions, however, was restricted to agriculture, industry, science, or literature; any discussion of religion or politics was forbidden.
The great fear of the government and of Napoleon III was that, if

they permitted a discussion of politics, France would revert to what it considered the dangerous situation of the political clubs of 1848; a situation the imperial government wished to avoid at all costs.

Laboulaye chaired one of the first public meetings held under the new law. It was held in the Faubourg Saint Marcel, and was a discussion of the state of the economy led by several prominent economists.[58] Laboulaye drew special comfort from the law on public meetings as it enabled him to speak on a variety of subjects for the Société du Travail and also on behalf of the Bibliothèques Populaires. As the noted historian of the Second Empire, Pierre de la Gorce, pointed out, Laboulaye, who embodied "le libéralisme pur,"[59] held a series of public meetings on a variety of subjects such as progress, duty, the family, love of one's profession, and the like. La Gorce termed this type of public meeting as one conducted with "une main élégante" [an elegant hand].[60] At these public meetings held in Paris at the Salle de la Rédoute or the Théâtre du Prince Impérial featuring such speakers as Laboulaye, Jules Simon, Jules Favre, Prince Albert de Broglie, Frédéric Passy, and others, a small subscription was charged that served to keep out the more militant of the so-called popular elements. But as La Gorce observed, under the camouflage of ambiguous topics, "the only aim of these meetings was to criticize the government, however, it was never a direct frontal attack."[61] Many of Laboulaye's speeches during this period were published in his *Discours populaires*.[62]

The Law of 11 May 1868, which granted the press its freedom,[63] began a series of virulent political attacks from the intransigent press against the government of Napoleon III. The best example of this level of journalism was Henri Rochefort, whose weekly, *La Lanterne,* "poked fun at every public figure from Napoleon III downwards."[64] With the freedom of reunion and the freedom of the press, the Empire moved further in the direction of a liberal state and political life was revived on many levels. In 1869 Napoleon III was able to secure the allegiance of a young republican deputy, Émile Ollivier, who would eventually become the first and only prime minister of the Liberal Empire. In December 1869 Ollivier was able to form a ministry, which marked a new direction for the Second Empire.[65] Many prominent liberals rallied to the Empire such as Prévost-Paradol,[66] who accepted a post as minister to the United States, François Guizot, who accepted a post on a committee to propose educational reforms,[67] Clément Duvernois, who accepted a cabinet post, and Édouard Laboulaye.

Laboulaye rallied to the Empire when a plebiscite was called for 8 May 1870 to vote on a new liberal constitution for the Empire. The plebiscite approved the new constitution by a vote of 7,358,786 against only 1,571,939. Laboulaye confronted one of the most traumatic experiences of his life when he chose to support the plebiscite; as La Gorce observed: "M. Laboulaye qui, plus familiarisé avec les coutumes suisses ou américaines qu'avec les pratiques de l'Angleterre, voyait dans l'appel au peuple un moyen de corriger les abus du parle-mentarisme" [Laboulaye more familiar with Swiss or American prac-tice than with English politics saw the plebiscite as a way to correct the abuses of parliamentarianism].[68] In a letter to John Bigelow writ-ten after the vote he said:

J'ai voté le plébiscite et conseillé de le voter pour deux raisons. La première c'est qu'il est toujours plus sage d'accepter la liberté présente que de courir les chances de l'inconnu, quand cet inconnu est une révolution; *la séconde* parce que le plébiscite, en restituant le pouvoir constituant au peuple, et en déclarant qu'on ne pourrait plus modifier la constitution que de l'aveu de la nation, m'a paru conforme aux vrais principes démocratiques, tels qu'ils sont entendus et pratiqués aux États-Unis

[I voted for the plebiscite and advised voting for it for two reasons. The first being that it is always wiser to accept an existing liberty than to risk the unknown when that unknown is a revolution; the second being that the plebiscite by restoring the constitutive power to the people, and by declaring that one can no longer make constitutions except by the will of the nation seemed to me in keeping with the democratic principles, such as they are understood and practiced in the United States].[69]

Laboulaye's fullest explanation of his role in the plebiscite was in-corporated as a chapter in his *Questions constitutionnelles*. In the de-bates over the plebiscite he stated, "on m'a calomnié à l'outrance" [I was outrageously slandered].[70] His position never varied as he said that the draft of the proposed constitution was not exactly what he would have wanted but to vote against it would be to bring about a revolution, an idea abhorrent to Laboulaye. The opponents of the plebiscite wished for an omnipotent assembly that was the fad of the revolutionary school. Laboulaye, on the contrary, claimed that he had always defended the true principles of democracy, "government of the people, by the people, and for the people."[71] He declared that although he had voted against the presidency of Louis Napoleon in 1851 and for the proclamation of the Empire in 1852, "je ne voyais dans la nouvelle Constitution qu'une seule chose, le retour de la liberté parle-mentaire" [I saw but one thing in the new constitution; the return of parliamentary liberty.][72] He also observed that for a constitution to be valid it had to be ratified by the people and, this, he argued, the plebiscite would accomplish.

The polemics over the plebiscite drew forth Laboulaye's greatest efforts. M. Labouchère, who had voted for him in 1869 in the Seine-et-Oise, asked his opinion of the plebiscite. He wrote a lengthy letter, which he permitted Labouchère to publish; it stands as his statement on the plebiscite.[73] The letter was reprinted widely in various newspapers. The most quoted expression in the letter was drawn from the early nineteenth-century historian, Daunou, who wrote, "La meilleure Constitution est celle qu'on a, pourvu qu'on s'en serve" [The best constitution is the one you have, as long as you use it].[74] He again warned that a negative vote meant revolution and affirmed that when a government is accepted by the vote of the nation the good citizen must submit to the national will. M. Martinelli in the newspaper, *La Gironde*, attacked Laboulaye for his letter to Labouchère, and Laboulaye replied that Martinelli's views would "push my country towards revolution."[75]

On 2 May 1870 Laboulaye attempted to speak on the plebiscite at a public meeting in Versailles. As he began to speak, a demonstration mounted against him; his supporters in turn mounted a counterdemonstration, the result being that for a long time he could not speak in spite of repeated attempts to do so. Laboulaye pleaded with his audience for tolerance and to be heard, finally one voice raised the matter of freedom in America and Laboulaye retorted, "En Amérique, on écoute tout le monde" [In America, one listens to everyone]."[76] Eventually he was able to be heard and his remarks contained numerous references to the political system of the United States, which he held up as a model for the French. He concluded his remarks with "Pas de révolution, pas de contre-révolution; la liberté, toute la liberté, rien que la liberté" [No revolution, no counterrevolution: liberty, total liberty, nothing but liberty]."[77]

Laboulaye's difficulties were not over when the results of the plebiscite were known; new ones arose when he attempted to resume his courses at the Collège de France on 23 May 1870 after the Easter vacation. Laboulaye asserted that he was in the midst of a series of lectures on Montesquieu when certain individuals aimed to drive him from the lecturn from which he had taught for twenty-two years "that liberty had two great enemies, despotism and revolution."[78] The *Journal des Débats*[79] reported on the affair that students shouted and dared Laboulaye to return the *l'encrier de Strasbourg* (the Strasbourg inkstand). Amidst the brouhaha he spoke with difficulty but managed to explain his Strasbourg candidacy. In spite of considerable heckling, he was able to quote a long passage from Constant declaring that "Les révolutions me sont odieuses . . . parce que la liberté m'est chère" [Revolutions are odious to me because I cherish liberty]."[80] After this tumultuous scene in the Collège de France where he abandoned his prepared lecture to reply to hecklers, Laboulaye went to his carriage to return to his home in Versailles; loyal students gathered about his carriage and sent him on his way with applause and shouts of support.

A few days later on 27 May 1870 the Collège de France was invaded, in Laboulaye's words, "par le ban et l'arrière ban des irréconcilⁱ iables" [the ban and the arrière ban of the irreconciliables].[81] The following inscription on the blackboard welcomed Laboulaye: "Laboulaye, apostat.—cours fermé pour cause d'apostasie" [Laboulaye, apostate—course closed by reason of apostasy].[82] There was such a tumult in Amphitheater Number 7 that Laboulaye could not speak and after three-quarters of an hour he left the amphitheater with dignity. Drumont, writing in *La Liberté,* expressed his scorn for "cette intolérance brutale on plaint moins la sympathique personnalité de M. Laboulaye que la cause de la liberté" [that brutal intolerance; our complaint is less for the agreeable personality of M. Laboulaye than for the cause of liberty], and he regretted the treatment of a man in such an odious fashion who was devoted to the cause of liberty. Drumont ended by observing that "Le côté triste, c'est le manque d'éducation libérale qui s'affirme chez la génération qui vient" [the sad thing is the lack of liberal education we see in the next generation].[83] After the events of 27 May Laboulaye returned to his home in Glatigny-Versailles and with a heavy heart addressed a letter to the administrator of the Collège de France in which he requested permission to suspend his courses temporarily.[84]

Many of Laboulaye's former students joined the students of 1870 who wrote him privately to express their admiration for the man and for his liberalism. Dozens of such letters are among his papers at Le Quesnay. *La Liberté* and the *Journal des Débats* published several of them including those bearing multiple signatures. In concluding his account of the fracas over the plebiscite, Laboulaye noted that on 27 May 1870 he was chased out of his chair at the Collège de France, but on 2 July 1871, just over a year later, the Parisian voters elected him to the National Assembly. In the meantime, France had gone through the Franco-Prussian War, the fall of the Empire, the proclamation of the Third Republic, and the Commune of Paris—a sad and difficult year for Laboulaye and his beloved France.

After the plebiscite, Émile Ollivier, the premier, formed a new cabinet in which he gave serious consideration to naming Laboulaye; however, he was dissuaded by the Emperor, who thought that Laboulaye's appointment to a cabinet post would cause difficulties in the Chamber.[85] His friend John Bigelow observed,

He thus so completely committed himself to the imperial régime, that, fortunately for him, it was not thought worth while to waste upon him any of those imperial favors which were supposed to have had their weight in seducing the other gentlemen from the ranks of the opposition, and which, if tendered, he could hardly have declined had he been so disposed.[86]

Scholarly Pursuits

In 1864 Laboulaye concluded his lectures on the American Constitution at the Collège de France and proceeded to give a series of lectures on English criminal procedure, the history of legislation and administration of France under Louis XVI during the years 1787–91.[87] The years 1865 through 1871 were spent on a lengthy analysis of Montesquieu's writings for an anotated seven-volume edition of his complete works that was published a decade later.[88]

His earlier interest in the American Civil War and also his friendship with Francis Lieber filled him with concern to alleviate the horrors of war. At the height of the Civil War Francis Lieber drew up *General Orders No. 100, Instructions for the Government of Armies of the United States in the Field,* which is usually referred to as General Orders No. 100. These orders were to remain, in the words of Richard Shelly Hartigan, "a benchmark for the conduct of an army toward an enemy army and population," and it became the first time in "western history in which a government established solid guidelines for the conduct of its army towards its enemies."[89] Lieber sent Laboulaye a copy of his General Orders No. 100 through the diplomatic pouch of John Bigelow.[90] Laboulaye acknowledged receipt and informed Lieber that he had sent the copy to M. Victor Foucher, who was in charge of drawing up the French military code.[91]

Lieber's General Orders No. 100 inspired Johan Kaspar Bluntschli to prepare a similar treatise that was in most respects a translation of Lieber's work into German. Soon Lieber's treatise became the basis for a code of the law of war drawn up by a congress of scholars, which in turn directly influenced the Hague Conferences and Conventions of 1899 and 1907.[92]

In 1869 Bluntschli's work was translated into French and was entitled, *Le droit international codifié;* Laboulaye wrote the Preface, in which he pointed out the value of Lieber's General Orders No. 100. For Laboulaye, the code was a stepping stone to international peace which he saw as a possible means of banishing war. He identified his own views with those of Lieber and Bluntschli and stated that in the arena of truth there are no frontiers and that one does not ask whether an idea comes from one country or another but rather the highest goal is "faire de tous les hommes une même famille, chasser de la terre la guerre qui l'a longtemps ensanglantée, c'est un rêve pour les sages du jour" [make of all men one family, banish from the earth the war that has bloodied it for so long; this is, the dream of today's wise man].[93] Laboulaye observed that in the late 1860s there was a general effort to establish a single monetary system, a common standard of weights and measures, common postal and telegraphic laws, as well as common maritime and commercial practices. He saw all as leading to unity and most certainly towards universal peace.[94]

Another matter of concern to Laboulaye in the late 1860s was the problem of the medical services in the French army. He wrote a lengthy article that was published in December 1869 in the *Revue des Deux Mondes* in which he compared the medical services in the French army with those of the American army. His essay was also published in the United States.[95] His basic thesis was that the medical services in the French army were woefully inadequate and, if no changes were made, this inadequacy would become painfully evident in a future war. The lessons of the Franco-Prussian War only proved the correctness of Laboulaye's views. The United States, he argued, had improved its medical services greatly as was attested to in the recent Civil War. This is but another example of the almost unlimited interests of Laboulaye in matters that would benefit and improve society. His boundless intellectual energy led him constantly into new fields of concern.

The Franco-Prussian War

When the Franco-Prussian War broke out in July 1870 Laboulaye resolutely defended France against the Prussian invader. He wrote John Bigelow, who was then in Berlin, "je suis prêt à tout sacrifier, ma fortune et ma vie pour aider à la défense de mon pays" [I am ready to sacrifice all, my fortune and my life to aid in the defense of my country].[96] Laboulaye, in a letter to George Bancroft, the American minister to Prussia, expressed the firm belief that France had not provoked the war but that it had stupidly declared war and that this was done by an incompetent government. Laboulaye added that war had been unavoidable since Sadowa.[97]

Bigelow expressed the view that Prussian military strength was very strong and that France could possibly lose the war; Laboulaye countered that many people also thought that the North would lose in the American Civil War; but that the North was victorious, and so France would be in the Franco-Prussian War. This was a letter written a few days before the Battle of Sedan and the abdication of Napoleon III. Laboulaye was desolated by the tragic turn of events. In a letter to Bigelow dated 6 September 1870 he expressed his horror at the events that had transpired and said that the humiliation of France would benefit no one. He was especially concerned with, what he termed, the radicals who had taken over the municipal government of Paris. He bid Bigelow adieu since he might not be able to write him again; as he wrote Bigelow, he feared both the political situation in Paris and the possibility of Paris being besieged by the Prussians. His patriotic fervor was very strong but he considered himself too old to fight and said that he hoped to serve by volunteering as an ambulance attendant.[98]

After the defeat at Sedan and the proclamation of the Republic on 4 September 1870, the Prussian troops approached Paris, which they would soon besiege. Laboulaye felt uncomfortable in Paris and decided that the only safe course of action was to leave the city; he went to Bolbec in Normandy where he organized ambulances. During the course of his stay at Bolbec he told Bigelow that he had observed the Prussians at close hand and said, "je conçus une haine profonde contre cette race hypocrite et perverse, incapable de noblesse et de générosité" [I conceived a profound hatred against this hypocritical and perverse race that is incapable of nobility and generosity].[99] As he predicted, the Prussian siege of Paris kept him away from that city and he was not able to return to his home at Glatigny-Versailles until 26 March 1871. Upon his return he found that it had been occupied by the Prussians during the seige of Paris. Although his wine cellar had been emptied by the Prussians and several small objects taken, his house was in very good shape compared to those of his neighbors. He observed that his wife's crucifix was placed in a prominent place by the Prussians and decorated with boughs. He concluded that they must have been Catholic!

In a letter written after his return to Versailles, he confided to Bigelow that he was old, tired, without ambition, and that he did not possess the necessary stamina to lead a political party.[100] Little did he realize that a whole new career was ahead of him in the Third Republic.

6

Senator for Life and the Statue of Liberty

Le monument de l'Indépendance sera exécuté en commun par les deux peuples associés dans cette oeuvre fraternelle comme ils le furent jadis pour fonder l'Indépendance.

Nous affirmerons ainsi par un souvenir impérissable l'amitié que le sang versé par nos pères avait scellée jadis entre les deux nations.

[This monument to independence will be executed in common by the two nations, joined together in this fraternal work as they once were to achieve independence.

We will thus affirm by an enduring souvenir, the friendship between the two nations that was sealed in a former time by the blood shed by our fathers.]

—Edouard Laboulaye

Laboulaye's concluding years were marked by success in several areas. First, in politics he served as a deputy and later as a senator for life, in fact, he became one of the founding fathers of the Third Republic. Then another honor was bestowed in March 1873 when he was made the *administrateur* of the Collège de France, a post he held until his death. Finally, his efforts as chairman of the Franco-American Commission to raise funds for the Statue of Liberty in France brought him much acclaim, although he died before the statue could be erected in New York Harbor. Finally, he continued his public lectures, his journalistic activities, and the other endeavors that he had begun earlier in his life. He was much in demand as a public speaker; for example, he delivered eulogies at the funerals of Edgar Quinet and Jules Michelet, among others, and gave the official eulogies for several deceased members of the Institut de France.

Hans Christian Anderson, a visitor to Paris, went to Glatigny-Versailles to visit Laboulaye on 2 June 1873; he has left us the following portrait:

I had the heartiest greetings from the eminent scholar. Scholar, do I say? Laboulaye is one of the few mortals that combine all intellectual excellences in themselves. As M. Jean Lemoine had told me that very morning, 'You will find in him a great jurist, a sagacious statesman, a brilliant orator, a sweet poet, a fascinating story-teller, and the most amiable of men.'

Laboulaye told Anderson that he had not written anything worth mentioning for several years, however, he added, "I believe, he said smilingly, I have done my share as a writer. The reviews, the *Journal des Débats,* and committee work in the Assembly absorb most of my time." Laboulaye told Anderson that his solution was to "work, work, work, from early dawn till late at night." He also told Anderson that "France was never more solidly republican than today." Anderson concluded, "I had spent one of the most delightful days of my whole journey."[1]

Senator for Life

Immediately after the signing of the armistice between France and the new German Empire in February 1871, the first and most pressing business was the election of members to a new national assembly, a single-chambered legislative body, which was designed as a temporary replacement for the parliamentary institutions of the Second Empire. In the elections held in February to elect members to the National Assembly the French voters returned a monarchist majority but the monarchists were divided on who should occupy the throne between the Legitimists who supported the Comte de Chambord (known to his followers as Henri V), the Orleanists who supported the grandson of Louis Philippe, the Comte de Paris, and the Bonapartists who wished for a restoration of Napoleon III. The deep divisions within the monarchist camp precluded any restoration and, in fact, facilitated the eventual acceptance of a republic.

In the by-elections held in July 1871, necessitated by the number of multiple candidacies in February, the republicans won 99 of the 114 seats up for election and Édouard Laboulaye, an avowed republican and a candidate in the Department of the Seine, received 107,773 votes, sufficient to be elected deputy. In his campaign he openly supported the establishment of a republic and clearly opposed the restoration of monarchy in any form. Also he supported the policies of Thiers. Laboulaye, thus in 1871, achieved his cherished objective of a seat in the national legislature after having been defeated four times during the Second Empire. Never again was he to lose an election.

As a republican deputy Laboulaye desired a government with conservative institutions, institutions that would guard against revolution in the Jacobin tradition, such as he had seen surface in the bloody Commune of Paris in 1871. This event was foremost in his mind; his loathing convinced him that the republic must possess a constitutional framework to prevent a repetition of the violence of the Commune. He also wished to avoid a return to authoritarian government. In short, his political position was midway between the extreme Right as seen in the Legitimists, who dreamed only of France before 1789, and the extreme Left led by Gambetta who drew their inspiration from the Jacobin Republic of the 1790s, the Second Republic in 1848, and the Commune. In the National Assembly he soon was drawn to a faction of the republicans called the *centre gauche* or the left center. He was elected vice-president of this faction that, by and large, came to support the policies of Thiers, who as chief of the executive power or provisional president, was also a member as well as titular head of this group.

The *centre gauche,* the most conservative of the republican parties in the Assembly, was comprised chiefly of former Orleanists who became moderate republicans during the Second Empire such as Casimir-Perier, Dufaure, Léonce de Lavergne, and Jules Simon. The moderate republicans, or the *gauche républicain,* formed a second and more radical grouping of republicans. Their leader was Jules Ferry and their chief members were Jules Grévy, Jules Favre, and later Jules Simon. The group of republicans comprising the extreme left were the most radical. They formed the *union républicaine* led by Léon Gambetta. Gambetta's closest colleagues were Freycinet, Challemel-Lacour, Ranc, Allain-Targé, Paul Bert and Scheurer-Kestner. During the decade of the 1870s the *gauche républicain* and the *union républicaine* gathered voting strength at the expense of the monarchist parties and the *centre gauche.* In fact, the election of 1879 was the last one in which the *centre gauche* played an important role.[2]

Laboulaye's first parliamentary appointment as chair of a committee to reorganize higher education reflected his vast experience in French higher education. As Jacques Gadille points out the Commission on Education appointed as *rapporteur* "une personnalité unanimement respectée dans l'Assemblée" [a person universally respected in the Assembly], Laboulaye.[3] Consequently, many of his early speeches in the Assembly were devoted to educational matters; his major speeches on education, however, were to be delivered after 1874.

Consistent with his previous scholarly interests, it was only natural that Laboulaye would begin his work in the National Assembly by making proposals for the future constitution of France. After all, he was one of France's leading authorities on constitutions and constitutional law and held the chair of professor of comparative legislation at the Collège de France. As early as May 1871 he wrote an article entitled, "La République constitutionnelle," which was published by his friend, Eugène Yung, in the *Journal de Lyon*.[4] Yung had asked him for his views. Laboulaye replied that a constitutional republic must guarantee the natural rights of man in society such as freedom of one's person and freedom to work, freedom of conscience, separation of church and state, freedom of speech and education, freedom of the press, the right of assembly, and the right to petition the government. As to the form of government he advocated a two-chambered or bicameral legislature, a president independent of the parliament, and an independent judiciary. Republican institutions would be further enhanced by administrative decentralization, a citizen army, free education for all children, and a reduction of the public debt.[5] He concluded his essay by stating "Arborons le drapeau de la *République constitutionnelle* et puissions-nous bientôt relever notre pays et lui rendre le rang qui lui appartient parmi les nations" [Let us raise the flag of the *Constitutional Republic* and may we soon raise our country to the rank among nations that belongs to her]![6]

Next Laboulaye wrote in June 1871 an article on "La question des deux chambres,"[7] where he underscored his great interest in a bicameral legislature, which he asserted would give France "un gouvernement libre, des institutions sages et des lois respectées" [a free government, wise institutions and respected laws].[8] This article was followed shortly thereafter by one published in The *Revue des Deux Mondes* in October 1871 on "Le pouvoir constituant," which was also included in his *Questions constitutionnelles*.[9] In this essay he surveyed the history of French constitution making during the past eighty years during which France had had eleven constitutions; France had passed from servitude to liberty and from liberty to servitude in a recurring pattern, a pattern that, he argued, must be stopped. The problem was that the French constitution framers had not drafted a proper and workable constitution; England had a workable but unwritten constitution; France, he asserted, must turn to America for the example of a written and workable constitution. Furthermore, America was a democracy and thus worthy of French emulation; to follow the American example would give France stable and free political institutions. Laboulaye received much favorable comment on this article.[10]

In May 1872 Laboulaye wrote "De la souveraineté," which was originally published in the *Journal de Lyon*.[11] It was published at the same time as the Assembly was voting on the matter of nominations of members to the Conseil d'État. In this essay he cautioned against setting up an omnipotent parliament, urging instead that the office of president possess significant powers. In support of this position he cited Benjamin Constant, who had also warned against "L'horrible route de l'omnipotence parlementaire" [The horrible path of parliamentary omnipotence].[12] He expressed the hope that his language would not offend anyone but he said that for twenty-five years "que je defends les principes de l'école libérale, c'est n'est pas au moment du danger que je pouvais abandonner mon drapeau" [during which I had defended the principles of the liberal school, it is not in a moment of danger that I could abandon my flag].[13]

In September 1872 Laboulaye published a pamphlet of some hundred pages, entitled *Lettres politiques*, in which he discussed the future constitution and also furnished a six-page draft of a model constitution. This pamphlet and constitutional draft, based on his previous writings, was intended for a wider audience, namely, the readers of the *Journal des Débats*.[14] Such were Laboulaye's published observations on the future constitution of the Third Republic. They were consistent with his previous writings on a proper constitution as well as an expansion of the views he had expressed in 1863 as part of the program for *l'école libérale* in his book, *Le Parti libéral*. It is no exaggeration to say that between 1871and 1875 he was in the thick of the fight to draft constitutional legislation. He strongly supported Thiers in 1873 when the royalist majority maneuvered to secure his resignation. According to Laboulaye, Thiers was committed to the Republic and would act to establish a liberal constitution. What was needed was for France and French parliamentarians to acknowledge that France was a republic.

In 1873 the National Assembly formed the so-called Committee of Thirty to draft constitutional legislation. Laboulaye was elected to this committee but initially it was dominated by the Orleanists who wished a restoration of the Comte de Paris. The final process of passing constitutional legislation would have to survive parliamentary infighting and bickering for another two years or until early 1875. In January 1875 Laboulaye was serving as *rapporteur* of the Committee of Thirty and in this capacity he proposed an amendment on 29 January, which began by stating "The Government of the Republic is composed of two chambers and a President." The word "Republic" was in the first line and the Right found this offensive; Laboulaye replied to these criticisms, "Mais vous n'êtes pas en monarchie, vous êtes en République" [you are not living in a monarchy, you are living in a republic].[15] He attempted to convince the right in the Assembly to accept the Republic and he repeated many times in his address, "Nous vivons en République" [we live in a republic].[16] The monarchist Right was unconvinced that France was actually living in a republic and Laboulaye's amendment was defeated by a vote of 359 to 366 with twenty abstentions.[17] As the result of the vote was announced Laboulaye cried "Ayez pitié de la France!" [Have pity for France!] and this cry of pain caused a sensation in the Assembly.[18]

The next day Laboulaye's colleague and friend, Henri Wallon,[19] a devout Catholic professor and well-known hellenist, drafted an amendment that was substantially the same as Laboulaye's, as the *Journal des Débats* editorialized, "qui diffère si peu de l'amendement de M. Laboulaye" [which differs so little from M. Laboulaye's amendment].[20] In Wallon's amendment the hated word "Republic" was only in the second line. Its second line read, "The Government of the Republic is composed of two Chambers and a President," and continued, "The President of the Republic is elected by a majority of votes by the Senate and the Chamber of Deputies sitting together as a national assembly." This amendment was passed 353 to 352, a majority of one. The Republic came into being with one vote to spare—a fact its opponents would never forget! When the final vote was taken Laboulaye voted enthusiastically for Wallon's amendment.[21]

One of the recurrent themes in the parliamentary debates on the constitutional laws was that the French were following the American example. The two-chambered legislature and the desire for a strong president are, however, but examples of, what was termed inappropriately we think, the strong influence of America. What the framers of the constitutional laws, including Laboulaye, did not see or grasp was the significance of the office of the premier in the French parliamentary system, or the dynamics of parliamentary government. The premier owed his office to a parliamentary majority and did not serve exclusively at the pleasure of the president. Since the office of premier was alien to the American political system, the founders of the Third Republic could not be said to be completely imitating the American system. It is difficult to see how such a misinterpretation could have been made, and the English historian, Denis Brogan, goes so far as to term Laboulaye's claim to be copying America as absurd.[22] What Laboulaye and his followers borrowed from the American system was, in the most simple terms, the office of a strong president and a legislature containing two houses. Also it must be remembered that the founders of the Third Republic passed a series of constitutional laws but never systematically drew up a constitution, which was a reflection of the intense political divisions of the time.

The establishment of an upper house to be called a Senate posed a major problem for the republicans. The more radical wished for direct elections of senators by universal suffrage and the more conservative wished for some senators to be elected for life by the Chamber of Deputies or appointed by the president while the majority of the senators would be elected indirectly. The law on the Senate was passed on 24 February 1875. Senators had to have reached the minimum age of forty, a third of the Senate's members would be replaced at a time, and seventy-five senators would have a life-time appointment. It was hoped that the senators for life would be conservative. Two hundred and twenty-five senators would be elected indirectly by departmental electoral colleges and not by universal suffrage. The distribution of seats and the method of election perpetuated the rural domination of the Senate, "the bastion of traditional France."[23] Laboulaye summed up the work of the constitutional laws as embodying "the common right of free peoples."[24] As Jean-Claude Lamberti states, "Central to his [Laboulaye's] thinking was the concept of a 'common law of free peoples' which spanned oceans and language in its expression of true liberty."[25]

When elections of senators for life took place in December, Laboulaye was the tenth senator elected to one of the seventy-five cherished and sought-after positions,[26] which required a majority of votes in the National Assembly. Laboulaye's early election is testimony to the esteem in which he was held by his colleagues in the National Assembly as well as the political support he enjoyed as a leader of the *centre gauche*. The hope of the founding fathers of the Third Republic was that the senators for life would be conservative. As the *Journal des Débats* observed Laboulaye and others elected with him would give France "les garanties conservatrices" [conservative guarantees] that one had the right to expect from senators for life.[27] In fact, the vast majority of them, although conservative, were dedicated republicans. The monarchists, who comprised the extreme Right, were routed as they only succeeded in electing eighteen senators for life.

The Struggle for Freedom of Education

Election as lifetime senator was the pinnacle of Laboulaye's political career; this did not mean, however, that he would relax for one moment his interest in political affairs. In fact, he was almost immediately in the center of the controversy over education, a subject that had been of great interest to Laboulaye from the beginning of his legislative career. He was particularly impressed by the German system of education, especially higher education, which was not bound by the centralizing features of the French educational system. The monopoly of the University did not exist east of the Rhine, in its place was competition. Laboulaye was also favorably impressed by the practice of the *Privatdozent*, or private instructor or tutor, in German higher education. Laboulaye reflected the view current in France that one of the reasons for the French defeat in the Franco-Prussian War was the inferior French educational system. Hence, a reform of the educational system was a high priority of the founding fathers of the Third Republic. It is only fair to add here that some of Laboulaye's educational views reflected his study of American educational institutions, especially the work of Horace Mann.

One of Laboulaye's first interests in education after his election as deputy was to support his former pupil, Émile Boutmy, in his efforts to establish a private faculty that would train the administrative elite of France.[28] Boutmy was much influenced by the British political tradition and also the curriculum in British higher education, which prepared its students for future roles in public service.[29] In addition to Laboulaye his efforts were supported by François Guizot, Hippolyte Taine, Edmond Scherer, Louis Wolowski, and others. Boutmy opened his school, the École Libre des Sciences Politiques, on 15 January 1872. At the opening ceremony Laboulaye gave a brief address and also agreed to serve the school in an advisory capacity and also to give occasional lectures. The founders of the École Libre hoped that their efforts would avoid the pitfalls of the earlier experiment in 1848–49. Their efforts were rewarded as the school trained the administrative elite of the Third Republic and remained in existence until 1939.[30]

In the closing year of the Second Empire, the minister of education, M. Segris, appointed Laboulaye to the extra parliamentary commission that was asked to propose reforms of French higher education. It was a distinguished body with Guizot serving as chairman and Prévost-Paradol and the Père Chaptier (shot as a hostage in the Commune) among its members. Laboulaye commented favorably on the commission's work, which was cut short by the Franco-Prussian War. The basic recommendations of the Guizot Commission were embodied in the first proposed educational reforms of the Third Republic. Count Jaubert, a member of the parliamentary committee on education, incorporated many of the commission's findings in an educational reform bill that he wished to have passed in the early years of the Third Republic. This reform would permit the establishment of nongovernmentally supported or private faculties that would be empowered to grant degrees. Laboulaye supported these proposals as he argued that they would guarantee liberty and remove the monopoly of the University in the matter of degrees and grades. In fact, Count Jaubert's proposals formed the basis of work for the parliamentary committee of which Laboulaye was *rapporteur*.[31]

Laboulaye's interest in education was sincere, profound, and tied to his liberalism. He once wrote, "Une démocratie ignorante est une démocratie condamnée" [an ignorant democracy is a doomed democracy] and he also loved to quote Daniel Webster who said, "Pour voir à l'instruction de la jeunesse est pour l'État un droit incontestable et un devoir rigoureux" [To see to the education of youth is for the State an uncontestable right and a rigorous duty].[32] In *Le Parti libéral* he asserted "L'État peut offrir l'enseignement, mais qu'il n'a le droit de l'imposer" [The State can offer instruction, but it does not have the right to impose it],[33] and he added, freedom of education was just and necessary because our soul belonged only to us. He concluded, "Le citoyen doit à l'État l'obéissance civile jusqu'au sacrifice de sa vie, il ne lui doit pas le sacrifice de sa raison et de sa conscience" [The citizen owes the state civil obedience as far as the sacrifice of his life, he does not owe the sacrifice of his reason or his conscience].[34] He also declared, "l'État enseignant est déjà un fait énorme, mais l'État prétendant au monopole de toute science et de tout enseignement, cela est odieux et ridicule" [A teaching state is already an enormous factor but a state monopolizing all knowledge and all learning, that is odious and absurd].[35] He decried the intellectual centralization of the French system and argued that there is nothing to justify entrusting the monopoly over education to either the church or the state.[36]

On 6 June 1875 he served as *rapporteur* for a bill on higher education, advocating freedom of higher education he said, "La liberté individuelle est notre principe. Et si pour nous la Révolution française à un côté respectable, c'est que précisément elle a fondé le droit sur le respect de la liberté individuelle" [Individual freedom is our principle. And if for us there is a respectable side of the French Revolution, it is precisely that it based law on respect for the individual].[37] Laboulaye underscored further his concept of liberty or freedom of teaching when he replied in the Chamber "Je crois . . . que sans religion il n'y a pas de liberté possible" [I believe . . . that without religion freedom is not possible][38]

The quotations cited above were central to Laboulaye's thought on education and explain his views and votes as a parliamentarian on that question. Simply stated, in education, neither the church nor the state should have a monopoly. He opposed centralization and the compulsory indoctrination of any system of thought, or more to the point, republican, laic, or anticlerical world views as well as clerical views. For him, an official ideology imparted in the schools would be an infringement of the individual liberty of its citizens. The line separating church and state, he argued, was a fine and difficult one, but it should be respected and treasured to prevent the tyranny of either. These views on liberty and education would eventually lead Laboulaye into a headlong clash with radical republicans such as Léon Gambetta and Jules Ferry who were intransigent in their wish to make republican and laic education compulsory. Furthermore, Laboulaye would be a leading opponent of Ferry's educational proposals in 1880.[39]

Laboulaye's first task on the Committee of Higher Education was to examine the law proposed by Count Jaubert, a law that Jaubert submitted on 31 July 1871. Laboulaye submitted the committee's report to the Chamber on 23 July 1873. The law dealt with a reform of higher education; it would permit the opening of free Catholic universities and allotted the awarding of degrees to mixed boards of examiners consisting of professors from the state educational institutions and from the free universities. Two years later it was debated in the Chamber and Laboulaye declared: "Je demande que les catholiques aient la liberté comme citoyens" [I ask that Catholics enjoy freedom as citizens].[40] In his report to the Assembly he declared, "La Liberté d'enseignement est généralement réclamée aujourd'hui" [Freedom of education is generally demanded today],[41] and he continued by stating that France was no longer living in the era of Royer-Collard, who declared in the Chamber during the Restoration that higher education belonged to the state and was under the "direction supérieure du roi."[42] In the debates in the Chamber, he said that without religion, liberty was impossible.[43] The law was passed on 12 July 1875 and the vote was accomplished with the aid of the votes of the royalist and clerical members in the Assembly.[44] In commenting on the Law the *Journal des Débats* termed it a law of liberty.[45] In the course of the debates Laboulaye made a stirring appeal for academic freedom when he recounted his own difficulties in developing a course on the American Constitution when he found that in order to lecture on the Constitution he had to study not only the American Revolution but also the early history of the colonies. He stated that, if a government inspector had come into his class on the American Constitution and found him lecturing on the arrival of the Pilgrims at Plymouth Rock, he would have been in serious trouble. Government inspectors should not come into the classroom as it violated academic freedom or, as he called it, *"liberté d'enseignement."*[46]

Although his declining health in the late 1870s forced him to restrict his activities as a senator and also to turn his courses at the Collège de France over to his *suppléant,* M. Flach (in the French system a deputy or stand-in instructor), Laboulaye, nevertheless maintained a keen interest in the various education laws that were proposed. In 1880, Jules Ferry, who was appointed minister of education and served from 4 February 1879 to 14 November 1881 and then from 30 January to 7 August 1882 and finally from 21 February to 20 November 1883, drafted a sweeping reform of the French educational system, which he proposed not in one all-encompassing law, but in peacemeal fashion, one law after another. The chief thrust of Ferry's reforms was to laicize the French educational system, to remove the influence of the church.[47] As Antoine Prost asserted, henceforth the French state would control primary education, which would be "compulsory, free, and lay."[48]

During the nineteenth century the Catholic church in France had been, by and large, allied politically with the French Right. During the Second Empire a small group of Catholics, the liberal Catholics, led by such men as the Count de Montalembert, Bishop Dupanloup, the Count de Falloux, Théophile Foisset, and Augustin Cochin, were liberals in politics and advocated a free church in a free state and opposed the close reliance of the French church with the state. Also they strongly opposed the conservative policies of Pope Pius IX, especially, as expressed in his *Syllabus of Errors,* issued in 1864, which explicitly condemned liberalism and many modern movements. Many liberal lay Catholics and several French bishops also opposed the definition of papal infallibility by the Vatican Council in 1870.

The conflict of the French church and state during the Third Republic must also be viewed in the context of the past history of the French church as well as certain problems unique to the decade of the 1870s and 1880s. First, Catholics were shocked by the excesses of the Paris Commune in 1871 when the archbishop of Paris and some fifty priests were held hostage and later shot. Coming as it did after the defeat in the Franco-Prussian War, the feeling of many churchmen and Catholics was, as Adrien Dansette states, that "France had sinned and was making satisfaction through her misfortunes."[49] Second, the majority of the French hierarchy and clergy were monarchists and, consequently, hostile to the Republic. Furthermore, the taking of Rome by the Kingdom of Italy, which caused not only the loss of papal temporal power but created the view of Pope Pius IX as being the Prisoner of the Vatican, evoked much sympathy from French Catholics who wished the restoration of temporal power. During the 1870s the Assumptionist Order organized numerous pilgrimages making use of the railways to Lourdes, La Salette, Paray-le-Monial, Pontmain, and Chartres. At the religious services at these shrines prayers were usually offered for the restoration of the temporal power, and often also for the restoration of the monarchy, or explicity for the

restoration of the Bourbon pretender, Henry V, the Count of Chambord. The view was also current that the defeat in the Franco-Prussian
War and the bloodshed of the Commune were caused by the sins of
the nation. French Catholics also began to build a basilica on the
summit of Montmartre in Paris to be dedicated to the Sacred Heart,
in expiation for the defeat of 1870 and the horrors of the Commune.
The land for Sacré Coeur required special legislation to be passed by
the National Assembly and Jules Simon, the minister of cults, introduced the necessary legislation, which the Assembly passed. The passage of this legislation infuriated the anticlericals.

The most explicit statement, however, of the hatred for the Republic was given by Pope Pius IX, who in a tactless letter, wrote the
Bishop of Quimper in 1873, "We are referring not to the enemies of
the Church for they are known to us, but to those who spread and
sow revolution under the pretence of reconciling Catholicism and
liberty."[50] Advocating French support for the restoration of temporal
sovereignty and the restoration of the monarchy did not please republicans who were also skeptical of the educational law of 1874, which
permitted Catholic schools of higher education to grant degrees.

Given the strong clerical influence in the early years of the Third
Republic, it is not surprising that French political life during the
first fifteen years of the Third Republic was dominated by a wave
of anticlericalism emanating, chiefly, from the dedicated republicans.
Gambetta in an oft-quoted speech told the Chamber of Deputies on
4 May 1877 in an impassioned speech: "Vous sentez donc, vous avouez
donc qu'il y a une chose qui, à l'égal de l'Ancien Régime, répugne à
ce pays, répugne aux paysans de France . . . c'est la domination du
cléricalisme" [You feel then, you vow then that there is one thing
which—equal to the Ancien Régime—disgusts this country, disgusts
the peasants of France . . . it is clerical domination]! and he concluded
his inflamatory speech with "Le cléricalisme? Voilà l'ennemi" [Cleri-
calism, there is the enemy]![51] Gambetta added the deadly words, "It
is rare indeed for a Catholic to be a patriot."[52] In the 1870s, as John
McManners asserted, "The menace of clericalism was the central
theme of the highly organized Republican propaganda."[53]

In the midst of this heated political climate of the clerical-anticleri-
cal controversy, Jules Ferry introduced new educational laws, which
in the words of John McManners had two objectives:

to prise the clergy out of influential positions in State education, and
to weaken the private system of education controlled by the Church.
Henceforward, ecclesiastics would be excluded from the national and departmental councils which supervised the official schools, and the name

of "university" and the right to confer degrees would be limited to public institutions.[54]

Laboulaye was not a clerical (not to mention his manner of dress)
although his votes on educational matters often coincided with the
clerical point of view. There is also no question that he was a sincere
Catholic whose writings also pointed out the good in Protestantism
as was evident in his championing of Channing's religious views at a
time when most Catholics were anything but ecumenical. He based
his opposition to the laic laws on the principle that they were an
infringement on the rights of the private schools and individuals; this
opposition was consistent with his abhorrence of an omnipotent state
that infringed upon the rights of its citizens. In opposing the educational laws he constantly returned to the necessity of maintaining the
liberties of all citizens. Today it may be difficult to understand those
republicans who thought that the church was the greatest enemy of
the Republic and Catholics who thought that the Republic was the
greatest enemy of the church. But it is an uncontestable fact that
anticlericalism became the battle cry in the 1870s and 1880s.

Central to an understanding of Ferry's proposed laws in 1880 was
the matter of unauthorized religious orders teaching in France. For an
order to be authorized it had to be specifically approved in the Concordat of 1802 signed between the church and Napoleon. Only five orders
of men possessed such authorization in 1879. By the 1870s many
orders of both men and women not specifically recognized by the
Concordat were teaching in the French school system at all levels. In
fact, many had been founded since the signing of the Concordat.
French governments between 1802 and the 1870s had tolerated this
practice, and not only had it become accepted practice that these
orders taught in France, but in fact, the educational system relied on
their services. One religious order that was not authorized in the
Concordat of 1802 was the Society of Jesus or the Jesuits. At the time
of the signing of the Concordat, the Jesuits did not exist in France.
They had been suppressed throughout the church in 1773 by Pope
Clement XIV and were only reinstated in 1814 by Pope Pius VII. In
the polemics of the day the Jesuits usually bore the brunt of the
anticlerical attacks.[55]

Ferry's proposed law stated in Article VII that only authorized
orders could teach in the schools; Laboulaye argued that this proposal
was directed against the Jesuits in particular and was a violation of
their rights. He also wrote that the law was based on a spirit of
intolerance that would turn the university into a war machine "pour
renverser ce qu'on appelle le cléricalisme, et ce que les catholiques

appellent la religion" [to overturn which is called clericalism, and what Catholics call religion].[56] Evelyn M. Acomb summed up Laboulaye's position by stating: "A group of liberal conservatives, including such men as Jules Simon, Laboulaye, Dufaure, Étienne Lamy, and Bardoux, was opposed to the laic laws as a violation of those principles of freedom of conscience, freedom of instruction, and freedom of association for which the republican party had long stood."[57] Jules Simon's and Laboulaye's positions on educational questions were strikingly similar.[58] Opposition to Article VII was sufficiently strong in the Senate to delay its passage for several years. Some of Laboulaye's friends and supporters considered his efforts against this legislation to have strained his delicate health and hastened his death, which occurred in 1883.

As part of his educational laws Ferry also succeeded in having repealed some provisions of the Law of 1875, which permitted the establishment of private and Catholic universities. Henceforth, these institutions could neither grant degrees nor call themselves universities. Degrees had to be awarded by the state, which also controlled the grades; this was but one more step in a movement towards the laic state.

Individual Catholics wrote to Laboulaye congratulating him on his opposition to Ferry's laws: a group of twenty-one Catholics from Montpellier and the bishop of Montpellier wrote of "son admiration et sa gratitude pour les services éminents qu'un vrai libéral à la cause sacrée de l'indépendance de l'enseignement chrétien" [his admiration and his gratitude for the eminent services of a true liberal in the sacred cause of the independence of Christian education].[59] The *Semaine religieuse de Paris* commented after Laboulaye's death that the moderate republic had lost one of its most brilliant defenders. The *Semaine* continued "On se rappelle encore avec quelle vigueur il défendit, en se séparant nettement de ses coreligionnaires politiques, la liberté de l'enseignement" [We still recall with what vigor he defended the freedom of education separating himself clearly from his political allies].[60] In his papers were dozens of calling cards left at his home by French bishops, often with a brief word of encouragement. Many of these calling cards are dated at the time of the debates on the Ferry Laws.

In conclusion, Laboulaye's opposition to Ferry's legislation was that it infringed on the rights of others. The state had the right to maintain a school system, but others also had the same right. Rigid centralized state control was, for Laboulaye, a violation of true liberal principles. The omnipotent state was for him inconsistent with liberal principles and harkened back to the worst days of the French Revolution. He also opposed the compulsory inculcation of a laic ideology.

Laboulaye continued to give public lectures on topics that were dear to his heart, especially at awards ceremonies and to adult education groups. Of special interest to him was the École Professionnelle Libre directed by M. Bertrand at Versailles, where he appeared every year at their awards ceremony. Four of these addresses were printed in his *Discours populaires* and ten were printed in his *Derniers discours populaires*. His first address to the students of the École Professionnelle Libre was in 1866 and his last in 1881, two years before his death. Laboulaye was the patron of this school and his addresses to the students form a course in morals for the young. From his introductory remarks given to these talks it is obvious that he enjoyed these appearances immensely.

Liberty Enlightening the World

Laboulaye is probably best remembered in America today as the person who served as president of the FrancoAmerican Union, which raised funds to erect the Statue of Liberty Enlightening the World in New York Harbor. To raise funds for such a gigantic endeavor was thoroughly consistent with his previous activities as France's leading Americanist. The story has often been told how the Alsatian sculptor Frédéric Bartholdi, Agénor de Gasparin, Henri Martin, and Charles de Rémusat were having dinner at Laboulaye's house in Versailles in 1865 and the idea of erecting a statue in America to celebrate the centennial of its independence in 1876 was conceived.[61]

Most writers agree that the idea of a statue of liberty came largely from Laboulaye. Catherine Hodeir asserted, "it is likely that Laboulaye approached the sculptor with his idea for a monument to be given by the French people to the United States to symbolize the friendship between the two countries as well as to celebrate the American political system."[62] The idea that it would be a colossal statue no doubt came from Bartholdi, who was strongly influenced by the colossal element in ancient and modern sculpture. Bartholdi wrote Laboulaye in 1871 that he wished a colossal statue and informed him that he had found the site in New York Harbor.[63] According to Hodeir, "Laboulaye played an important part in the subsequent story, especially since he is the one who gave final shape to the image, and since he held firmly to the whole symbolic meaning of the project. Bartholdi must have understood that immediately in 1865."[64]

From the time the idea was first conceived until the concerted campaign to raise funds, ten years elapsed. One must remember that during these ten years a site had to be found, which necessitated

Bartholdi visiting the United States to seek one out. Also the design and general shape of the statue had to be decided and the model/maquette executed. Delays were caused as well by events of the period such as the Franco-Prussian War, the fall of the Second Empire, the Commune, the postwar disruption in France, and the reluctance of monarchists to honor a republic.

After his military service in the Franco-Prussian War, Bartholdi wrote Laboulaye from his native Colmar that he hoped soon to have a maquette of his monument in honor of independence and liberty. He added: "J'ai relu et relis encore vos oeuvres à ce sujet [liberté] et j'espère faire honneur à votre amitié qui me patronera. Je tâcherai de glorifier la République et la Liberté là bas" [I have reread and am still rereading your works on the subject "liberty," and I hope to honor your friendship, which will subsidize me. I will endeavor to glorify the Republic and liberty over there].[65] In 1871, at his own expense, Bartholdi sailed to New York to look for a site. He was armed with letters of introduction from Laboulaye to Miss Mary Booth, Senator Sumner, Colonel Forney, Francis Lieber, and others.[66] During his voyage in America Bartholdi met Longfellow, who told him he wished him every success and offered his help in erecting the statue of friendship.[67]

Only in 1875 was the Franco-American committee organized to raise funds for the Statue of Liberty. Fund raising was delayed until after France had paid her indemnities to the German Empire thereby ending the occupation of parts of France. It was considered inappropriate to mount a major fund-raising campaign until after the indemnity had been paid. It was also decided to wait until France was officially a republic with a constitution. The royalists, who were dominant until 1875, did not always look kindly on a monument praising liberty in the American republic. Most of the committee members to raise funds for the statue were drawn from Laboulaye's own political group in the National Assembly, the *centre gauche,* and included several prominent freemasons. The committee was officially formed on 26 September 1875 and hoped to raise the funds within a year so that in 1876 France would have the amount needed to erect the statue in the centennial year of the Declaration of Independence. Unfortunately, the campaign dragged on until 1880.

The newly formed Comité de l'Union Franco-Américaine had Laboulaye serving as president and Henri Martin, the historian and senator, and Dietz Monin, Bartholdi's cousin, as vice-presidents. Descendants of Lafayette, Rochambeau, and Noailles, whose ancestors had fought in the American Revolution, all served on the committee in varying capacities as did Tocqueville's brother, the Comte de

Tocqueville. Leading members of the *centre gauche* such as Wad-
dington and Wolowski also served on the committee as did Guizot's
son-in-law Cornelis de Witt, a political conservative, who had, after
all, written a life of Washington that no doubt qualified him for
membership. The major campaign for funds featured appeals in the
press and also advertisements.

The committee envisioned three major events to publicize their project: a banquet at the Hotel du Louvre on 6 November 1875; a fête at
the Palais de l'Industrie on the Champs Elysées, 19 November 1875;
and a reception and concert at the Paris Opera on 25 April 1876. At
the committee's kick-off banquet, speeches were made by Henri Martin, the American minister to France, Elihu B. Washburne, John W.
Forney, and Laboulaye. Laboulaye's speech was described in the *Evening Telegram* as "being remarkable for its chaste eloquence and thrill-
ing *résumé* of the life and character of Lafayette."[68] The *Journal des
Débats* commented that "M. Laboulaye est chez lui en Amérique
comme en France, et, en l'écoutant parler, on songeait à Franklin qui
n'était pas moins chez lui en France qu'en Amérique" [M. Laboulaye
is at home in America as he is in France, and to listen to him is to
think of Franklin who was no less at home in France than in
America].[69] This banquet was one of the first large banquets held
during the Third Republic, a period during which the institution of
the banquet was to become a hallowed ritual. This one successfully
raised over 40,000 francs or about one-tenth of the Statue of Liberty's cost.[70]

After Henri Martin had delivered a lengthy toast to the United
States and President Grant, Elihu Washburne replied with a toast to
Marshal MacMahon and France. Then the featured speaker, Édouard
Laboulaye, spoke. One of the secretaries described it as "un modèle
achevé d'éloquence, de sagesse politique et patriotique, de tact, de
spirituelle et fine ironie" [A perfect model of eloquence, of political
and patriotic wisdom, of tact, of witty and refined irony].[71] Laboulaye's address, interrupted numerous times with applause, traced Franco-American relations from American independence to 1875 with
special emphasis upon Franklin, Washington, and Lincoln. He concluded his remarks with a toast that he said summed up the feelings,
hopes, and desires of his audience. It was "À l'amitié, à l'éternelle
amitié de la France et de l'Amérique" [to the friendship, to the eternal
friendship of France and America].[72] After Laboulaye, John W. Forney spoke briefly in his capacity as the representative in Europe of
the Centennial Exposition, which was to take place in Philadelphia
in 1876. At this exposition Bartholdi would exhibit the maquette of
the gigantic right hand of the statue to help raise funds in the United

States for the pedestal of the statue. At the conclusion of the banquet, telegrams were sent to Presidents MacMahon and Grant and it was hoped that by the magic of telegraph Grant would receive his telegram with his dinner![73]

The fête at the Palais de l'Industrie was a failure; it drew a small audience, which disappointed its sponsors. The concert at the Palais de l'Opéra was an extraordinary event although the performers and the orchestra apparently almost outnumbered the audience. When the curtain was raised, a group of men were seated on stage around one man "dressed in kind of a high-necked tunic buttoned to the top and revealing only the line of the white neck; clean shaven; the hair grey, worn long and brushed back."[74] This was Édouard Laboulaye who looked for all the world like a "Quaker," but whose brief address was "to the point and often witty."[75] The program was an extravaganza that included all that we have come to understand as the worst aspects of nineteenth-century taste. It is worth a look for that reason alone. A musical program followed Laboulaye's remarks and included selections by Aubert, Fauré, Rossini, and Gounod's "Ave Maria." Charles Gounod, the noted opera composer, wrote a choral work especially for the occasion sung by a male chorus of some seven hundred men drawn from the ranks of the people. The hymn dedicated to the Statue of Liberty was entitled, "La liberté éclairant le Monde" [liberty illuminating the world], with words by Émile Guiard (Gounod had first sought to have Victor Hugo write the words but the poet declined this honor). The musical portion of the program concluded with the massed choruses singing "Hail Columbia," which was identified as the American national anthem. The musical portion of the program was understandably severely criticized in the press and the financial success of the program was equally disappointing: only 8,291 francs were raised not the projected 22,000 francs that a full house would have brought in.

After its first fund-raising attempts in 1876, the committee realized that it would take time to raise the money; it was not until 1880 that the campaign was concluded. To spur the interest of prospective donors Bartholdi exhibited the head of the statue at the Universal Exposition in Paris in 1878. At the same time, admission was charged to visit a diorama showing the statue in the Tuileries Gardens. It was, however, only when the committee resorted to a national lottery to raise funds that the campaign for funds reached its goal. The lottery campaign opened with the exhibition of prizes in Paris on 27 June 1879 and the drawing of the lottery took place on 20 June 1880.[76] On 7 July 1880 at a banquet in the Hôtel Continental, the committee announced that its fund raising had reached its goal and the members of the committee present sent official notification to the United States. Four days after the banquet Laboulaye wrote Mary L. Booth to tell of their success and also to say that his health was such that he would not live to see the statue erected in New York.[77]

One of the tourist attractions of Paris was the construction site of the statue. The most prominent American tourist was General Grant, who toured Europe after he left office, and visited the construction site on 21 November 1877; in a letter to Laboulaye he expressed the hope that the statue would soon be completed.[78] Laboulaye replied that "Votre visite a été une sorte de consécration du momument qui doit attester aux générations les plus lontaines l'amitié de la France et des États-Unis" [Your visit has been a sort of consecration of the monument and ought to bear witness for future generations to the friendship of France and the United States].[79]

The statue was first erected in Paris, and on 24 October 1881 a ceremony was held at the construction site on the Rue de Chazelles near the Place de l'Étoile to drive the first rivet that would tie the statue to its pedestal or plinth. The American minister, Levi Parsons Morton, attended the ceremony and he was received by Laboulaye as president of the Union Franco-Américaine.[80] The ceremony was held on the centennial of the surrender of Yorktown. In a brief address Laboulaye introduced Morton and expressed his hope that in the next century "cette vision fraternelle que le temps n'a fait que fortifier la perpetuelle amitié de la France et de l'Amérique" [this fraternal symbol that in time will only fortify the perpetual friendship of France and America]. Morton in his reply accepted the statue and concluded by paying tribute to Laboulaye "le nom de votre éminent président, le savant interprète, en France, de nos institutions politiques et de notre Constitution nationale, M. Laboulaye" [the name of your distinguished president, the learned interpreter, in France, of our political institutions and our national Constitution, M. Laboulaye].[81]

As the erection of the statue proceeded it became a major tourist attraction and Parisians noted, when it was finished, that it was higher than the Vendôme Column. When the right foot was completed a rather bizarre event occurred as a banquet was held in the completed foot for Bartholdi's friends; later an intimate dinner was also held in the knee when it was finished. After approximately three years of work the statue was completed. It was officially dedicated in Paris on 4 July 1884, and Ferdinand de Lesseps, who had succeeded to the presidency of the Franco-American Union after Laboulaye's death gave the principal address. On 28 October 1886 the statue would be dedicated in New York Harbor—twenty-one years after the idea was first conceived at Laboulaye's dinner party in 1865!

On 21 May 1884, at a banquet given by an American resident in Paris, Mr. Henry F. Gillig delivered the following toast in tribute to Laboulaye:

M. Laboulaye was a born friend of America—and I say "born" because from his birth he was American, although he had never been in America. He described America as only a few would do it, not even an American. I was astonished at it when, after having read his works—and many of them—on America, I went there for the first time. He had never been there, but he defined America so well that I do not believe any one could better define the honor of American character, the love of the people for civilisation, and the openhanded manner, full of generosity, frankness, and even innocence with which they practise "Liberty." No one could better describe American characteristics—and I was struck with it—than M. Laboulaye. It is to him that I owe my knowledge of America, and I have only known America through him, even after having been there. M. Laboulaye thus deserves all our thoughts. He was an honest man above all, *savant*, amiable, and affectionate, and I drink to his memory, which is joined to that of liberty, of honor, and of the greatness of America.[82]

His Death and Legacy

Laboulaye, whose health had been failing for many years as attested to in his letters, declined dramatically in the three or four years before his death on 25 May 1883. In 1878 he suffered a psychological defeat when his candidacy for election to the seat vacated by Silvestre de Sacy in the Académie Française was unsuccessful; Maxime du Camp was elected to a seat among the forty *immortels*. Émile Littré wrote Laboulaye in 1880 and told him that he should be in the Académie Française and that he would support his candidacy; however, Laboulaye did not present himself again.[83] Thus his most cherished goal of a seat in the Académie Française was denied him. His disappointment was bitter. He did, however, in 1878 draw some consolation from being promoted to the rank of grand officer in the Legion of Honor.[84]

After 1871 his courses at the Collège de France were usually taught by his *suppléant*, M. Flach, as his duties as a parliamentarian interfered with his teaching duties. He did, however, resume his teaching in December 1877 and taught until 1879 when ill health forced him to turn his courses once more over to his *suppléant*. Two years later he was able to resume his courses for a brief period of time; however, his last lecture at the Collège de France was given on 15 May 1882 just a year before his death. In these last years his visits to the Senate grew fewer as he seemed spent after the exhausting debates over the

Ferry laws.[85] His frequent speeches of former years were but a memory.

Death came swiftly. He was struck with an attack of apoplexy at three o'clock on the afternoon of Wednesday, 23 May, and he died the next morning at 5:00 A.M., Thursday, 24 May 1883,[86] after having received the last sacraments of the church.[87] His expressed wish was for a simple funeral with no eulogies. He lay in state at the Collège de France; three floral wreaths were placed on the casket: one from the Union Franco-Américaine, one from his friends in Boston, and the third from the École Professionnelle de Versailles.[88] On Monday, 28 May, his remains were transported to the nearby Church of Saint Étienne du Mont for the Mass of the Dead. After the Mass, the funeral cortège made its way through the streets of Paris to Père Lachaise Cemetery where he was interred. His wishes were carried out and there were no eulogies or speeches either at the church or the cemetery. A large crowd attended the funeral and took part in the procession to Père Lachaise, among them an American admirer, Susan B. Anthony. Her biographer, Ira Hudsted Harper wrote, "At noon we went to the Collège de France to witness the last honors to Laboulaye, the scholar and Liberal. Saw his little study and sadly watched the priests perform the services over his coffin."[89] Elizabeth Cady Stanton in her memoirs recounted that one of the things that made the "deepest impression on Miss Anthony, during her stay in Paris," was the interrment of Laboulaye who she described as "the friend of the United states and of the woman (*sic*) movement." Also Miss Anthony fulfilled another cherished objective of her Paris visit by meeting Jules Ferry at Laboulaye's funeral.[90]

After his death, tributes to his life and activities abounded. *Le Monde* editorialized that "La République modérée et vraiment libérale perd en lui l'un de ses plus brillants défenseurs" [The moderate and truly liberal Republic loses in him one of its brightest defenders].[91] The *New York Herald* described him as "always a firm and warm friend of America, and did perhaps more than any other European to enlighten France concerning the United States."[92] The *Troy Daily Times* said "France loses one of its most profound scholars, an able statesman and a liberal, broadminded man, and America one of its warmest and most influential friends."[93] The influential Brussels news-paper, *L'Indépendance Belge,* declared "M. Laboulaye avait beaucoup d'amis en Amérique, qui avait en lui un de ses meilleurs amis" [M. Laboulaye had many friends in America, they had in him one of their best friends].[94] Agénor Bardoux, writing in the *Journal des Débats,* lamented that the *Journal* had lost a distinguished collaborator and that Laboulaye was not only the leader of the liberals but in reality the theoretician of liberty. Bardoux continued by noting that for La-boulaye "la liberté était chose individuelle, qu'elle était le droit appar-tentant à chacun, en sa qualité d'homme, d'exercer et de développer son intelligence et son corps sans que l'État intervienne autrement que pour le maintien de la paix et de la justice" [For Laboulaye, free-dom was an individual thing, the right belonging to everyone as a human being, to exercise and develop his intelligence and his body without State intervention except to maintain peace and justice].[95] The American government telegraphed its condolences to his eldest son, Paul de Laboulaye. An anonymous writer to *The American Regis-ter* commented on the telegram: "This was certainly a most appro-priate and well-deserved tribute of respect, and one that I am sure will be most heartily approved by the whole people of the United States."[96]

On 12 December 1883 the Société de Législation Comparée offi-cially commemorated the death of one of its founding and most distin-guished members with a eulogy delivered by its president, Henri Barboux. This eulogy, in reality, was a comprehensive examination of Laboulaye's contributions to comparative law.[97] The Société du Trav-ail at its General Assembly of 17 May 1884 listened to a lengthy eulogy, certainly the lengthiest published (eighty pages in print), from its President Frédéric Passy.[98] Although Laboulaye was unable, be-cause of his health, to preside at its meetings for several years, the members, officers, and Frédéric Passy were grateful for Laboulaye's efforts on behalf of workers' education in the past as well as the society's efforts at mutual aid and assistance to its members. Labou-laye's successor at the Collège de France, M. Flach, devoted his first lecture to Laboulaye, and the Société Franklin heard a eulogy from M. Thierry-Mieg.[99]

* * *

In the tributes to Laboulaye several words resonate: liberal, liberty, America, democracy, and religion. His heroes, Washington, Franklin, Lincoln, Lafayette, Mann, and Channing, were also cited as exemplars of his world view. Also numerous tributes in America echoed the theme of his support for the North during the Civil War and his opposition to slavery.

Laboulaye's cherished aim was to see liberty and freedom estab-lished in France and embodied in her political institutions; and, in this, he could derive a certain amount of comfort, for as a founding father of the Third Republic, he was a consistent supporter and advo-cate for its liberal political institutions. As France's leading Ameri-canist he not only interpreted America for his countrymen, but he also wished for and was partially successful in establishing American democracy in France. His greatest achievement was to demonstrate to his countrymen that American democracy could serve as a useful model: however, one has to await the Constitution of the Fifth Republic to see further developments on the lines originally sketched by Édouard Laboulaye in the nineteenth century.

One of the most moving assessments of Laboulaye was written by his friend, Ernest Renan:

> Il eût voulu être ministre et membre de l'Académie Française; il eût été excellent ministre, et il avait plus de titres à l'Académie que la moitié de ceux qui en sort. Il se consola en réalisant dans sa vie, par un effort continu, l'idéal d'un honnête homme. Je ne crois pas que personne ait compris et pratiqué mieux que Laboulaye le règle du parfait libéral. S'il a jamais péché, c'est par trop d'amour de la liberté. Oh! la belle faute, et que je fais mon compliment à ceux qui n'en ont jamais commis d'autre

> [He wanted to become a minister and a member of the Académie Française; he would have been an excellent minister, and he had more right to be in the Académie than half of its present members. He consoled himself in his own life by practicing continuously the role of an honest man. I do not think that anyone understood or practiced better the role of the perfect liberal. Oh! what a beautiful fault, and I offer my compliments to those who have never commited any other]![100]

In the same volume his pupil, Émile Boutmy spoke of Laboulaye's love of life and of his individuality, his spontaneity, his originality, and above all of his devotion to liberty and noted approvingly his abhorrence of the routine, the pedestrian, the conventional, and the artificial. He began his essay by writing "Laboulaye était un homme de grand savoir, un homme d'esprit et un homme de bien" [Laboulaye was a man of great knowledge, a man of genius, and a good man].[101] These words of Renan and Boutmy draw a fitting portrait as well as an assessment of Laboulaye.

In conclusion, Laboulaye, America's friend, would certainly have been justifiably proud that two of his direct descendants, his great grandson, André de Laboulaye, and his great-great grandson, François de Laboulaye, became ambassadors of France to the United States, thereby continuing within the family Édouard's interest in America!

Notes

Chapter 1. Introduction

1. Alexandre Delamarre, "Libéralisme: un "Laissez-faire"? Pas forcément . . . ," *Le Figaro Magazine,* 17 January 1987, p. 48.

2. Serge-Christophe Kolm, "Libéralisme classique et renouvelé," in *Nouvelle histoire des idées politiques,* ed. Pascal Ory (Paris: Hachette, 1987), pp. 575–89.

3. Jean-Claude Casanova, "From the Ancients to the Moderns: The Reasons for the Liberal Revival," in *Liberty/Liberté The French and American Experiences,* ed. Joseph Klaits and Michael Haltzell (Washington, D.C.: Woodrow Wilson Center Press; Baltimore and London: The Johns Hopkins University Press, 1991), p. 173.

4. André Jardin, *Histoire du libéralisme politique de la crise de l'absolutisme à la constitution de 1875* (Paris: Hachette Littérature, 1985).

5. Louis Girard, *Les Libéraux français, 1814–1875* (Paris: Aubier, 1985).

6. Pierre Manent, *Histoire intellectuelle du libéralisme, dix leçons* (Paris: Calmann-Lévy, 1987).

7. Pierre Manent, *Les Libéraux,* 2 vols. (Paris: Hachette/Pluriel, 1986). Manent's article "Situation du Libéralisme," *Commentaire* 35 (1986): 388–99 summarizes his views on contemporary liberalism.

8. Cheryl B. Welch, *Liberty and Utility, The French Idéologues and the Transformation of Liberalism* (New York: Columbia University Press, 1984), pp. 28–29.

9. Ibid., p. 29. In footnote 91, p. 206, Welch lists the following as Idéologues: Cabanis, Tracy, Volney, Garat, Dégerando, Maine de Biran, Laromiguière, Roederer, Say, Jacquemont, Thurot, Ginguené, Chénier, Andrieux, and Lakanal.

10. Emmet Kennedy, *A Philosophe in the Age of Revolution: Destutt de Tracy and the Origins of "Ideology"* (Philadelphia: American Philosophical Society, 1978).

11. Martin S. Staum, *Cabanis: Enlightenment and Medical Philosophy in the French Revolution* (Princeton: Princeton University Press, 1980).

12. Philippe Raynaud, "Le Libéralisme français à l'épreuve du pouvoir," in *Nouvelle histoire des idées politiques,* ed. Ory, pp. 166–67.

13. According to André Jardin, Albert Thibaudet accorded her this title. Jardin, *Histoire du libéralisme,* p. 210.

14. Mme de Staël, *Considérations sur les principaux événements de la Révolution Française* (Paris: Taillandier, 1983). Renee Winegarten, *Mme de Staël* (Leamington Spa, England: Berg, 1985).

15. Mme de Staël, *Delphine,* 2 vols. (Paris: des Femmes, 1981), 2: 222.

16. Jardin, *Histoire du libéralisme,* p. 210.

17. Stephen Holmes, *Benjamin Constant and the Making of Modern Liberalism,* (New Haven and London: Yale University Press, 1984), p. 21.

18. François Guizot, *Histoire de la civilisation en Europe depuis la chute de l'Empire romain jusqu'à la Révolution française suivie de philosophie politique: de la souveraineté* presented, edited, and annotated by Pierre Rosanvallon (Paris: Hachette, 1985), p. 14.

19. James K. Kieswetter, *Étienne-Denis Pasquier, The Last Chancellor of France* (Philadelphia: American Philosophical Society, 1977) and Alexis de Tocqueville, *Oeuvres complètes tome XI Correspondance d'Alexis de Tocqueville et de Pierre-Paul Royer-Collard, Correspondance d'Alexis de Tocqueville et de Jean-Jacques Ampère* (Paris: Gallimard, 1970). This volume is edited by André Jardin and contains an excellent Introduction by him. An old but still useful study of Royer-Collard is Roger Langeron, *Un conseiller secret de Louis XVIII, Royer-Collard* (Paris: Hachette, 1956). On Fiévée see Jean Tulard, *Joseph Fiévée, conseiller secret de Napoléon* (Paris: Fayard, 1985).

20. Jean-Claude Lamberti, *Tocqueville and the Two Democracies* (Cambridge: Harvard University Press, 1989), p. 6.

21. Alan B. Spitzer, *The French Generation of 1820* (Princeton: Princeton University Press, 1987). See also his "Restoration Political Theory and the Debate over the Law of the Double Vote," *Journal of Modern History* 55 (1983): 54–70.

22. H. A. C. Collingham with R. S. Alexander, *The July Monarchy, A Political History of France, 1830–1848* (London and New York: Longman, 1988), p. 112.

23. David H. Pinkney, *Decisive Years in France, 1840–1847* (Princeton: Princeton University Press, 1986).

24. Ibid., pp. 23–49.

25. Pierre Rosanvallon, *Le moment Guizot* (Paris: Gallimard, 1985), J. P. T. Bury and R. R. Tombs, *Thiers, 1797–1877, A Political Biography* (London: Allen and Unwin, 1986) and Pierre Guiral, *Adolphe Thiers ou la necessité en politique* (Paris: Fayard, 1986).

26. Jules Michelet, *Oeuvres complètes*, ed. Paul Viallaneix (Paris: Flammarion, 1971–   ) and also his *Journal, texte intégral, établi sur les manuscrits autographes et publié pour la première fois, avec une introduction, des notes et de nombreux documents inédits, par Paul Viallaneix*, 4 vols. (Paris: Gallimard, 1959–76).

27. Jean-Claude Lamberti, *Tocqueville et les deux démocraties* (Paris: Presses Universitaires de France, 1983) recently translated into English as *Tocqueville and the Two Democracies* (Cambridge: Harvard University Press, 1989). Lamberti's study is the first state doctorate (doctorat d'état) ever done on Tocqueville in a French university. Of interest also is his earlier work *La notion de invidiualisme chez Tocqueville* (Paris: Presses Universitaires de France, 1970). Two American scholars writing on Tocqueville are: James T. Schleifer, *The Making of Tocqueville's "Democracy in America"* (Chapel Hill: University of North Carolina Press, 1980); and Roger Boesche, *The Strange Liberalism of Alexis de Tocqueville* (Ithaca: Cornell University Press, 1987). Schleifer's work traces the intellectual origins of Tocqueville's work by studying his working manuscript and his rough drafts in the Beinecke Library at Yale University. Françoise Melonio, an assistant to the commission publishing Tocqueville's works, has written many excellent introductions to the various volumes of Tocqueville's *Oeuvres complètes*. The major full-length biography of Tocqueville is André Jardin, *Alexis de Tocqueville, 1805–1859* (Paris: Hachette, 1984).

28. Philippe Raynaud in his Preface to his edition of Constant's *De la force du gouvernement actuel de la France et de la Nécessité de s'y rallier* and *Des réactions politiques des effets de la Terreur* (Paris: Flammarion, 1988), p. 7 remarks "Un des aspects les plus heureux de l'évolution intellectuelle récente aura sans doute été la redécouverte progressive, depuis bientôt, de l'oeuvre des grands libéraux du XIXe siècle français" [One of the most pleasant aspects of the recent intellectual revolution is the progressive rediscovery of the work of the French liberals of the nineteenth century].

29. Jean Rivero, "The Jacobin and Liberal Traditions," in *Liberty/Liberté*, ed. Klaits and Haltzell, p. 121.

30. George Armstrong Kelly, "The Jacobin and Liberal Contributions to the Founding of the Second and Third French Republics (with an Epilogue on America)," in *Liberty/Liberté*, ed. Klaits and Haltzell, p. 137.

31. Pierre Guiral, *Prévost-Paradol, 1829–1870, pensée et action d'un libéral sous le Second Empire* (Paris: Presses Universitaires de France, 1955), Theodore Zeldin, *Émile Ollivier and the Liberal Empire of Napoleon III* (Oxford: The Clarendon Press, 1963), and Philip A. Bertocci, *Jules Simon, Republican Anticlericalism and Cultural Politics in France, 1848–1886* (Columbia: University of Missouri Press, 1978).

32. An example of this prejudice is illustrated in the preface of Pierre Guiral to his recent biography of Thiers who recounts how friends and colleagues wondered why he was writing a biography of Thiers, who was associated with so much tawdry politics. Guiral, *Thiers*, p. 8.

33. No book-length biography or study of Laboulaye exists. There are, however, several useful brief studies of him by his pupils and colleagues. His former pupil, Émile Boutmy, in his *Taine, Scherer, Laboulaye* (Paris: A. Colin, 1901) included a sympathetic essay written shortly after Laboulaye's death. The official eulogy for the Institut de France was delivered by H. Wallon, "Notice sur la vie et les travaux de M. Édouard-René Lefebvre-Laboulaye, membre ordinaire de l'Académie des Inscriptions et Belles-Lettres," *Mémoires de l'Institut National de France, Académie des Inscriptions et Belles-Lettres*, 25:286–321, is helpful and contains a detailed bibliography of Laboulaye's writings. John Bigelow's, *Some Recollections of the Late Edouard Laboulaye* (New York: G. P. Putnam's Sons, 1889), is the brief testimony of an American friend and admirer. Bigelow included the sections dealing with Laboulaye in his multivolumed work, *Retrospections of an Active Life*, 5 vols. (New York and Garden City, N.J.: The Baker and Taylor Company, 1909–13). A brief work by Alkan Ainé, *Un fondeur en caractères, membre de l'Institut* (Paris: Au Bureau de "la Typologie-Tucker," 1886), contains a useful bibliography and some anecdotes concerning Laboulaye's youth and early career as a typesetter. A scholarly analysis of his political thought is Jean de Soto, "Édouard Laboulaye," *Revue internationale d'histoire politique et constitutionnelle* 5 (1955): 114–50. See also Walter D. Gray, "Edouard Laboulaye: 'Liberal' Catholic and 'Americanist' during the Second Empire," *Cithara* 3 (1964): 3–15, and his "Liberalism in the Second Empire and the Influence of America: Edouard Laboulaye and his Circle," in *Liberty/Liberté*, ed. Klaits and Haltzell, pp. 71–85. Also the late Jean-Claude Lamberti's, "Laboulaye and the Common Law of Free Peoples," in *Liberty, The French American Statue in Art and History*, ed. Provoyeur and Hargrove (New York: Harper and Row, 1986), pp. 20–25.

34. In reply to an anonymous query Laboulaye wrote, "Je suis né le 18 janvier 1811, et mon nom complet, que je ne prends jamais est Lefebvre de Laboulaye, Édouard René" [I was born on 18 January 1811, and my complete name, which I never use, is Lefebvre de Laboulaye, Édouard René]. Bibliothèque Nationale, N. A. F. 20507, Laboulaye to Monsieur [no name given], Paris, 4 February 1855. Laboulaye did not use the "de," the "particule de noblesse," in his name as was customary with some of his generation as Napoleon had banned the use of the "de" unless there was a specific patent entitling the person to use the "de." Laboulaye's sons, however, used it somewhat to the consternation of some American admirers.

35. *Recherches sur la condition civile et politique des femmes depuis les romains jusqu'à nos jours* (Paris: A. Durand, 1841).

36. Mme Édouard Laboulaye, *Vie de Jeanne d'Arc* (Paris: H. Pelagaud, 1877). The book was reprinted in 1880 and 1895.

37. The author wishes to express his gratitude to M. André Dauteribes of Dijon, France, for the information he has furnished him on the Laboulaye family.

38. New York Historical Society, Laboulaye to mon cher collègue [someone in the Loyal Publication Society, probably James McKay], Paris, 30 December 1863.

39. René Rémond, *Les États-Unis devant l'opinion française, 1815–1852* (Paris: Presses Universitaires de France, 1962), 2:245.

40. Theodore Zeldin, *France, 1848–1945* (Oxford: At the Clarendon Press, 1973–77), 2:129.

41. Édouard Laboulaye, "Horace Mann," *Revue des cours littéraires de la France et de l'étranger,* 27 February 1869, pp. 198–99.

42. Émile Boutmy, ed., *Le Livre du centenaire du Journal des Débats* (Paris: E. Plon, Nourrit et Cie., 1889), p. 253.

43. "Élection de M. Laboulaye," *Revue de législation et de jurisprudence* 17 (1845): 146.

44. Karen Offen discusses this book as well as Laboulaye's views on women's history in Karen Offen, "The Beginnings of 'Scientific' Women's History in France, 1830–1848," *Proceedings of the Eleventh Annual Meeting of the Western Society for French History, 3–5 November 1983* (Lawrence: University of Kansas, 1984), pp. 255–71.

45. Wolowski was a political exile from the abortive Polish Rebellion of 1830. Laboulaye maintained a long friendship with him and both will end their careers serving in the Senate of the Third Republic.

46. Laboulaye discusses this change in the Foreword to his *Considérations sur la constitution* (Paris: A. Durand, 1848) reprinted in his *Questions constitutionnelles* (Paris: Charpentier, 1873), pp. 3–4.

47. Henry Blumenthal in his *American and French Culture, Interchanges in Art, Science, Literature, and Society* (Baton Rouge: Louisiana State University Press, 1975), p. 77 incorrectly states that Laboulaye was dismissed with Michelet.

48. Laboulaye's career on the *Journal des Débats* is discussed by his former pupil, Émile Boutmy, "Laboulaye," *Le livre du centenaire du Journal des Débats* pp. 253–60.

49. Rodolphe Dareste in his Preface to Édouard de Laboulaye, *Trente ans d'enseignement au Collège de France, 1818–1882 publiés par ses fils avec le concours de M. Marcel Fournier, Préface de M. Rodolphe Dareste* (Paris: L. Larose et Forcel, 1888), p. xi.

50. Édouard Laboulaye, *La liberté religieuse* (Paris, 1858).

51. Édouard Laboulaye, "Horace Mann," *Revue des cours littéraires de la France et de l'étranger,* 27 February 1869, p. 202.

52. Édouard de Laboulaye, *Trente ans d'enseignement au Collège de France,* pp. xviii–xix.

53. Édouard Laboulaye, "Cours de législation comparée de la constitution des États-Unis," *Revue Nationale* 15 (10 January 1864): 385.

54. "Edouard Laboulaye," *Appleton's Journal of Popular Literature, Science, and Art,* 4 September 1869, pp. 84–85.

55. "M. Edouard Laboulaye," *Every Saturday,* 8 March 1873, p. 275.

56. Bigelow, *Some Recollections of the Late Edouard Laboulaye,* p. 14.

57. Ibid., pp. 3–4.

58. *L'Événement,* 27 April 1876, as quoted in Catherine Hodeir, "The French Campaign," in *Liberty,* ed. Provoyeur and Hargrove, p. 126.

59. *Le Figaro,* 26 April 1876 as quoted in Hodeir, "The French Campaign," p. 126.

60. *Le Petit Journal,* 27 May 1883.
61. Émile Boutmy, *Taine, Scherer, Laboulaye,* p. 111.

Chapter 2. Laboulaye, the Liberal

1. Alexis de Tocqueville, *The Recollections of Alexis de Tocqueville,* ed. J. P. Mayer (New York: Meridian Books, 1959), p. 78.
2. Jean Rivero, "The Jacobin and Liberal Traditions," *Liberty/Liberté,* ed. Klaits and Haltzell, p. 122.
3. Roger Price, *The Second Republic, A Social History* (London: B. T. Batsford, 1972).
4. John Merriman, *The Agony of the Republic: Repression of the Left in Revolutionary France, 1848–1851* (New Haven: Yale University Press, 1978).
5. Maurice Agulhon, *La République au village* (Paris: Plon, 1970). Agulhon has also written a general history of the period, *1848 ou l'apprentissage de la République, 1848–1852* (Paris: Seuil, 1973), which has been translated into English as *The Republican Experiment, 1848–1852* (Cambridge: Cambridge University Press, 1983).
6. Ted W. Margadant, *French Peasants in Revolt, The Insurrection of 1851* (Princeton: Princeton University Press, 1979).
7. Thomas R. Forstenzer, *French Provincial Police and the Fall of the Second Republic: Social Fear and Counterrevolution* (Princeton: Princeton University Press, 1981).
8. Edward Berenson, *Populist Religion and Left-Wing Politics in France, 1830–1852* (Princeton: Princeton University Press, 1984) covers a much wider period but does treat in considerable detail and with great insight the démo-socs.
9. Laboulaye, *Questions constitutionnelles,* p. 3.
10. Ibid.
11. Ibid., pp. 5–103.
12. Preface to *Considérations sur la constitution,* in *Questions constitutionnelles,* pp. iv–vi. For a clear and concise definition of the two schools see George Armstrong Kelly, "The Jacobin and Liberal Contributions to the Founding of the Second and Third French Republics (with an Epilogue on America)," in *Liberty/Liberté,* ed. Klaits and Haltzell, pp. 134–38.
13. Laboulaye, Foreword to *La Révision da la constitution,* in *Questions constitutionnelles,* p. 107.
14. Édouard Laboulaye, *Histoire des États-Unis,* 1:20.
15. Laboulaye, Foreword to *La Révision de la constitution,* in *Questions constitutionnelles,* p. 107.
16. Laboulaye, *Questions constitutionnelles,* pp. 105–251.
17. Laboulaye, Foreword to *La Révision de la Constitution,* in *Questions constitutionnelles,* p. 109.
18. Laboulaye, *Questions constitutionnelles,* p. 111.
19. Édouard Laboulaye, "Cours de législation comparée—De la constitution des États-Unis," *Revue Nationale* 15 (10 January 1864): 385.
20. Bigelow, *Some Recollections of the Late Edouard Laboulaye,* p. 14.
21. Édouard de Laboulaye, *Trente ans d'enseignement au Collège de France, 1848–1882, publiés par ses fils avec le concours de M. Marcel Fournier, Préface de M. Rodolphe Dareste,* pp. xix–xx.
22. Donald R. Kelley, *Historians and the Law in Postrevolutionary France* (Princeton: Princeton University Press, 1984).

23. Ibid., p. 73.

24. Friedrich Karl von Savigny, *Vom Beruf unserer Zeit für Gesetzgebung und Rechtswissenschaft* (Heidelberg: Mohr und Zimmer, 1814).

25. Kelley, *Historians and the Law*, p. 78.

26. It is interesting to note that one of Laboulaye's most devoted correspondants was Francis Lieber, who was a student and protégé of Niebuhr.

27. Édouard Laboulaye, *Études contemporaines sur l'Allemagne et les pays slaves*, 2d ed. (Paris: Charpentier, 1865), pp. i–ii. On 23 January 1856 Saint-Marc Girardin expressed his thanks to Laboulaye. Laboulaye Papers, Saint-Marc Girardin to Laboulaye, Paris, 23 January 1856.

28. Kelley, *Historians and the Law*, p. 83.

29. Félix Ponteil, *Histoire de l'enseignement en France, les grandes étapes, 1789–1964* (Paris: Sirey, 1966), p. 165.

30. Édouard Laboulaye, "Frédéric-Charles de Savigny," *Études contemporains de l'allemagne et des pays slaves*, p. 224.

31. Thomas R. Osborne, *A Grande Ecole for the Grands Corps, The Recruitment and Training of the French Administrative Elites in the Nineteenth Century* (Boulder, Colo.: Social Science Monographs, 1983), p. 30. See also Victor Cousin, "Huit mois au ministère de l'Instruction Publique," *Revue des Deux-Mondes*, ser. 4, 25 (1841): 388.

32. Laboulaye's complete report, "De l'enseignement et du noviciat administratif en Allemagne," is printed in *Revue de législation et de jurisprudence* 2 (1843): 513–611.

33. Ponteil, *Histoire de l'enseignement*, pp. 166–67. The educational policy of the July Monarchy is also discussed in H. A. C. Collingham with R. S. Alexander, *The July Monarchy, A Political History of France, 1830–1848* (London: Longman, 1988), pp. 309–16.

34. Edouard Laboulaye, "Quelques Réflections sur l'enseignement du droit en France, à l'occasion des réponses faites par les facultés proposées par M. le Ministre de l'Instruction Publique," *Revue de législation et de jurisprudence* 24 (1845): 289.

35. Laboulaye's friendship and scholarly association with Wolowski lasted until Wolowski's death when both were serving as members of the *centre gauche* in the Senate of the Third Republic.

36. "De l'enseignement et du noviciat administratif en Allemagne," 2 (1843): 513–611 (his report on his trip to Germany); "Quelques réflexions sur l'enseignement du droit en France, à l'occasion des réponses faites par les facultés proposées par M. le ministre de l'Instruction Publique [Salvandry]," 24 (1845): 289–370; "Enseignement de droit, concours,—Quelques mots sur un article de M. Bonnier," 24 (1845): 532–38; "Lettre de M. Laboulaye à M. Valette avocat et professeur à l'école de droit de Paris," 25 (1846): 205–11; and "De l'admission dans les services publics à l'occasion de la proposition de M. de Gasparin," 25 (1846): 257–85.

37. Édouard Laboulaye, "Réponse de M. Laboulaye," *Revue de législation et de jurisprudence* 17 (1845): 154. The complete text is found on pp. 155–60.

38. "Élection de M. Laboulaye," *Revue de législation et de jurisprudence* 22 (1845): 146.

39. See Vincent Wright, "L'École Nationale d'Administration de 1848 à 1849: un échec révélateur," *Revue historique* 196 (1976): 21–42; Howard Machin and Vincent Wright, "Les Éleves de l'école nationale d'administration de 1848 à 1849," *Revue d'histoire moderne et contemporaine* 36 (1989): 605–39; and Ponteil, *Histoire de l'enseignement*, 226–27.

40. Osborne, *A Grande Ecole for the Grands Corps*, pp. 53–59; and Robert Cha-

banne, *Les Institutions de la France de la fin de l'ancien régime à l'avenement de la IIIe République (1789–1875)* (Lyon: Éditions l'Hermes, 1977), pp. 360–62.

41. Three new chairs were created at the Collège de France in 1831: a chair in comparative law for Lerminier, one in archeology for Champollion Le Jeune, and one in political economy for Jean-Baptiste Say. Dareste, Preface to Laboulaye, *Trente ans d'enseignement au Collège de France*, p. vi.

42. Bonnie G. Smith, in her excellent article, "The Rise and Fall of Eugène Lerminier," *French Historical Studies* 12 (1982): 377–400, traces the incredible career of Lerminier as a savant, professor, and boulevardier.

43. Kelley, *Historians and the Law*, p. 53.

44. Letter of von Savigny to Bethmann-Hollweg, 2 February 1842 in Adolf Stoll, *Friedrich von Savigny, ein Bild seines Leben mit einer Sammlung seiner Briefe* (Berlin: Ed. C. Heyman, 1917–29), 3:199. See also Laboulaye's, *Essai sur la vie et les doctrines de Frédéric-Charles de Savigny* (Paris: Ed. A. Durand, 1843).

45. Friedrich Karl von Savigny, *Vom Beruf unser Zeit für Gesetzgebung und Rechtwissenschaft*, 3d ed. (Freiburg am Breisgau: Mohr, 1892), p. 9.

46. J. K. Bluntschli, *The Theory of the State*, 2d ed. (Oxford: The Clarendon Press, 1892), p. 7.

47. Édouard Laboulaye, *Histoire des États-Unis*, 5th ed. (Paris: Charpentier, 1870), 1:212.

48. Kelley, *Historians and the Law*, p. 80.

49. Boutmy, *Taine, Scherer, Laboulaye*, p. 102.

50. Guizot as quoted in Douglas Johnson, *Guizot, Aspects of French History, 1787–1874* (London: Routledge and Kegan Paul, 1963), p. 51.

51. Daniel Coit Gilman, *Bluntschli, Lieber and Laboulaye* (Baltimore: J. Murphy & Co., 1884), p. 1. The portion of this work devoted to Laboulaye is a long quotation from John Bigelow and is a summary of observations about Laboulaye later published by Bigelow in his *Some Recollections of the Late Edouard Laboulaye*.

52. John Emerich Edward Dalberg-Acton, First Baron Acton, "German Schools of History," in *Historical Essays and Studies*, ed. John Neville Figgis and Reginald Vere Lawrence (London: Macmillan & Co., 1919), p. 347.

53. On the significance of this edition see George Armstrong Kelly, "Constant Commotion: Avatars of a Pure Liberal," *Journal of Modern History* 54 (1982): 497. Kelly remarks, "Constant is the most consequent, balanced, and articulate spokesman for 'pure liberalism' that we have. As such, he deserves a seat among the mighty" p. 518.

54. Charles Auguste Sainte-Beuve, *Nouveaux lundis* (Paris: Calman Lévy, 1890), 1:412. Sainte-Beuve was named a senator on 29 April 1865.

55. Bibliothèque Spoelberch de Louvenjoul, Chantilly, Laboulaye to Sainte-Beuve, Paris, 28 January 1862.

56. "Discours de M. Guizot," 24 January 1861, cited in Laboulaye's edition of Constant's *Cours de politique*, 1:xlvi.

57. Ibid.

58. Constant, *Cours de politique* 1:viii.

59. Ibid.

60. Laboulaye's essay, "Le Liberté antique et la liberté moderne," is reprinted in *L'État et ses limites, suivis d'essais politiques sur Alexis de Tocqueville, Instruction publique, les finances, le droit de pétition, etc.* (Paris Charpentier, 1863), pp. 103–37.

61. Constant, *Cours de politique*, 1:ix; Laboulaye, *L'État et ses limites*, p. 137.

62. Laboulaye as quoted in Lamberti, *Tocqueville and the Two Democracies*, p. 291, n. 92; Laboulaye, *L'État et ses limites*, pp. 110–11.

63. Constant, *Cours de politique,* 1:ix.
64. On this point see Mona Ozouf's essay, "Liberty," in *A Critical Dictionary of the French Revolution,* ed. Furet and Ozouf, p. 726.
65. Constant's view of religious liberty is stated in *Cours de politique,* 1:128–45.
66. Ibid., 1:144–45.
67. H. Gouhier, *Benjamin Constant, les écrivains devant Dieu* (Paris: Desclée et Brouwer, 1967), pp. 43, 61, 106–7 as quoted in Lamberti, *Tocqueville and the Two Democracies,* p. 290, footnote 77.
68. Laboulaye, Introduction to Constant, *Cours de politique,* 1:xv.
69. Constant's view on freedom of the press is in *Cours de politique,* 1:125–27.
70. See Édouard Laboulaye, "Benjamin Constant et les Cent-Jours," *Revue nationale* 15 (1 October 1866): 385–411; 16 (1 November 1866): 53–77; 18 (1 January 1867): 404–31.
71. Constant, *Cours de politique,* 1:101.
72. Bibliothèque Spoelberch de Louvenjoul, Chantilly, Laboulaye to Sainte-Beuve, Paris, 28 January 1862.
73. Charles Dollfus, "Chronique Parisienne," *Revue Germanique* 4 (1858): 427, contains a favorable review of the book and refers to the moderation of Laboulaye in religious thought.
74. Lieber Papers, Huntington Library, Laboulaye to Lieber, Paris, 25 September 1863.
75. Laboulaye Papers, Lieber to Laboulaye, New York, 14 November 1863.
76. Laboulaye, *Le Parti libéral,* p. 308.
77. The letter although addressed to the editor of *Le Siècle,* M. Havin, was published in the *Journal des Débats,* 14 May 1863.
78. Laboulaye, *Le Parti libéral,* p. 13.
79. Ibid., p. 14.
80. Laboulaye's indebtedness to Channing was profound. He edited, translated, and wrote introductions to the following works: *Oeuvres sociales de W.-E. Channing, traduites de l'anglais, précédées d'un essai sur la vie et les doctrines de Channing et d'une introduction par M. Édouard Laboulaye* (Paris: Comon, 1854); and *Oeuvres de W.-E. Channing. De l'esclavage précédé d'un préface et d'une étude sur l'esclavage aux États-Unis* (Paris: Lacroix-Comon, 1855); *Oeuvres de W.-E. Channing, Traités religieux, précédées d'une introduction par M. Édouard Laboulaye* (Paris: Lacroix-Comon, 1856); *Oeuvres de W.-E. Channing, le christianisme unitaire, suites des traités religieux par M. Édouard Laboulaye* (Paris: Dentu, 1862). As a measure of his esteem he reprinted his essays on Channing in *La liberté religieuse,* pp. 210–51. For another view of Channing see Ernest Bersot's review of Charles de Rémusat's, *Channing, sa vie et ses oeuvres* in *Journal des Débats,* 27 November 1861.
81. On Vinet see Alexandre Vinet, *Outlines of Philosophy and Literature* (London, 1867). For Vinet's views on separation of church and state see pp. 173–404.
82. On both Tocqueville's and Laboulaye's indebtedness to America see, Philippe Raynaud, "La Révolution Américaine," *Dictionnaire critique de la Révolution Française* ed. Furet and Ozouf (Paris: Flammarion, 1988), p. 870.
83. Lamberti, *Tocqueville and the Two Democracies,* p. 54.
84. Laboulaye as quoted in Lamberti, *Tocqueville and the Two Democracies,* p. 79. Lamberti is quoting from Roland Pierre-Marcel, *Essai politique sur Alexis de Tocqueville* (Paris: Alcan, 1910), p. 180.
85. Lamberti, *Tocqueville and the two democracies,* pp. 79–80.
86. Lieber Papers, Huntington Library, Lieber to Laboulaye, New York, 7 July 1863.

87. Lieber Papers, Huntington Library, Laboulaye to Lieber, Paris, 15 September 1863.
88. Laboulaye's reverence for Tocqueville is evident in an essay written shortly after Tocqueville's death and published in *L'État et ses limites, pp. 138–201.*
89. Constant, *Cours de politique,* 1:ix.
90. Laboulaye, *L'État et ses limites,* p. 28.
91. Laboulaye pointed out that as early as 1830 Lammenais, Montalembert, and Lacordaire advocated separation of church and state in *L'Avenir* but that they drew forth the condemnation of Pope Gregory XVI. *Le Parti libéral,* p. 52.
92. Laboulaye, *Le Parti libéral,* p. 46.
93. Ibid., p. 63.
94. Ibid., p. 62.
95. Laboulaye lectured frequently at the meetings of this society where he also served as honorary president.
96. Georges Duveau, *La vie ouvrière en France sous le Second Empire* (Paris: Gallimard, 1946), p. 35.
97. In *Le Parti libéral,* there are frequent references to Fiévée's work. On Fiévée's political career during the Restoration see Jean Tulard, *Joseph Fiévée, conseiller secret de Napoléon* (Paris: Fayard, 1985), pp. 181–223.
98. Laboulaye, *Le Parti libéral,* p. 115–16.
99. Ibid., p. 125.
100. Ibid., pp. 130–33.
101. Laboulaye, "Horace Mann," *Revue des cours littéraires de la France et l'étranger* (27 February 1869): 198–204. On popular education see R. D. Anderson, *Education in France, 1848–1870* (Oxford: Clarendon Press, 1975), pp. 144–52. Also Georges Duveau, *La vie ouvrière en France sous le Second Empire,* pp. 434–62.
102. Laboulaye, *Le Parti libéral,* p. 167.
103. Ibid., p. 191.
104. Ibid., p. 200.
105. Ibid., pp. 209–10.
106. Ibid., p. 247.
107. Ibid., p. 248.
108. Ibid., p. 255.
109. Ibid., pp. 260–61.
110. Ibid., p. 262.
111. Ibid., p. 253.
112. Ibid., p. 270.
113. Ibid., p. 272.
114. *Journal des Débats,* 19 November 1863.

Chapter 3. Laboulaye, the Americanist

1. Adolph Robert, Edgar Bourloton, and Gaston Cougny, *Dictionnaire des parlementaires français comprenant tous les membres des Assemblées Françaises et tous les Ministres français depuis le 1 mai 1789 jusqu'au 1er mai 1889 ...* (Paris: Bourloton, 1889–90), 3:484.
2. Laboulaye Papers, Lowell to Laboulaye, Boston, 15 December 1865; Henry Villard to Laboulaye, Boston, 18 December 1865; Daniel Coit Gilman to Laboulaye, 8 April 1875; Andrew D. White to Laboulaye, Paris, 28 April 1868.
3. The teaching of American history in the lycées was only made mandatory in

a decree signed by President Adolphe Thiers on 12 August 1872. See Henry Blumen-thal, *American and French Culture, 1800–1900, Interchanges in Art, Science, Litera-ture and Society* (Baton Rouge: Louisiana State University Press, 1975), p. 77. On the teaching of American history see also "America at the Continental Universities," *Appleton's Journal of Literature, Science and Art* 9 (12 April 1873): 494–95. Sigmund Skard, *American Studies in Europe* (Philadelphia: University of Pennsylvania Press, 1958), 1:130–50 discusses the evolution of American studies in France during the Second Empire and the early years of the Third Republic.

    4. René Rémond, *Les États-Unis devant l'opinion française, 1815–1852* 1:349–50. Laboulaye was influenced by Lafayette when he was a young man; he wrote later in life to Robert C. Winthrop, "I saw him many times." Laboulaye to Robert C. Winthrop, Paris, 10 October 1882, *Proceedings of the Massachusetts His-torical Society* 20 (June 1883), p. 263.

    5. See Douglas Johnson, *Guizot, Aspects of French History, 1787–1874,* pp. 366–67. In 1851 Guizot published his essay as a book. According to Johnson, Guizot "contributed in a small way to the Washington Legend, the picture of a man who had none of the faults but only the virtues of his courage, sagacity and modesty," p. 366.

    6. Rémond, *Les États-Unis devant l'opinion française,* 1:12.

    7. Most of his lectures were published in the *Revue des cours littéraires de la France et de l'étranger* in 1863 and 1864 prior to being published in book form in 1866.

    8. The lectures form the first chapter of his *Histoire* and are also printed sepa-rately as a pamphlet, *De la constitution américaine et de l'utilité de son étude. Discours prononcé le 9 décembre 1849 à l'ouverture du cours de législation comparée* (Paris: Hennuyer, 1850).

    9. In the Laboulaye papers there are thirteen letters from Walsh to Laboulaye written between 1850 and 1856. From these letters it is obvious that Walsh was a major source of information about the United States as well as a provider of recently published works. Walsh was a journalist who represented several American news-papers. Sr. M. Frederick Lochmenes, *Robert Walsh: His Story* (New York: American Irish Historical Society, 1941), pp. 195–271 discusses Walsh's activities as consul-general in Paris, 1844–51. For the remainder of his life in Paris until his death in 1859 see pp. 218–27.

    10. Édouard Laboulaye, *Histoire des États-Unis,* 1:iv–v.

    11. Laboulaye's correspondence with Bancroft ended with the Franco-Prussian War as Bancroft, who was serving as American minister to Prussia in 1870, sided with the Prussians in the conflict. Laboulaye, ever a loyal Frenchman, severed all ties with Bancroft.

    12. Laboulaye, *de la Constitution américaine,* p. 7.

    13. Laboulaye, *Histoire des États-Unis,* 1:19.

    14. *Ibid.,* 1:23.

    15. *Ibid.,* 1:40.

    16. *Ibid.,* 1:35.

    17. *Ibid.,* 1:34.

    20. Alkan Aîné, *Un Fondeur en caractères,* p. 16. Laboulaye gave further evidence of his views on religious liberty when he wrote in *L'État et ses limites,* p. 28, "La liberté religieuse, c'est l'âme des sociétés modernes, c'est la racine de toutes les au-tres libertés."

    21. Laboulaye, *Histoire des États-Unis,* 1:156.

    21. *Ibid.,* 1:256.

    22. Laboulaye's essay on Locke forms two lectures in his *Histoire des États-Unis,*

1:328–64. He also published his lectures on Locke in a separate pamphlet, *Locke, législateur de la Caroline* (Paris: Durand, 1850).

22. Laboulaye, *Oeuvres de W.-E. Channing, De l'esclavage, précédé d'une préface et d'une étude sur l'esclavage aux États-Unis.*

23. Laboulaye Papers, Edward Everett to Laboulaye, Boston, 9 October 1855.

24. Ernest Renan, *Questions contemporaines*, p. 142, as quoted in Christophe Charle, "Le Collège de France," in *Les Lieux de mémoire*, ed. Pierre Nora, (Paris: Gallimard, 1986), 2:397.

25. Laboulaye, *Histoire*, 2:x.

26. Édouard Laboulaye, *Oeuvres complètes de Montesquieu avec les variantes des premières éditions, un choix des meilleurs commentaires et des notes nouvelles par M. Édouard Laboulaye*, 7 vols. (Paris: Garnier, 1875–79).

27. Laboulaye, *Histoire*, 3:289.

28. William Alexander Duer, *A Course of Lectures on the Constitution* (New York: Harper and Brothers, 1843); Joseph Story, *Commentaries on the Constitution of the United States* (Boston: Brown, Shattuck, and Co., 1833); James Kent, *Commentaries on American Law* (New York: O. Huested, 1826–30); George Tricknor Curtis, *History of the Origins, Formation, and Adoption of the Constitution of the United States*, 2 vols. (New York: Harper and Brothers, 1854–58); James A. Bayard, *A Brief Exposition of the Constitution of the United States* (Philadelphia: Hogan and Thompson, 1833); and Furman Sheppard, *The Constitutional Textbook; a Practical and Familiar Exposition of the Constitution of the United States* (Philadelphia: Childs and Peterson, 1855). Most of these works went through numerous editions but I have cited only the first edition of each work as Laboulaye does not indicate which edition he consulted.

29. The lectures were published in 1866, 1867, and 1869.

30. The lecture "L'Amérique et la Révolution Française" was published twelve years later in *Études morales et politiques*, pp. 279–306.

31. Montesquieu, *Oeuvres complètes*, 3:xvi–xvii. Laboulaye makes frequent reference to Greek writers such as Plato and Aristotle and, no doubt drawing on his early publications on Roman history and Roman law, he never tires of citing the precedent or practices of Roman law and the writings of the Roman legists. In this he was consistent with the historical school.

32. Laboulaye, "Cours de législation comparée—De la constitution des États-Unis," *Revue Nationale* 15 (10 January 1864): 385.

33. Laboulaye *Histoire*, 3:328.

34. Laboulaye, *Recherches sur la condition civile et politique des femmes depuis les Romains jusqu'à nos jours* (Paris: A. Dyrand, 1843).

35. Elizabeth Cady Stanton, *Eighty Years and More (1815–1897); Reminiscences of Elizabeth Cady Stanton* (New York: European Publishing Company, 1898), p. 177.

36. New York Historical Society, Laboulaye to "Mon Cher Collègue," Paris, 30 December 1863.

37. Alkan Ainé, *Un Fondeur en caractères*, p. 8.

38. Edmond Dreyfus-Brisac, "Édouard Laboulaye," *Revue internationale de l'enseignement* 5 (1883): 596.

39. Vacherot's thought is discussed in Jardin, *Histoire du libéralisme politique*, pp. 388–89 and in Girard, *Les Libéraux français*, pp. 183–84.

40. Laboulaye, *Histoire*, 3:66.

41. Édouard Laboulaye, "Cours de législation comparée—De la constitution des États-Unis," *Revue Nationale* 15 (10 January 1864): 385.

42. It is interesting to note here the similarity to Montesquieu's *Persian Letters*, which used a similar strategy to criticize contemporary Parisians.

43. Seward to Bigelow, Washington, 31 March 1863, in Bigelow, *Retrospections of an Active Life*, 1:616–17.

44. Bigelow, *Some Recollections of the Late Edouard Laboulaye*, p. 7.

45. Laboulaye Papers, Everett to Laboulaye, Boston, 19 January 1864.

46. Laboulaye Papers, Laboulaye to Lieber, Paris, 25 September 1863.

47. Laboulaye Papers, Lieber to Laboulaye, New York, 14 November 1863.

48. New York Historical Society, Laboulaye to "mon cher collègue," Paris, 30 December 1863.

49. *New York Tribune*, 1 January 1864.

50. "Paris en Amérique," *Revue des cours littéraires de la France et de l'étranger*, 1 (5 December 1863): 69.

51. Courcelle-Seneuil, "Paris en Amérique," *Journal des Économistes*, 40 (1863): 348, as quoted in Gavronsky, *The French Liberal Opposition and the American Civil War*, p. 199.

52. James McKay, Preface to Édouard Laboulaye, *Separation: War Without End* (New York: Loyal Publication Society, 1864), p. 3.

53. James McKay, Introduction, to Laboulaye, *Separation: War Without End* pp. 4–5.

54. Laboulaye, *Oeuvres sociales de Channing, traduites de l'Anglais, précédées d'uressai sur la vie et les doctrines de Channing et d'une introduction par M. Édouard Laboulaye* (Paris: Comon, 1854).

55. *Oeuvres de W.-E. Channing, De l'esclavage précédé d'une préface et d'une étude sur l'esclavage aux États-Unis*, his essay on "L'esclavage aux États-Unis," is printed in *Études morales et politiques*, pp. 186–241.

56. Laboulaye, *La Liberté religieuse* (Paris: Charpentier, 1858), pp. 241–51.

57. Laboulaye Papers, Walsh to Laboulaye, Paris, 6 January 1854. Earlier Walsh had sent Laboulaye three letters of Channing to read and return to him. Walsh to Laboulaye, Paris, 6 December 1852.

58. Laboulaye, *Études morales et politiques*, p. 220. See also Barbara Karsky, "Les libéraux français et l'émancipation des esclaves aux États-Unis, 1852–1870," *Revue d'histoire moderne et contemporaine* 21 (1974): 575–90; and Serge Gavronsky, "American Slavery and the French Liberals, An Interpretation of Slavery in French Politics during the Second Empire," *Journal of Negro History* 51 (1966): 36–52.

59. Laboulaye, *Les États-Unis et la France*, p. 338.

60. Printed in *La Science de Bonhomme Richard ou le chemin de la fortune par Benjamin Franklin suivie d'extraits de ses mémoires et de sa correspondance et précédée de la jeunesse de Franklin par Édouard Laboulaye* (Paris: Hachette et cie., 1872). See pp. 11–46 for Laboulaye's essay "La Jeunesse de Franklin."

61. *Ibid.*, p. 9.

62. Édouard Laboulaye, *Mémoires de Benjamin Franklin écrits par lui-même, traduits et annotés par Édouard Laboulaye*, 2d ed. (Paris: Hachette, 1866).

63. James Parton, *The Life and Times of Benjamin Franklin*, 2 vols. (New York, 1864.) Laboulaye acknowledged his indebtedness to Jared Sparks in a letter to Lieber, Lieber Papers, Huntington Library, Laboulaye to Lieber, Paris, 12 July 1864.

64. Bigelow recounts the finding and purchase of the original manuscript of the Franklin *Autobiography*, in *Some Recollections of the Late Edouard Laboulaye*, pp. 25–42.

65. Édouard Laboulaye, *Essais de morale et d'économie politique de Benjamin*

Franklin traduits de l'anglais et annotés par Édouard Laboulaye de l'Institut de France et des sociétés historiques de New-York et de Massachusetts, 2d ed. (Paris, 1869).

66. Ibid., p. 15.

67. Laboulaye, *La science de Bonhomme Richard ou le chemin de la fortune.*

68. Alfred Sirven, *Journaux et journalistes, Journal des Débats* 3d ed. (Paris: F. Cournol, 1865), p. 310.

69. Laboulaye, *La Jeunesse de Franklin*, pp. 45–46.

70. Laboulaye, "L'Éducation en Amérique," *Études morales et politiques*, pp. 169–85.

71. Édouard Laboulaye, "Horace Mann," *Revue des cours littéraires de la France et de l'étranger* (27 February 1869): 198–204.

72. Jonathan Messerli, *Horace Mann, A Biography* (New York: Knopf, 1972), pp. 248–49. On Mann's career see also Robert B. Downs, *Horace Mann, Champion of Public Schools* (New York: Twayne Publishers, 1974).

73. Victor Cousin, *De l'Instruction publique dans quelques pays de l'Allemagne et particulièrement en Prusse*, 2 vols. (Paris: Pitois-Levrault, 1840).

74. Edward L. Pierce, *Memoirs and Letters of Charles Sumner* (New York, Arno Press, 1969), 1:265. For Cousin's influence on Mann see Messerli, *Horace Mann*, p. 255.

75. Laboulaye, "Horace Mann," p. 200.

76. Ibid., pp. 200–201.

77. Ibid., p. 202.

78. Ibid., p. 203.

79. Laboulaye, *Discours populaires* (Paris: Charpentier, 1869), pp. 205–25.

80. Édouard Laboulaye, *Mann (Horace), De l'importance de l'éducation dans une république traduit de l'américain, avec extraits de la vie de Mann* (Paris: Charpentier, 1873).

Chapter 4. Defender of the North

1. James McPherson, *Battle Cry of Freedom, The Civil War Era* (New York: Oxford University Press, 1988), p. 235.

2. Bigelow, *Some Recollections of the Late Edouard Laboulaye*, p. 1.

3. On Dayton see, Joseph Bradley, "A Memorial of the Life and Character of Hon. William L. Dayton, Late U.S. Minister to France," *Proceedings of the New Jersey Historical Society*, 2d ser., 4 (1875); 70–118. On Dayton's appointment see Lynn M. Case and Warren F. Spencer, *The United States and France: Civil War Diplomacy* (Philadelphia: The University of Pennsylvania Press, 1970), p. 37 and for an evaluation of Dayton see pp. 558–60, 603–4.

4. Paris, Dayton to Seward, 27 May 1861, quoted in Margaret Clapp, *Forgotten First Citizen: John Bigelow* (Boston: Little, Brown, 1947), pp. 150–51.

5. For an account of the negotiations over Bigelow's appointment see Clapp, *Forgotten First Citizen* pp. 146–48.

6. Case and Spencer, *The United States and France: Civil War Diplomacy*, p. 175.

7. Clapp, *Forgotten First Citizen*, pp. 158–59. On the Trent Affair see Case and Spencer, *The United States and France: Civil War Diplomacy*, pp. 190–249.

8. Serge Gavronsky, *French Liberals and the American Civil War* (New York: The Humanities Press, 1968), p. 20.

9. Mary L. Booth, "Translator's Preface," *Paris in America*, p. iii.

10. The hostility of much of French public opinion to the South is discussed in Charles P. Cullop, "Edwin de Leon, Jefferson Davis' Propagandist," *Civil War History* 8 (1962): 391–92. The reports of the procurators general in France during the Civil War are printed in Lynn M. Case, *French Opinion on the United States and Mexico, 1860–1867* (New York: D. Appleton Century, 1936). These reports filed regularly by the procurator's general provide an excellent indication of French public opinion during the Civil War.

11. Andrew D. White, *Autobiography of Andrew Dickson White* (New York: The Century Company, 1905), 1:96.

12. Laboulaye, "La guerre civile aux États-Unis," *Journal des Débats,* 2–3 October 1861. It is reprinted in Laboulaye, *Études morales et politiques* pp. 253–78. The books reviewed were Agénor de Gasparin, *Un grand peuple qui se relève* (Paris: Michel Lévy Frères, 1861) [the American translation was published (New York, 1861)]: and Xavier Eyma, *La République américaine: ses institutions, ses hommes* 2 vols. (Paris: Michel Lévy Frères, 1861).

13. Booth translated this 263-page book in a week. See Harold Howland, "Mary Louise Booth," *Dictionary of American Biography,* 2:454–55.

14. Agénor de Gasparin, *America Before Europe: Principles and Interests* (New York: C. Scribner, 1862).

15. Laboulaye received a letter of thanks from Eyma who was happy and flattered by Laboulaye's review. Laboulaye Papers, Xavier Eyma to Laboulaye, Paris, 14 October 1861.

16. *Journal des Débats,* 2 October 1861.

17. Laboulaye, "La Guerre civile aux États-Unis," pp. 259–62.

18. Edward L. Pierce, *Memoirs and letters of Charles Sumner,* 3:607. A full account of the speech is found on 3:607–14.

19. Laboulaye, "La Guerre civile aux États-Unis," p. 266.

20. Carey as quoted by Eric Foner, *Free Soil, Free Labor, Free Men: The Ideology of the Republic Party before the Civil War* (New York: Oxford University Press, 1970), p. 19.

21. Laboulaye, "La Guerre civile aux États-Unis," pp. 169–220.

22. Laboulaye Papers, George A. Matile to Laboulaye, 10 May 1857 informed Laboulaye that Carey was coming to Paris. An undated letter of Matile to Laboulaye commented favorably on Carey's visit and contains his impressions of Laboulaye.

23. H. W. Bellows, *A Sermon Preached in All Souls Church, New York, April 21, 1861* (New York: Miller, 1861) as quoted in Laboulaye, "La Guerre Civile," p. 274.

24. *Journal des Débats,* 3 October 1861.

25. Bigelow, *Some Recollections,* p. 2.

26. Ibid., p. 7.

27. A revised and enlarged version was printed as a pamphlet—Édouard Laboulaye, *Les États-Unis et la France* (Paris: E. Dentu, 1862), p. 324. This version was reprinted in Laboulaye, *L'État et ses limites,* pp. 323–75. References are to this later edition.

28. Laboulaye Papers, Sumner to Laboulaye, Boston, 14 November 1863.

29. It is interesting to note that a recent book on the Civil War stated a view similar to Laboulaye's, "At the root of the crisis that produced the Civil War lay slavery, the 'peculiar institution' of the Old South." Eric Foner and Olivia Mahony, *A House Divided, America in the Age of Lincoln* (New York: Chicago Historical Association in association with W. W. Norton & Company, 1990), p. ix.

30. Agénor de Gasparin, *L'Amérique devant l'Europe* (Paris: Michel Lévy Frères,

1862) An English translation by Mary L. Booth was published as *America Before Europe. Principles and Interests* in 1862.

31. Charles Sumner, *The Rebellion: Its Origin and Main-Spring, An Oration delivered by the Hon. Charles Sumner under the auspices of the Young Men's Republican Union of New York, November 27, 1861* (New York: Young Men's Republican Union, 1862).

32. George Fisch, *Les États-Unis en 1861* (Paris: C. Meyrueis, 1862). An English translation was published, *Nine Months in the United States during the Crisis* (London, 1863). Fisch was the pastor of the French Evangelical church in Paris and was a partisan of the north.

33. Laboulaye Papers, Bigelow to Laboulaye, Paris, 28 August 1862. Bigelow was a friend not only of Laboulaye but also of such leading savants as Guizot, Renan, Taine, Martin, Berryer, Montalembert, and Cochin. See Margaret Clapp, *Forgotten First Citizen,* p. 173.

34. Bigelow, *Retrospections of an Active Life,* 1:533.

35. Bigelow to Seward, Paris, 29 August 1862, in Bigelow, *Retrospections of an Active Life,* 1:539.

36. François Barbé-Marbois, *Histoire de la Louisiane* (Paris: Impr. de F. Didol, 1829), p. 282, as quoted by Laboulaye in *The United States and France,* p. 13. Also Laboulaye, *Les États-Unis et la France,* pp. 372–73.

37. Duc d'Aumale to Cuvillier-Fleury, Twickenham, 15 January 1862, *Correspondance du Duc d'Aumale et de Cuvillier-Fleury* (Paris: Plon, 1910–1912), 3:205.

38. Donaldson Jordan and Edwin J. Pratt, *Europe and the American Civil War* (Boston: Houghton Mifflin Company, 1931), p. 243.

39. Laboulaye, *L'État et ses limites,* p. 349.

40. Ibid., p. 325. On the diplomatic maneuverings of the Union to prevent French intervention see Henry Blumenthal, *A Reappraisal of Franco-American Relations, 1830–1871* (Chapel Hill: University of North Carolina Press, 1959), pp. 130–56. Also Clapp, *Forgotten First Citizen,* pp. 149 et seq.; Case and Spencer, *The United States and France,* pp. 333–73.

41. Laboulaye, *Les États-Unis et la France,* p. 338.

42. Ibid., p. 339.

43. Ibid., p. 339.

44. Dayton Papers, Princeton University Library, Dayton to Laboulaye, Paris, 16 September 1862; Laboulaye to Dayton, Versailles, 24 October 1862.

45. Dayton Papers, Princeton University Library, Laboulaye to Dayton, Versailles, 24 September 1862.

46. Frank Freidel, "The Loyal Publication Society: A Pro-Union Propaganda Agency," *Mississippi Valley Historical Review* 26 (1939): 369.

47. Laboulaye, "Pourquoi le Nord ne peut accepter la séparation," was first published on 10 December 1862 in the *Revue nationale* 12 (1862): 481–90. It was revised and published in *L'État et ses limites,* pp. 376–91 and later translated as *Separation: War Without End* (New York: Loyal Publication Society, 1864). This American edition was published by the Loyal Publication Society whose president was Laboulaye's admirer, Francis Lieber. References are to the American edition.

48. Laboulaye, *Separation: War Without End,* p. 19.

49. Ibid., p. 16.

50. Laboulaye, *L'État et ses limites,* p. 391.

51. "Pourquoi le Nord ne peut accepter la séparation," in Laboulaye, *L'État et ses limites,* p. 391.

52. Laboulaye Papers, Lieber to Laboulaye, New York, 7 July 1863.

53. Laboulaye, *Les États-Unis et la France*, pp. 361–62.
54. McPherson, *Battle Cry of Freedom*, p. 545.
55. Ibid., p. 557.
56. Case and Spencer, *Civil War Diplomacy*, p. 327.
57. McPherson, *Battle Cry of Freedom*, p. 558.
58. Case and Spencer, *Civil War Diplomacy*, p. 329.
59. Freidel, "Loyal Publication Society," p. 372.
60. *Address of the Loyal National League to Messrs. Agénor de Gasparin, Édouard Laboulaye, Augustin Cochin, Henri Martin, and other Friends of America in France* (New York: Loyal Publication Society, 1863). An account of the Sumter meeting is in the *New York Tribune*, 1 January 1864.
61. *Address of the Loyal National League* pp. 3–4.
62. *Address of the Loyal Publication Society*, p. 4.
63. Laboulaye Papers, Lieber to Laboulaye, New York, 7 July 1863.
64. Lieber Papers, Huntington Library, Laboulaye to Lieber, Paris, 31 July 1863.
65. Laboulaye Papers, Cochin to Laboulaye, St. Benoît d'Azy, 17 October 1863.
66. Laboulaye Papers, Lieber to Laboulaye, New York, 10 December 1863.
67. *Reply of Messrs. Agénor de Gasparin, Édouard Laboulaye, Henri Martin, Augustin Cochin to the Loyal National League of New York* (New York: Loyal Publication Society, 1863), p. 3.
68. Laboulaye Papers, Geo. P. Putnam to Laboulaye, New York, 16 April 1864 and Francis Lieber et al. to Laboulaye, New York, 30 June 1865, which informed Laboulaye that the books will be hand delivered by William T. Blodgett. The books were intended for those "who have remained faithful to the cause of Freedom and Humanity for which we have struggled when manful friends in Europe were but few."
69. On the similar memberships of the two organizations see Frank Freidel, ed., *Union Pamphlets of the Civil War, 1861–1865* (Cambridge: Belknap of Harvard University Press, 1967), 1:9–14.
70. *Letters from Europe touching the American Contest and Acknowledging the Receipt, from Citizens of New York, of presentation sets of the "Rebellion Record" and Loyal Publication Society publications* (New York: Loyal Publication Society, 1864), p. 20.
71. McPherson, *Battle Cry of Freedom*, p. 610.
72. Lieber Papers, Huntington Library, Laboulaye to Lieber, Paris, 31 July 1863.
73. This is the thesis of Christian Schefer, *La Grande pensée de Napoléon III: les origines de l'expédition du Mexique (1858–1862)* (Paris: M. Rivière et Cie., 1939).
74. On the background to the Mexican venture see Nancy Nichols Barker, *The French Experience in Mexico, 1821–1861: A History of Constant Misunderstanding* (Chapel Hill: University of North Carolina Press, 1979).
75. Lieber Papers, Huntington Library, Laboulaye to Lieber, Paris, 25 September 1863.
76. Laboulaye Papers, Lieber to Laboulaye, New York, 27 May 1864; Lieber Papers, Huntington Library, Laboulaye to Lieber, Paris, 12 July 1864.
77. Laboulaye Papers, Edward Everett to Laboulaye, Boston, 19 January 1864.
78. Bigelow, *Some Recollections*, p. 17.
79. For the work of the Commission see, William Quentin Maxwell, *Lincoln's Fifth Wheel: The Political History of the United States Sanitary Commission* (New York: Longman's Green, 1956).
80. Laboulaye Papers, Lieber to Laboulaye, New York, 12 July 1864.
81. Lieber Papers, Huntington Library, Laboulaye to Lieber, Paris, 12 July 1864.
82. Laboulaye Papers, Lieber to Laboulaye, New York, 14 September 1864.

83. Édouard Laboulaye, *Professor Laboulaye, the Great Friend of America, on the Presidential Election. The Election of the President of the United States* (Washington: Union Congressional Committee, 1864). Laboulaye's statement was sent to the Department of State by the American Consul-General, James Bigelow.

84. Ibid., p. 3. Laboulaye's own summary of his arguments is contained in a letter to Lieber, Lieber Papers, Huntington Library, Laboulaye to Lieber, 4 October 1864.

85. Ibid., p. 3.

86. Ibid., p. 4.

87. Lieber Papers, Huntington Library, Laboulaye to Lieber, Glatigny-Versailles, 14 October 1864.

88. Laboulaye, *Professor Laboulaye*, p. 14.

89. Case and Spencer, *Civil War Diplomacy*, p. 559. On the death of Dayton see also Poultney Bigelow, "John Bigelow and Napoleon III," *New York History* 13 (1932); 154–65.

90. Bigelow, *Some Recollections*, p. 19. The entire eulogy is printed on pp. 18–19.

91. "Speech of Édouard Laboulaye: on the Death of Mr. Lincoln," *Lincolniana, In Memoriam* (Boston: William V. Spencer, 1865), pp. 320–26. This was published in a limited edition of 250 copies.

Chapter 5. Last Years of the Empire

1. Laboulaye Papers, Lieber to Laboulaye, New York, 7 July 1865.

2. Lieber Papers, Huntington Library, Laboulaye to Lieber, Paris, 25 September 1865.

3. Édouard Laboulaye, *Discours populaires* (Paris: Charpentier, 1869 [a second edition was published in 1870]) and *Derniers discours populaires* (Paris: Charpentier, 1881). For an account of these public lectures see Frédéric Passy, *Édouard Laboulaye, Conférence faite à la société du travail par Frédéric Passy* (Paris: Librarie Guillaumin, 1884), pp. 36–37, 48, 56–57. Passy gave the official eulogy for Laboulaye at the Société du Travail on 17 May 1884.

4. Laboulaye Papers, Sumner to Laboulaye, Boston, 4 August 1865.

5. George A. Matile served during the Civil War as a member of the United States Sanitary Commission. Previously he had enjoyed a distinguished career as a legal scholar and judge in Switzerland before the Revolutions of 1848. It was through their mutual interest in legal studies and the historical school that Laboulaye and Matile became correspondents.

6. Seward Papers, University of Rochester, Matile to Seward, 31 May 1865.

7. Laboulaye Papers, Seward to George A. Matile, Washington, 11 June 1865. Of interest also is the letter in the Seward Papers, University of Rochester Library, Matile to Seward, Washington, 5 June 1865 in which Matile urged that Laboulaye be named an honorary citizen of the United States! He argued, "Lafayette became a citizen for having fought for liberty on our soil—Laboulaye is courageously and perseveringly fighting abroad against elements hostile to us."

8. Seward Papers, University of Rochester Library, Laboulaye to Seward, Paris, 31 August 1865. One must point out to the historians of contemporary America the prophetic nature of Laboulaye's prediction on the after-effects of the abolition of slavery.

9. "Meeting en faveur des esclaves affranchis aux États-Unis," *Revue des cours littéraires de la France et de l'étranger*, 11 November 1865, pp. 809–12.

10. Laboulaye Papers, Seward to Laboulaye, Washington, 19 September 1865.

11. Olive Risley Seward, ed., *William H. Seward's Travels around the World* (New York: D. Appleton and Company, 1873), p. 703.

12. *The Washington Daily Chronicle*, Washington, 17 April 1866. Laboulaye's American translator, Mary L. Booth, urged him to become involved in American politics in 1868. Laboulaye Papers, Mary L. Booth to Laboulaye, New York, 24 March 1868, 18 June 1868, and 17 July 1868.

13. Laboulaye Papers, Richard H. Crittenden to Laboulaye, New York, 4 May 1868.

14. *Le Messager Franco-Américain*, New York, 16 October 1868.

15. Laboulaye Papers, Forney to Laboulaye, Philadelphia, 8 September 1868. Forney asked Laboulaye, whom he had met at the Exposition in 1867, to write in behalf of Grant's election. The draft of Laboulaye's letter to Forney, is dated 28 September 1868 and the text was printed in *Le Messager Franco-Américain* 16 October 1865. The letter was also published in an English translation in *The Press*, on 12 October 1868.

16. *The Press*, Philadelphia, 17 October 1868, and *Le Messager Franco-Américain*, New York, 16 October 1868.

17. Laboulaye Papers, Forney to Laboulaye, Philadelphia, 15 October 1868. Also George A. Blanchard to Laboulaye, Philadelphia, 29 October 1868, informed Laboulaye that he had read Forney's letter to him and was enclosing a portrait of General Grant.

18. *The Press*, Philadelphia, 16 October 1868.

19. Laboulaye Papers, Bigelow to Laboulaye, Highland Falls, N.Y., 18 April 1868.

20. The list of officers of the Comité is printed in *Revue des cours*, 28 September 1867, p. 689. For information on the founding of the Comité see Laboulaye Papers, Augustin Cochin to Laboulaye, Plessis Chenet (Seine-et-Oise), 12 May 1865; 18 May 1865, and 28 May 1865.

21. Barbara Karsky, "Les Libéraux français et l'émancipation des esclaves aux États-Unis, 1852–1870," *Revue d'histoire moderne et contemporaine* 21 (1974): 589.

22. Laboulaye constantly refers in letters to eye problems in the 1860s and 1870s and gives his *mal d'yeux* as an excuse for being unable to do various things such as travel to the United States. It is not clear what the nature of his eye difficulty was but it did leave him in need of rest. It was even feared in 1865 that his eyes were so bad that he would be unable to resume his teaching that academic year at the Collège de France. *Revue des cours* 11 November 1865, p, 809.

23. "Meeting en faveur des esclaves affranchis des États-Unis," Ibid., p. 810.

24. Ibid., p. 816.

25. Ibid., p. 820.

26. According to Augustin Cochin, Mme Laboulaye was active in the women's committee for the freed slaves. The Catholic bishop of Charleston was coming to Paris to seek funds from the committee of women to aid the 700,000 freed slaves in his diocese. Cochin asked Laboulaye to inform his wife of this impending visit. Laboulaye Papers, Augustin Cochin to Laboulaye, Plessis Chenet (Seine-et-Oise), 28 May 1865. Mme Laboulaye also secured the assistance of Mme Cochin in the work of the Comité. See Laboulaye Papers, Cochin to Laboulaye, Plessis Chenet (Seine-et-Oise), undated [probably in 1865].

27. Ibid., pp. 811–12.

28. The speeches delivered are printed in "Meeting sur l'abolition de l'esclavage aux États-Unis et à Cuba," *Revue des cours*, 27 January 1866, pp. 149–66.

29. Ibid., p. 150.

30. Laboulaye Papers, Augustin Cochin to Laboulaye, Paris, 28 February 1866.

31. "Le traité et l'esclavage," *Revue des cours,* 28 September 1867, p. 689.

32. Laboulaye Papers, Sumner to Laboulaye, Boston, 12 August 1867. In this letter Sumner recommended Palfrey to Laboulaye and praised him as a member of Congress who worked for emancipation.

33. In a letter to Laboulaye Chamerovzov arranged a meeting to plan for the conference. Laboulaye Papers, Chamerovzov to Laboulaye, Neuilly, 6 February 1867.

34. *Revue des cours,* 28 September 1867, p. 690.

35. The resolutions are to be found in Ibid., 25 September 1867, pp. 196–97.

36. Ibid., 2 November 1867, pp. 769–73.

37. Ibid., pp. 777–78.

38. Ibid., p. 784.

39. Laboulaye Papers, Cochin to Laboulaye, Paris, 7 September 1868 writes of their mutual efforts with the British emancipation society to abolish slavery in the Spanish colonies. Also a letter of 8 March 1869 refers to a proposed mass meeting at the Château d'Eau in Paris with Laboulaye presiding that will discuss the freed slaves and their needs in America. Barbara Karsky in her article, "Les libéraux français et l'émancipation des esclaves aux États-Unis, 1852–1870," p. 509 states that the French Emancipation Society ended its work at the end of the American Civil War. Such was obviously not the case.

40. On Laboulaye's proposed candidacy in 1863 see Émile Ollivier, *L'Empire libéral: études, récits, souvenirs* (Paris: Garnier Frères, 1895–1918), 4:232–38, and Pierre de la Gorce, *Histoire du Second Empire* (Paris: Librairie Plon, 1894–1905), 4:214. La Gorce said Laboulaye was part of "la faction libérale."

41. *Journal des Débats,* 16 May 1863.

42. Ollivier, *L'Empire libéral,* 4:237.

43. Laboulaye Papers, campaign poster for 1864 election. The poster is published in the *Journal des Débats,* 8 March 1864.

44. *Journal des Débats,* 9 March 1864. See also the editorial of Émile de Girardin, 13 March 1864, where he urges a vote for Laboulaye and notes that his *Parti libéral,* published in December 1863, was his election manifesto.

45. *Journal des Débats,* 16, 19, 20, and 21 March 1864.

46. *Journal des Débats,* 23 March 1864.

47. Laboulaye, *Questions constitutionnelles,* p. 266. Laboulaye included a lengthy discussion of the plebiscite in a chapter entitled "Le plébiscite de 1870" in his *Questions constitutionnelles,* pp. 255–305.

48. Émile Ollivier, *Journal, 1846–1869,* texts chosen and edited by Theodore Zeldin (Paris: René Juillard, 1961), 2:242.

49. "Chronique de la Quinzaine," 14 April 1866, *Revue des Deux Mondes* 62 (1866): 1064. For the reaction of an opponent of the Empire to Laboulaye's defeat see Allain-Targé, *La République sous l'Empire, Lettres (1864–1870)* (Paris: Éditions Bernard Grasset, 1939), p. 72.

50. Laboulaye, *Questions constitutionnelles,* p. 266.

51. Laboulaye to Bigelow, Glatigny-Versailles, 23 October 1868, in Bigelow, *Some Recollections of the Late Edouard Laboulaye,* pp. 43–45.

52. Ibid.

53. Édouard Laboulaye, *Le Prince Caniche* (Paris: Charpentier, 1878).

54. Frédéric Passy. *Société du Travail, Assemblée générale tenue le 17 mai 1884,* p. 55. Passy succeeded Laboulaye as president of the Société du Travail and these comments were part of his official eulogy after Laboulaye's death.

55. La Gorce, *Histoire du Second Empire,* 5:478.

56. See Laboulaye, *Addresse aux électeurs de la première circonscription de Seine-et-Oise* (Paris: n.p., 1869), for a statement of his platform.

57. Theodore Zeldin, *The Political System of Napoleon III*, (London: Macmillan, 1958), pp. 135–42.

58. La Gorce, *Histoire du Second Empire*, 5:436.

59. Ibid., 5:478.

60. Ibid., 5:461.

61. Ibid., 5:461–462.

62. Édouard Laboulaye, *Discours populaires* (Paris, Charpentier, 1869).

63. On the press law and its importance see Irene Collins, *The Government and the Newspaper Press in France, 1814–1881* (Oxford: Oxford University Press, 1959), pp. 147–63.

64. Ibid., p. 155. On Rochefort's career see Roger L. Williams, *Henri Rochefort, Prince of the Gutter Press* (New York: Charles Scribner's Sons, 1966).

65. On Emile Ollivier and the Liberal Empire see Theodore Zeldin, *Emile Ollivier and the Liberal Empire of Napoleon III* (Oxford: Clarendon Press, 1963). For the establishment of the Liberal Empire see pp. 105–19.

66. Prévost-Paradol's rallying to the Empire is treated in Pierre Guiral, *Prévost-Paradol, 1829–1870, pensée et action d'un libéral sous le Second Empire*, pp. 645–702.

67. Ollivier's description of Guizot's rallying to the Empire is found in *L'empire libéral*, 13:460–61.

68. La Gorce, *Histoire du Second Empire*, 6:107.

69. Laboulaye to John Bigelow, Glatigny-Versailles, 7 June 1870, printed in Bigelow, *Some Recollections of the Late Edouard Laboulaye*, p. 49.

70. Laboulaye, *Questions constitutionnelles*, p. 257.

71. Ibid.

72. Ibid., p. 258.

73. The letter is published in Laboulaye, *Questions constitutionnelles*, pp. 261–63.

74. Ibid., p. 262. Also published separately under the title *Plébiscite du 8 mai 1870. Lettre addressée par M. Édouard Laboulaye . . . au comité plébiscitaire du Rueil* (Paris: Impr. de E. Blot, 1870).

75. Laboulaye, *Questions constitutionnelles*, p. 265. Also published as *Lettre à un électeur de la commune de Jouy-en-Josas (Seine-et-Oise)* (Le Cateau: Impr. J. de Lempereur, 1870).

76. Laboulaye, *Questions constitutionnelles*, p. 272. An account of the entire meeting is printed on pp. 268–85.

77. Ibid., pp. 284–85.

78. Ibid., p. 285.

79. *Journal des Débats*, 23 May 1870 gives a full account of the event and it is also summarized by Laboulaye in *Questions constitutionnelles*, pp. 286–92.

80. Laboulaye, *Questions constitutionnelles*, p. 289. Laboulaye was quoting from his edition of Constant's *Cours de politique*, 2:70.

81. Laboulaye, *Questions constitutionnelles*, p. 292.

82. Ibid. Laboulaye cites the account of the events of 27 May from an article of Édouard Drumont in *La Liberté* of 29 May 1870.

83. Laboulaye, *Questions constitutionnelles*, pp. 293–94.

84. Ibid., pp. 295–96.

85. Ollivier, *Journal, 1846–1869*, 2:443.

86. Bigelow, *Some Recollections of the Late Edouard Laboulaye*, p. 47.

87. His lectures on France were published during 1865 and 1866 in each issue of the *Revue des cours*.

88. Édouard Laboulaye, ed., *Oeuvres complètes de Montesquieu, avec les variantes des premières éditions, un choix des meilleurs commentaires et des notes nouvelles* 7 vols. (Paris: Garnier Frères, 1875).

89. Richard Shelly Hartigan, *Lieber's Code and the Law of War* (Chicago: Precedent, 1983), pp. 1–2. The text of General Orders No. 100 is printed on pp. 45–71. On General Orders No. 100 see also Freidel, *Francis Lieber*, pp. 317–41.

90. Laboulaye Papers, Lieber to Laboulaye, 24 August 1863.

91. Lieber Papers, Huntington Library, Laboulaye to Lieber, Glatigny-Versailles, 25 September 1863.

92. Hartigan, *Lieber's Code*, p. 22.

93. M. Bluntschli, *Le Droit international codifié traduit de l'Allemand par M. C. Lardy précédé d'une préface par M. Édouard Laboulaye* 2d ed. (Paris: Librarie de Guillaumin, 1874), p. xxiii.

94. Bluntschli, *Le Droit international codifié*, pp. xxiv–xxv.

95. Edouard Laboulaye, "The French Army," *Old and New*, 11 October 1870, 516–29.

96. Laboulaye to Bigelow, Paris, 27 August 1870, printed in Bigelow, *Some Recollections of the Late Edouard Laboulaye*, p. 61. Laboulaye also had a house in Paris, 34 Rue Taitbout.

97. M. A. de Wolfe Howe, *The Life and Letters of George Bancroft* (New York: Da Capo Press, 1970), 2:237.

98. Laboulaye to Bigelow, Paris, 6 September 1870, printed in Bigelow *Some Recollections of the Late Edouard Laboulaye*, pp. 63–65.

99. Laboulaye to Bigelow, Glatigny-Versailles, 28 July 1871, printed in Bigelow, *Some Recollections of the Late Edouard Laboulaye*, p. 67.

100. Ibid., pp. 68–69.

Chapter 6. Senator for Life and the Statue of Liberty

1. Hans Christian Anderson, "Laboulaye," *Appleton's Journal of Literature, Science, and Art* 11 (1874): 151.

2. On the strengths of the various republican factions see R. D. Anderson, *France, 1870–1914, Politics and Society* (London: Routledge and Kegan Paul, 1977), pp. 163–67. Also Jean-Marie Mayeur and Madeleine Rebérioux, *The Third Republic from its Origins to the Great War, 1871–1914* (Cambridge: Cambridge University Pres, 1987), pp. 8–13.

3. Jacques Gadille, *La Pensée et l'action politiques des évêques français au début de la IIIe République, 1870–1883* (Paris: Hachette, 1967), 1: 340.

4. Laboulaye, *Questions constitutionnelles*, pp. 309–29.

5. Ibid., pp. 326–27, contains an outline of a model constitution.

6. Ibid., p. 328.

7. Ibid., pp. 333–66.

8. Ibid., p. 366.

9. "Le pouvoir constituant," *Revue des Deux Mondes* 95 (1871): 792–814; Laboulaye, *Questions constitutionnelles*, pp. 369–405. References are to the later text.

10. Laboulaye Papers. Favorable comments were received from Émile Faguet to Laboulaye, La Rochelle, 26 November 1871; François Chauneau, avocat à la cour d'appel (Paris), to Laboulaye, Paris, 24 October 1871; K. Eckstrom to Laboulaye, Stockholm, 28 October 1871; and B. Chaunu to Laboulaye, Paris, 19 October 1871.

11. *Journal de Lyon*, 22 September 1872, also printed in Laboulaye, *Questions constitutionnelles*, pp. 409–21. References are to the later text.

12. Laboulaye, *Questions constitutionnelles*, p. 421.

13. Ibid.

14. Édouard Laboulaye, *Lettres Politiques, Esquisse d'une constitution républicaine suivie d'un projet de constitution* (Paris: Charpentier et Cie., 1872). The pamphlet is in the form of a series of nine letters to the editor of the *Journal des Débats*, Jules Bapst, who published them in September 1872. The draft of the constitution is appended to the text of the letters.

15. *Journal Officiel*, 29 January 1875, p. 769.

16. Ibid.

17. Ibid., p. 770.

18. Jacques Chastenet, *Gambetta* (Paris: Fayard, 1968), p. 239.

19. Wallon gave the official eulogy for Laboulaye at the Institut de France in 1887.

20. *Journal Officiel*, 31 January 1875, p. 798.

21. *Journal Officiel*, 30 January 1875, p. 779. For the politics of the early years of the Third Republic see, Jacques Chastenet, *Histoire de la Troisième République* (Paris: Librairie Hachette, 1952), vol. 1, "L'Enfance de la Troisième République, 1870–1879"; Maurice Deslandres, *Histoire constitutionnelle de la France* (Paris: Édouard Duchemin, 1977), vol. 3, "L'Avenement de la Troisième République"; J. P. T. Bury, *Gambetta and the Making of the Third Republic* (London: Longman, 1973); Guy Chapman, *The Third Republic of France, The First Phase, 1871–1894* (London: Macmillan, 1962).

22. D. W. Brogan, *The Development of Modern France (1870–1939)* (Gloucester, Mass.: Peter Smith, 1970), p. 111.

23. Jean-Marie Mayeur and Madeleine Rebérioux, *The Third Republic from its Origins to the Great War, 1871–1914* (Cambridge: Cambridge University Press, 1987), p. 25.

24. Laboulaye as quoted in Marcel Prélot, *Institutions politiques et droit constitutionnel* (Paris: Dalloz, 1969), p. 450.

25. Jean-Claude Lamberti, "Laboulaye and the Common Law of Free Peoples," in *Liberty, The French-American Statue in Art and History* ed. Provoyeur and Hargrove, p. 20.

26. *Journal Officiel*, 10 December 1875, p. 10215.

27. *Journal des Débats*, 12 December 1875.

28. Laboulaye Papers, Boutmy to Laboulaye, Paris, 1 December 1871, acknowledges Laboulaye's support. See also Boutmy, *Taine, Scherer, Laboulaye*, p. 10, also André Dauteribes, "Laboulaye et la réforme de droit," *Revue d'histoire des facultés de droit et de la science juridique*, 10 (1990): pp. 53–57.

29. On Boutmy see Louis Voskuil, "Émile Boutmy: The Political Education of the Third Republic" (Ph.D. diss., Loyola University of Chicago, 1977).

30. Osborne, *A Grande Ecole for the Grands Corps*, pp. 57–59 discusses the founding of the École Libre. See also Pierre Rain, *L'École Libre des Sciences Politiques, 1871–1939* (Paris: Fondation Nationale des Sciences Politiques, 1963), p. 16.

31. *Journal Officiel*, 6 June 1875, p. 4048. Laboulaye recounts his work on the two commissions.

32. Laboulaye as quoted in Edmond Dreyfus-Brisac, "Édouard Laboulaye," *Revue internationale de l'enseignement* 5 (1883): 599.

33. Laboulaye, *Le Parti libéral*, p. 62.

34. Ibid., p. 61.

35. Ibid., p. 75.

36. Ibid., p. 62.

37. *Journal Officiel,* 6 June 1875, p. 4048.

38. *Journal Officiel,* 8 July 1875, p. 5077.

39. Édouard Laboulaye, *La Liberté d'enseignement et les projets des lois de M. Jules Ferry* (Paris: L. Larose, 1880), summarizes his views on education as well as Ferry's proposals.

40. *Journal Officiel,* 29 May 1875, p. 3820.

41. Ibid.

42. Laboulaye as quoted in Édmond Dreyfus-Brisac, "Édouard Laboulaye," *Revue internationale de l'enseignement* 5 (1883): 600.

43. *Journal Officiel,* 8 July 1875, p. 3819.

44. *Journal Officiel,* 13 July 1875, p. 5218. On the law of 1875 see Antoine Prost, *L'Enseignement en France, 1800–1967* (Paris, Armand Colin, 1968), pp. 184–85.

45. *Journal des Débats,* 14 July 1875.

46. *Journal Officiel,* 13 July 1875, p. 5281.

47. On Ferry's views on laicity and education see Jean-Marie Mayeur, "Jules Ferry et la laïcité," in *Jules Ferry, fondateur de la République. Actes du colloque organisé par l'école des Hautes Études en Sciences Sociales,* ed. François Furet (Paris: Éditions de l'École des Hautes Études en Sciences Sociales, 1985), pp. 147–60 and in the same collection Antoine Prost, "Jules Ferry, ministre de l'instruction publique ou de l'administration de la pédagogie," pp. 161–69. Also of interest is Pierre Chevallier, *La Séparation de l'Église et de l'école, Jules Ferry et Léon XIII* (Paris: Fayard, 1981), pp. 61–70.

48. Prost, *L'Enseignement en France,* p. 193.

49. Adrien Dansette, *Religious History of Modern France* (New York: Herder and Herder, 1961), 1: 324.

50. Ibid., 1: 326.

51. *Journal Officiel Chambre des Députés,* 4 May 1877 also printed in Léon Gambetta, *Discours et plaidoyers politiques de M. Gambetta* (Paris: G. Charpentier, 1880–85), 6: 344–45. On the question of anticlericalism see, René Rémond, *L'Anticléricalisme en France de 1815 à nos jours* (Paris: Fayard, 1976), pp. 175–87.

52. John McManners, *Church and State in France, 1870–1914* (New York: Harper and Row, 1972), p. 41.

53. Ibid., p. 42. McManners asserts that Gambetta also said, "It is rare for a Catholic to be a patriot," p. 41.

54. Ibid., p. 50.

55. On the Jesuits see John W. Padberg, S. J., *Colleges in Controversy, The Jesuit Schools in France from Revival to Suppression, 1814–1880* (Cambridge: Harvard University Press, 1969), pp. 249–72.

56. Laboulaye, *La liberté d'enseignement et les projets des lois de M. Jules Ferry,* p. 86.

57. Evelyn Martha Acomb, *The French Laic Laws (1879–1889), The First Anti-Clerical Campaign of the Third French Republic* (New York: Octagon, Books, 1967), p. 250.

58. Philip A. Bertocci, *Jules Simon, Republican Anticlericalism and Cultural Politics in France, 1848–1886* (Columbia: University of Missouri Press, 1978), p. 194 states: "Simon's arguments against Article 7 rested on his conviction that although laicity was an important republican principle, liberty of conscience took precedence. Liberal principle, that is, respect for liberty of conscience, and by extension, for liberty of education, required the rejection of a measure that contradicted republican tradition," pp. 194–95.

59. Laboulaye Papers, letter signed by twenty-one citizens of Montpellier to La-

boulaye, Montpellier, 23 February 1880; François-Marie-Anatole de Cabrières, évêque de Montpellier to Laboulaye, Montpellier, 25 February 1880.

60. "Nécrologie, M. Édouard Laboulaye," *La Semaine religieuse de Paris*, 3 June 1883.

61. The only evidence for this dinner is in Bartholdi's book, *The Statue of Liberty Enlightening the World*, ed. A. T. Rice (New York: North American Review, 1885). According to Bartholdi they met to discuss Bartholdi sculpting a bust of Laboulaye, possibly to be placed in the Collège de France. Bartholdi received the commission and exhibited the bust of Laboulaye in the Salon of 1866. On the building of the Statue of Liberty see Marvin Trachtenberg, *The Statue of Liberty* (New York: Viking Press, 1976). The catalogue issued for the centennial exposition honoring the Statue of Liberty contains many excellent articles: *Liberty, The French-American Statue in Art and History*, ed. Provoyeur and Hargrove.

62. Catherine Hodeir, "The French Campaign," in *Liberty*, ed. Provoyeur and Hargrove, p. 121.

63. Laboulaye Papers, Bartholdi to Laboulaye, New York, 15 July 1871. Bartholdi wrote, "J'ai trouvé un emplacement admirable, J'ai fait un dessin de l'oeuvre en place, c'est Bedloe's Island au milieu de la baie." [I have found an admirable site for the statue and I made a sketch of it in place, it is Bedloe's Island in the middle of the bay.]

64. Hodeir, "The French Campaign," in *Liberty*, ed. Provoyeur and Hargrove, p. 121.

65. Laboulaye Papers, Bartholdi to Laboulaye, Colmar, 8 May 1871.

66. Laboulaye Papers, Bartholdi to Laboulaye, New York, 15 July 1871.

67. Laboulaye Papers, Bartholdi to Laboulaye, San Francisco, 20 April 1872.

68. *Evening Telegram—New York*, 29 July 1876.

69. *Journal des Débats*, 8 November 1875.

70. Hodeir, "The French Campaign," in *Liberty*, ed. Provoyeur and Hargrove, pp. 124–25.

71. *Union Franco-Américaine. Discours de Mm. Henri Martin, E.-B. Washburne, Édouard Laboulaye, et J.-W. Forney prononcés au banquet du 6 novembre 1875* (Paris: Bibliothèque Charpentier, 1875), p. 25.

72. Ibid., p. 41.

73. Ibid., pp. 45–46.

74. *L'Évenement*, 27 April 1876 as quoted by Hodeir, "The French Campaign," in *Liberty*, ed. Provoyeur and Hargrove, p. 126.

75. *Le Figaro*, 26 April 1876, as quoted by Hodeir, "The French Campaign," in *Liberty*, eds. Provoyeur and Hargrove, p. 126. Laboulaye's address is printed in *Derniers discours populaires*, pp. 167–82.

76. Union Franco-Américaine, *Notice sur L'Union Franco-Américaine inauguration de l'exposition des lots de la loterie Franco-Américaine discours de Mm. Bozérian et Henri Martin, sénateurs, divers documents, liste des lots* (Paris: Au Siège du Comité, 1879) contains information on the lottery as well as its prizes.

77. Laboulaye to Mary Booth, Glatigny-Versailles, 11 July 1880, in Édouard Laboulaye, "La Statue de la Liberté. Lettre inédite à Mary Booth," *French-American Review* 2 (1949): 233–36.

78. General Grant to Laboulaye, Paris, 21 November 1877, in Union Franco-Américaine, *Notice sur L'Union Franco-Américaine*, p. 27.

79. Laboulaye to General Grant, Paris, 22 November 1877, in Union Franco-Américaine, *Notice sur L'Union Franco-Américaine*, p. 28.

80. In accepting Laboulaye's invitation Morton stated that he was "happy to assist at a ceremony which will, I doubt not, tend to cement still closer the friendship

which has so long existed between the governments and peoples of France and the United States." Laboulaye Papers, Levi Parsons Morton to Laboulaye, Paris, 19 October 1881.

81. *Le Moniteur universel*, 25 October 1881.

82. *Completion of the Mammoth Statue of "Liberty Enlightening the World." Banquet given by Mr. Henry F. Gillig in Honor of M. August Bartholdi, the Sculptor, Wednesday Evening, May 21, 1884* (Paris: Waterlow and Sons, Publishers, 1884), pp. 9–10.

83. Laboulaye Papers, Émile Littré to Laboulaye, Paris, 12 January 1880.

84. *Le Figaro*, 29 May 1883.

85. Dareste, Preface to Laboulaye, *Trente ans d'enseignement au Collège de France*, p. xxii.

85. *Le Figaro*, 29 May 1883.

87. *Semaine religieuse de Paris*, 3 June 1883.

88. *Le Monde Illustré*, 2 June 1883.

89. Ira Husted Harper, *The Life and Work of Susan B. Anthony, Including Public Addresses, her own Letters and Many from her Contemporaries during Fifty Years* 3 vols. (Indianapolis: Bowen-Merril, 1898–1908), 2: 561. This was her diary entry for 28 May 1883.

90. Elizabeth Cady Stanton, *Eighty Years and More (1815–1897) Reminiscences* (New York: European Publishing Company, 1898), p. 177.

91. *Le Monde*, 26 May 1883.

92. *New York Herald*, 25 May 1883.

93. *Troy Daily Times*, 26 May 1883.

94. *L'Indépendance Belge* (Brussels), 27 May 1883.

95. *Journal des Débats*, 10 June 1883. Other major obituaries are to be found in *Le Soleil*, 27 and 29 May 1883; *Le Figaro*, 29 May 1883; *Le Parlementaire, Journal de la République libérale*,26 May 1883; *Le Petit Journal*, 27 May 1883; *L'Illustration*,2 June 1883; *L'Univers Illustré*, 2 June 1883; *Gazette des Hôpitaux Civils et Militaires*, 26 May 1883; and *The New York Times*, 27 May 1883.

96. Letter signed "One of the Old Guard," *The American Register*, 9 June 1883.

97. Henri Barboux, *Discours et plaidoyers* (Paris: Librairie Nouvelle de droit et de jurisprudence, Arthur Rousseau, 1889), 2: 89–106.

98. *Société du Travail, Assemblée Générale, Tenue le 17 mai 1884* (Paris: Société du Travail, 1884) pp. 21–86.

99. Ibid., p. 26.

100. Ernest Renan, "Le *Journal des Débats* sous le Second Empire," in *Le Livre du centenaire du Journal des Débats*, ed. Boutmy, p. 240.

101. Émile Boutmy, "Laboulaye," in *Le Livre du centenaire du Journal des Débats*, pp. 253, 256.

Bibliography

Manuscript Sources

The Laboulaye Papers, in the possession of Ambassador François de Laboulaye, are housed at Le Quesnay (Normandy) and contain the correspondence received by Laboulaye and drafts of some letters he sent. This collection is particularly rich for the years of the 1850s and 1860s.

Letters of Laboulaye are found in the following repositories:

Archives Nationales, Paris
Bibliothèque Nationale, Paris
Bibliothèque Spoelberch de Louvenjoul, Chantilly
Houghton Library, Harvard University
Huntington Library, Pasadena, Francis Lieber Papers
Massachusetts Historical Society, Boston
New York Historical Society
New York Public Library
Pennsylvania Historical Society, Philadelphia
University of Rochester Library

Works by Laboulaye

De la Constitution américaine et de l'utilité de son étude. Discours prononcé le 9 décembre 1849 à l'ouverture du cours de législation comparée. Paris: Hennuyer, 1850.

Cours de politique constitutionnelle ou collection des ouvrages publiés sur le gouvernement représentatif par Benjamin Constant avec une introduction et notes par M. Édouard Laboulaye.; 2 vols. Paris: Librairie de Guillaumin, 1872.

Derniers discours populaires. Paris: Charpentier, 1881.

Discours populaires. Paris: Charpentier, 1869.

Essai sur la vie et les doctrines de Frédéric-Charles de Savigny. Paris: A. Durand, 1842.

Essais de morale et d'économie politique de Benjamin Franklin traduits de l'anglais et annotés par Édouard Laboulaye de l'Institut de France et des sociétés historiques de New York et de Massachusetts. 2d ed. Paris: L. Hachette, 1869.

Essais sur les lois criminelles des Romains concernant la responsabilité des magistrats. Paris: A. Durand, 1845.

L'État et ses limites, suivi d'essais politiques sur Alexis de Tocqueville, instruction publique, les finances, le droit de pétition, etc. Paris: Charpentier, 1863.

Les États-Unis et la France. Paris: E. Dentu, 1862. English translation, *The United States and France*. Boston: Boston Daily Advertiser, 1862.

Études contemporaines sur l'Allemagne et les pays slaves. Paris: Durand, 1855.

Études morales et politiques. 5th ed. Paris: Charpentier, 1871.

Histoire des États-Unis. 5th ed. 3 vols. Paris: Charpentier, 1870.

Histoire du droit de propriété foncière en Occident. Paris: de l'auteur, 1839.

Lettre de M. Éd. Laboulaye à un électeur de la commune de Jouy-en-Josas (Seine-et-Oise). Le Cateau: Impr. J. de Lempereur, 1870.

Lettres politiques. Esquisse d'une constitution républicaine suivie d'un projet de constitution. Paris: Charpentier, 1872.

La Liberté antique et la liberté moderne. Paris: Impr. de P.-A. Bournier, 1863.

La Liberté d'enseignement et les projets des lois de M. Jules Ferry. Paris: L. La Rose, 1880.

La liberté religieuse. Paris: Charpentier, 1858.

Mann (Horace). De l'importance de l'éducation dans une république traduit de l'américain, avec extraits de la vie de Mann. Paris: Charpentier, 1873.

Mémoires de Benjamin Franklin écrits par lui-même, traduits et annotés par Édouard Laboulaye. 2d ed. Paris: Hachette, 1866.

Oeuvres complètes de Montesquieu avec les variantes des premières éditions. Un choix des meilleurs commentaires et des notes nouvelles par M. Édouard Laboulaye. 7 vols. Paris: Garnier, 1875–79.

Oeuvres sociales de W.-E. Channing, traduites de l'anglais, précédés d'une essai sur la vie et les doctrines de Channing et d'une introduction par M.Édouard Laboulaye. Paris: Comon, 1854.

Oeuvres de W.-E. Channing, le christianisme unitaire, suite des traités religieux par M. Édouard Laboulaye. Paris: Dentu, 1862.

Oeuvres de W.-E. Channing. De l'esclavage précédé d'une préface et d'une étude sur l'esclavage aux États-Unis. Paris: Comon, 1855.

Oeuvres de W.-E. Channing, Traités religieux, précédés d'une introduction par M. Édouard Laboulaye. Paris: Lacroix-Comon, 1856.

Paris en Amérique, par le doc. René Lefebvre, parisien. Paris: Charpentier, 1863. English edition entitled *Paris in America by Dr. René Lefebvre, parisian*. Translated by Mary L. Booth. New York: Charles Scribner's, 1863.

Le Parti libéral. Paris: Charpentier, 1863.

Plébiscite du 8 mai 1870. Lettre adressée par M. Édouard Laboulaye . . . au comité plébiscitaire de Rueil. Paris: Impr. de E. Blot, 1870.

Le Prince Caniche. Paris: Charpentier, 1878.

Professor Laboulaye, the Great Friend of America, on the Presidential Election, The Election of the President of the United States. Washington: Union Congressional Committee, 1864.

Questions constitutionnelles. Paris: Charpentier, 1873.

Recherches sur la condition civile et politique des femmes depuis les Romains jusqu'à nos jours. Paris: A. Durand, 1843.

La science de Bonhomme Richard ou le chemin de la fortune par Benjamin Franklin suivi d'extraits de ses mémoires et de sa correspondance et précédée de la jeunesse de Franklin par Édouard Laboulaye. Paris: Hachette et Cie., 1872.

Separation: War Without End. New York: Loyal Publication Society, 1864.

"La Statue de la Liberté, Lettre inédite à Mary Booth." *French-American Review* 2 (1959): 233–36.

Trente ans d'enseignement au Collège de France, 1848–1882, publiés par ses fils avec le concours de M. Marcel Fournier, Préface de M. Rodolphe Dareste. Paris: L. Rose et Forcel, 1888.

Periodicals and newspapers wherein Laboulaye published frequently and his articles are too numerous to list separately; however, they are indicated in the notes.

Journal des Débats, 1854–83
Revue des cours littéraires de la France et de l'étranger, 1863–70
Revue de législation et de jurisprudence, 1843–53
Revue nationale et étranger, politique, scientifique, et littéraire, 1860–68

Laboulaye served on the editorial boards of the following journals:

Revue Germanique
Revue historique du droit français et étranger
Revue internationale de l'enseignement
Revue de législation et jurisprudence
Revue nationale et étranger, politique, scientifique et littéraire

Newspapers Consulted

Le Figaro
Journal des Débats
Journal Officiel
Le Moniteur Impériale
New York Times
New York Tribune

Other Published Works Cited

Acomb, Evelyn M. *The French Laic Laws (1879–1889). The First Anti-Clerical Campaign of the Third Republic.* New York: Archon Books, 1967.

Address of the Loyal National League to Messrs. Agénor de Gasparin, Édouard Laboulaye, Augustin Cochin, Henri Martin, and other Friends of America in France. New York: Loyal Publication Society, 1863.

Agulhon, Maurice. *1848 ou l'apprentissage de la République, 1848–1852.* Paris: Seuil, 1973. There is an English translation, *The Republican Experiment, 1848–1852,* trans. Janet Lloyd. Cambridge: Cambridge University Press, 1983.

———. *La République au village.* Paris: Plon, 1970.

Alkan Ainé. *Un Fondeur en caractères, membre de l'Institut.* Paris: Au Bureau de "la Typologie Tucker," 1886.

Allain-Targé, François-Henri. *La République sous l'Empire. Lettres (1864–1870)*. Paris: Éditions Bernard Grasset, 1939.

"America at the Continental Universities." *Appleton's Journal of Literature, Science and Art* 9 (1873): 494–95.

Anderson, Hans Christian. "Laboulaye." *Appleton's Journal of Literature, Science and Art* 11 (1874): 150–51.

Anderson, R. D. *Education in France, 1848–1870*. Oxford: Clarendon Press, 1975.

Aumale, Henri d'Orléans, duc d'. *Correspondance du Duc d'Aumale et de Cuvillier-Fleury (1848–1871)*. 4 vols. Paris: Plon, 1910–14.

Auspitz, Katherine. *The Radical Bourgeoisie, The Ligue d'Enseignement and the Origins of the Third Republic, 1866–1885*. Cambridge: Cambridge University Press, 1982.

Barbé-Marbois, François, marquis de. *Histoire de la Louisiane*. Paris: impr. de F. Didot, 1829.

Barboux, Henri, *Discours et plaidoyers*. 2 vols. Paris: Librairie Nouvelle de Droit et de Jurisprudence, Arthur Rousseau, 1889.

Barker, Nancy Nichols. *The French Experience in Mexico, 1821–1861: A History of Constant Misunderstanding*. Chapel Hill: University of North Carolina Press, 1979.

Barral, Pierre. *Jules Ferry, une volonté pour la République*. Nancy: Presses Universitaires de Nancy—Éditions Serpenoise, 1985.

Bartholdi, Frédéric. *The Statue of Liberty Enlightening the World*. Edited by A. T. Rice. New York: North American Review, 1885.

Bellows, H. W. *The State and the Nation—Sacred to Christian Citizens: A Sermon Preached in All Souls Church, New York, April 21, 1861*. New York: Miller, 1861.

Bertocci, Philip A. *Jules Simon, Republican Anticlericalism and Cultural Politics in France, 1848–1886*. Columbia: University of Missouri Press, 1978.

Bigelow, John. *Retrospections of an Active Life*. 5 vols. New York and Garden City, N.J.: the Baker and Taylor Company, 1909–13.

———. *Some Recollections of the Late Edouard Laboulaye*. New York: G. P. Putnam's, 1889.

Bigelow, Poultney. "John Bigelow and Napoleon III." *New York History* 13 (1932): 154–65.

Blumenthal, Henry. *American and French Culture. Interchanges in Art, Science, Literature and Society*. Baton Rouge: Louisiana State University Press, 1975.

———. *A Reappraisal of Franco-American Relations, 1830–1871* Chapel Hill: University of North Carolina Press, 1959.

Bluntschli, J. K. *Le Droit international codifié. traduit de l'allemand par M. C. Lardy précédé d'une préface par M. Édouard Laboulaye*. 2d ed. Paris: Librairie de Guillaumin, 1874.

———. *The Theory of the State*. 2d ed. Oxford: The Clarendon Press, 1892.

Boutmy, Émile, ed. *Le Livre du centenaire du Journal des Débats*. Paris: E. Plon, Nourrit et Cie., 1889.

———. *Taine, Scherer, Laboulaye*. Paris: A. Colin, 1901.

Bradley, Joseph. "A Memorial of the Life and Character of Hon. William L. Dayton, Late U. S. Minister to France." *Proceedings of the New Jersey Historical Society*, 2d ser., 4 (1875): 70–118.

Brogan, D. W. *The Development of Modern France (1870–1939).* Gloucester, Mass.: Peter Smith, 1970.

Bury, J. P. T. *Gambetta and the Making of the Third Republic.* London: Longman, 1973.

Bury, J. P. T., and R. R. Tombs. *Thiers, 1797–1877, A Political Biography.* London: Allen and Unwin, 1986.

Caperan, Louis. *Histoire contemporaine de la laïcité française.* 2 vols. Paris: Librairie Marcel Rivière et Cie., 1957.

Case, Lynn M. *French Opinion on the United States and Mexico, 1860–1867.* New York: D. Appleton Century, 1936.

Case, Lynn M., and Warren F. Spencer. *United States and France: Civil War Diplomacy.* Philadelphia: University of Pennsylvania Press, 1970.

Chabanne, Robert. *Les Institutions de la France de la fin de l'ancien régime à l'avènement de la IIIe République (1789–1875).* Lyon: Éditions l'Hermes, 1977.

Chapman, Guy. *The Third Republic of France, the First Phase, 1871–1894.* London: Macmillan, 1962.

Chastenet, Jacques. *Histoire de la Troisième République.* 7 vols. Paris: Librairie Hachette, 1952–63.

———. *Gambetta.* Paris: Fayard, 1968.

Chevalier, Pierre. *La Séparation de l'Église et de l'école, Jules Ferry et Léon XIII.* Paris: Fayard, 1981.

Clapp, Margaret. *Forgotten First Citizen: John Bigelow.* Boston: Little, Brown, 1947.

Cochin, Henry, ed. *Augustin Cochin, 1833–1872, ses lettres et sa vie.* 2 vols. Paris: Bloud et Gay, 1926.

Collingham, H. A. C., and R. S. Alexander. *The July Monarchy, A Political History of France, 1830–1848.* London: Longman, 1988.

Collins, Irene. *The Government and the Newspaper Press in France, 1814–1881.* Oxford: Oxford University Press, 1959.

Completion of the Mammoth Statue of "Liberty Enlightening the World." Banquet given by Mr. Henry F. Gillig in Honor of M. August Bartholdi, the Sculptor, Wednesday evening, May 21, 1884. Paris: Waterlow and Sons, Publishers, 1884.

Constant, Benjamin. *De la force du gouvernement actuel et la France et de la nécessité de s'y rallier* and *Des réactions politiques des effets de la Terreur.* Edited by Philippe Raynaud. Paris: Flammarion, 1988.

Cousin, Victor. "Huit mois au ministère de l'Instruction Publique." *Revue des Deux-Mondes,* ser. 4, 25 (1841): 377–96.

———. *Rapport sur l'état de l'instruction publique dans quelques pays d'Allemagne, et particulièrement en Prusse.* Paris: F.-G. Levrault, 1833.

Cullop, Charles P. "Edwin de Leon, Jefferson Davis' Propagandist." *Civil War History* 8 (1962): 386–400.

Dalberg-Acton, John Emmerich Edward. *Historical Essays and Studies.* Edited by John Neville Figgis and Reginald Vere Lawrence. London: Macmillan & Co. 1919.

Darimon, Alfred. *Histoire de douze ans (1857–1869), notes et souvenirs.* Paris: Dentu, 1883.

Dauteribes, André, "Laboulaye et la Réforme des Études de droit," *Revue historique des facultés de droit et de la science juridique.* 10 (1990): 13–57.

Delamarre, Alexandre. "Libéralisme: un 'Laissez-faire'? Pas forcément . . ." *Le Figaro Magazine*, 17 January 1987.

Deslandres, Maurice. *Histoire constitutionnelle de la France*. 3 vols. Paris: Édouard Duchemin, 1977.

Dollfus, Charles. "Chronique Parisienne." *Revue Germanique* 4 (1858): 427–33.

Downs, Robert B. *Horace Mann, Champion of Public Schools*. New York: Twayne Publishers, 1974.

Dreyfus-Brisac, Edmond. "Édouard Laboulaye." *Revue internationale de l'enseignement* 5 (1883): 593–602.

Duveau, Georges. *La Vie ouvrière en France sous le Second Empire* Paris: Gallimard, 1946.

"Edouard Laboulaye." *Appleton's Journal of Popular Literature, Science and Art* (4 September 1869): 84–85.

"M. Edouard Laboulaye." *Every Saturday*, 8 March 1873, pp. 274–75.

Foner, Eric. *Free Soil, Free Labor, Free Men: The Ideology of the Republican Party before the Civil War*. New York: Oxford University Press, 1970.

————, and Olivia Mahony. *A House Divided, America in the Age of Lincoln*. New York: Chicago Historical Association in association with W. W. Norton & Company, 1990.

Forstenzer, Thomas R. *French Provincial Police and the Fall of the Second Republic. Social Fear and Counterrevolution*. Princeton: Princeton University Press, 1981.

Friedel, Frank. *Francis Lieber: Nineteenth-Century Liberal*. Baton Rouge: Louisiana State University Press, 1947.

————. "Francis Lieber: Transmitter of European Ideas to America." *Bulletin of the John Rylands Library, Manchester* 38 (1955–56): 342–59.

————. "The Loyal Publication Society: A Pro-Union Propaganda Agency." *Mississippi Valley Historical Review* 26 (1939): 359–76.

————, ed. *Union Pamphlets of the Civil War, 1861–1865*. 2 vols. Cambridge: Belknap Press of Harvard University Press, 1967.

Furet, François, and Mona Ozouf, eds. *A Critical Dictionary of the French Revolution*. Cambridge: Belknap Press of Harvard University Press, 1989.

Furet, François. *Jules Ferry, fondateur de la République. Actes du colloque organisé par l'école des Haute Études en Sciences Sociales*. Paris: Éditions de l'École des Hautes Études en Sciences Sociales, 1985.

Gadille, Jacques. *La Pensée et l'action politiques des évêques français au début de la IIIe République, 1870–1883*. 2 vols. Paris: Hachette, 1967.

Gaillard, Jean-Michel. *Jules Ferry*. Paris: Fayard, 1989.

Gambetta, Léon. *Discours et plaidoyers politiques de M. Gambetta*. 11 vols. Paris: G. Charpentier, 1880–85.

Gasparin, Agénor de. *Un Grand peuple qui se relève*. Paris: Michel Lévy Frères, 1861.

Gavronsky, Serge. "American Slavery and the French Liberals, An Interpretation of Slavery in French Politics during the Second Empire." *Journal of Negro History* 51 (1966): 36–52.

————. *French Liberals and the American Civil War*. New York: The Humanities Press, 1968.

Gilman, Daniel Coit. *Bluntschli, Lieber and Laboulaye*. Baltimore: J. Murphy & Co., 1884.

Girard, Louis. _Les Libéraux français, 1814–1875_. Paris: Aubier, 1985.

Gorce, Pierre de la. _Histoire du Second Empire_. 7 vols. Paris: Plon, 1894–1905.

Gouhier, H. _Benjamin Constant, les écrivains devant Dieu_. Paris: Desclée et Brouwer, 1967.

Gray, Walter D. "Edouard Laboulaye: 'Liberal' Catholic and 'Americanist' during the Second Empire.'" _Cithara_ 3 (1964): 3–15.

Guiral, Pierre. _Adolphe Thiers ou la necessité en politique_. Paris: Fayard, 1986.

———. _Prévost-Paradol, 1829–1870, pensée et action d'un libéral sous le Second Empire_. Paris: Presses Universitaires de France, 1955.

Guizot, François. _Histoire de la civilisation en Europe depuis la chute de l'empire romain jusqu'à la Révolution française suivie de philosophie politique: de la souveraineté_. Presented, edited, and annotated by Pierre Rosanvallon. Paris: Hachette, 1985.

Harper, Ira Husted. _The Life and Work of Susan B. Anthony, Including Public Addresses, her own Letters and Many from her Contemporaries during Fifty Years_. 3 vols. Indianapolis: Bowen-Merril, 1898–1908.

Hartigan, Richard Shelly. _Lieber's Code and the Law of War_. Chicago: Precedent, 1983.

Holmes, Stephen. _Benjamin Constant and the Making of Modern Liberalism_. New Haven: Yale University Press, 1984.

Howe, M. A. de Wolfe, ed. _The Life and Letters of George Bancroft_. 2 vols. New York: Da Capo Press, 1970.

Howland, Harold, "Mary Louise Booth." _Dictionary of American Biography_, 2:454–55.

Jardin, André. _Alexis de Tocqueville, 1805–1859_. Paris: Hachette, 1984.

———. _Histoire du libéralisme politique de la crise de l'absolutisme à la constitution de 1875_. Paris: Hachette Littérature, 1985.

Johnson, Douglas. _Guizot, Aspects of French History, 1787–1874_. London: Routledge and Kegan Paul, 1963.

Jordan, Donaldson, and Edwin J. Pratt. _Europe and the American Civil War_. Boston: Houghton Mifflin Company, 1931.

Karsky, Barbara. "Les Libéraux français et l'émancipation des esclaves aux États-Unis, 1852–1870." _Revue d'histoire moderne et contemporaine_ 21 (1974): 575–90.

Kelley, Donald R. _Historians and the Law in Postrevolutionary France_. Princeton: Princeton University Press, 1984.

Kelly, George Armstrong. "Constant Commotion: Avatars of a Pure Liberal." _Journal of Modern History_ 54 (1982): 497–518.

Kennedy, Emmet. _A Philosophe in the Age of Revolution: Destutt de Tracy and the Origins of "Ideology"_. Philadelphia: American Philosophical Society, 1978.

Kieswetter, James K. _Etienne-Denis Pasquier, The Last Chancellor of France_. Philadelphia: American Philosophical Society, 1977.

Kloocke, Kurt. _Benjamin Constant, une biographie intellectuelle_. Geneva: Librairie Droz, 1984.

Kolm, Serge-Christophe. "Libéralisme classique et renouvelé." _Nouvelle histoire des idées politiques_. Edited by Pascal Ory, pp. 575–89. Paris: Hachette, 1987.

"Laboulaye on the United States of America." _American Presbyterian Review_, n.s., 1 (1863): 70.

Laboulaye, André. "La Statue de la liberté." *The Franco-American Review* 2 (1937–38): 71–86.

Laboulaye, Madame Édouard. *Vie de Jeanne d'Arc*. Paris: H. Pelagaud, 1877.

Lamberti, Jean-Claude. "Laboulaye and the Common Law of Free Peoples." In *Liberty, The French American Statue in Art and History*, eds. Provoyeur and Hargrove, pp. 20–25. New York: Harper and Row, 1986.

———. *La Notion de l'individualisme chez Tocqueville*. Paris: Presses Universitaires de France, 1970.

———. *Tocqueville et les deux démocraties*. Paris: Presses Universitaires de France, 1983. English translation: *Tocqueville and the Two Democracies*, trans. Arthur Goldhammer. Cambridge: Harvard University Press, 1989.

Langeron, Roger. *Un Conseiller secret de Louis XVIII, Royer-Collard*. Paris: Hachette, 1956.

Larregola, Jean-Guy. "Le gouvernement français face à la guerre de sécession." *Revue d'histoire diplomatique* 83 (1969); 314–37.

Letters from Europe touching the American Contest and Acknowledging the Receipt, from Citizens of New York, of Presentation Sets of the "Rebellion Record" and Loyal Publication Society Publications. New York: Loyal Publication Society, 1864.

Liberté/Liberty: The French and American Experience, eds. Joseph Klaits and Michael Haltzell. Washington, D.C.: Woodrow Wilson Center Press, 1991; and Baltimore and London: The Johns Hopkins Press, 1991.

Lincolniana, In Memoriam. Boston: William V. Spencer, 1865.

Lochmenes, Sr. M. Frederick. *Robert Walsh: His Story*. New York: Irish American Historical Society, 1941.

McManners, John. *Church and State in France, 1870–1914*. New York: Harper and Row, 1972.

McPherson, James. *Battle Cry of Freedom, The Civil War Era*. New York: Oxford University Press, 1988.

Manent, Pierre. *Histoire intellectuelle du libéralisme, dix leçons*. Paris: Calmann-Lévy, 1987.

———. *Les Libéraux*. 2 vols. Paris: Hachette/Pluriel, 1986.

Margadant, Ted W. *French Peasants in Revolt. The Insurrection of 1851*. Princeton: Princeton University Press, 1979.

Maxwell, William Quentin. *Lincoln's Fifth Wheel: The Political History of the United States Sanitary Commission*. New York: Longman's Green, 1956.

Mayer, Jean-Marie, and Madeleine Rebérioux. *The Third Republic from Its Origins to the Great War, 1871–1914*. Cambridge: Cambridge University Press, 1987.

Merriman, John. *The Agony of the Republic: Repression of the Left in Revolutionary France, 1848–1851*. New Haven: Yale University Press, 1978.

Messerli, Jonathan. *Horace Mann, A Biography*. New York: Knopf, 1972.

Michel, Henry. *L'Idée de l'état, essai critique sur l'histoire des théories sociales et politiques en France depuis la Révolution*. Paris: Hachette, 1896.

Michelet, Jules. *Journal, texte intégral, établi sur les manuscrits autographes et publié pour la première fois, avec une introduction, des notes et de nombreux documents inédits, par Paul Viallaneix*. 4 vols. Paris: Gallimard, 1959–76.

———. *Oeuvres complètes*. Edited by Paul Viallaneix. Paris: Flammarion, 1971–.

Notice sur l'Union Franco-Américaine inauguration de l'exposition des lots de la loterie

Franco-Américaine discours de Mm. Bozérian, Henri Martin, Sénateurs, divers documents, liste des lots. Paris: au Siège du Comité, 1879.

Offen, Karen. "The Beginnings of 'Scientific' Women's History in France, 1830–1848." *Proceedings of the Eleventh Annual Meeting of the Western Society for French History, 3–5 November 1983.* Lawrence: The University of Kansas, 1984. pp. 255–71.

Ollivier, Émile. *L'Empire libéral: études, récits, souvenirs.* 18 vols. Paris: Garnier Frères, 1895–1918.

———. *Journal, 1846–1869, texte choisi et annoté par Theodore Zeldin et Anne Troisier de Diaz.* 2 vols. Paris: Julliard, 1961.

Osborne, Thomas R. *A Grande Ecole for the Grands Corps: The Recruitment and Training of the French Administrative Elite in the Nineteenth Century.* Boulder, Colo: Social Science Monographs, 1983.

Padberg, John W., S. J. *Colleges in Controversy. The Jesuit Schools in France from Revival to Suppression, 1814–1880.* Cambridge: Harvard University Press, 1969.

Passy, Frédéric. *Édouard Laboulaye, Conférence faite à la Société du Travail par Frédéric Passy.* Paris: Librairie Guillaumin, 1884.

———. *Société du Travail, Assemblée générale tenue le 17 mai 1884.* Paris: Société du Travail, 1884.

Pierce, Edward L., ed. *Memoirs and Letters of Charles Sumner.* 4 vols. New York: Arno Press, 1969.

Pierre-Marcel, Roland. *Essai politique sur Alexis de Tocqueville.* Paris: Alcan, 1910.

Pinkney, David H. *Decisive Years in France, 1840–1847.* Princeton: Princeton University Press, 1986.

Poinsatte, Charles, and Anne Marie Poinsatte. "Augustin Cochin's 'L'Abolition de l'esclavage' and the Emancipation Proclamation." *Review of Politics* 46 (1984): 410–27.

Ponteil, Félix. *Histoire de l'enseignement en France, les grandes étapes.* Paris: Sirey, 1966.

Prélot, Marcel. *Histoire des idées politiques.* 2d ed. Paris: Dalloz, 1961.

———. *Institutions politiques et droit constitutionnel.* Paris: Dalloz, 1969.

Prévost-Paradol, Lucien. *Quelques pages d'histoire contemporaine, lettres politiques.* 4 vols. Paris: Michel Lévy, 1868.

Price, Roger. *The Second Republic, A Social History.* London: B. T. Batsford, 1972.

Prost, Antoine. *L'Enseignement en France, 1800–1967.* Paris: Armand Colin, 1968.

Provoyeur, Pierre, and June Hargrove, eds. *Liberty, The French-American Statue in Art and History.* New York: Harper and Row, 1986.

Rain, Pierre. *L'École Libre des Sciences Politiques, 1871–1939.* Paris: Fondation Nationale des Sciences Politiques, 1963.

Raynaud, Philippe. "Le Libéralisme français à l'épreuve du pouvoir." In *Nouvelle histoire des idées politiques,* edited by Pascal Ory. Paris: Hachette, 1987.

Rémond, René. *L'Anticléricalisme en France de 1815 à nos jours.* Paris: Fayard, 1976.

———. *Les États-Unis devant l'opinion française, 1815–1852.* 2 vols. Paris: Presses Universitaires de France, 1962.

Rémusat, Charles de. "Les élections de 1863." *Revue des Deux Mondes* 46 (1863): 257–77.

————. *Mémoires de ma vie*. Edited by Charles H. Pouthas. 5 vols. Paris: Librairie Plon, 1958–67.

Robert, Adolph, Edgar Bourloton, and Gaston Cougny. *Dictionnaire des parlementaires français comprenant tous les membres des Assemblées Françaises et tous les Ministres français depuis le 1 mai 1789 jusqu'au 1er mai 1889. . . .* 5 vols. Paris: Bourloton, 1889.

Rosanvallon, Pierre. *Le Moment Guizot*. Paris: Gallimard, 1985.

Saint-Beuve, Charles Auguste. *Nouveaux Lundis*. 13 vols. Paris: Calmann Lévy, 1890.

Savigny, Friedrich Karl von. *Vom Beruf unserer Zeit für Gesetzgebung ein Rechtswissenschaft*. 3d ed. Freiberg am Breisgau: Mohr, 1892.

Schefer, Christian. *La Grande pensée de Napoléon III: les origines de l'expédition du Mexique (1858–1862)*. Paris: M. Rivière et Cie., 1939.

Schliefer, James T. *The Making of Tocqueville's "Democracy in America."* Chapel Hill: University of North Carolina Press, 1980.

Seward, Olive Risley, ed. *William H. Seward's Travels around the World*. New York: D. Appleton Century and Company, 1873.

Simon, Jules. *La Liberté politique*. Paris: Hachette, 1881.

————. *Thiers, Guizot, Rémusat*. Paris: Calmann Lévy, 1885.

Sirven, Alfred. *Journaux et journalistes, Journal des Débats*. 3d ed. Paris: F. Cournol, 1865.

Skard, Sigmund. *American Studies in Europe*. 2 vols. Philadelphia: University of Pennsylvania Press, 1958.

Smith, Bonnie G. "The Rise and Fall of Eugène Lerminier." *French Historical Studies* 12 (1982): 377–400.

Société Franklin pour la propagation des bibliothèques populaires et des bibliothèques de l'armée discours de M. Éd. Laboulaye sur l'éducation du pays par l'armée. Paris: Librairie Ch. Delagrave et Cie, 1874.

Société Franklin pour la propagation des bibliothèques populaires, séance générale du jeudi 27 avril 1865. Paris: Siège de la Société, 1865.

Soto, Jean de. "Édouard Laboulaye." *Revue internationale d'histoire politique et constitutionnelle* 5 (1955): 114–50.

Spitzer, Alan, B. *The French Generation of 1820*. Princeton: Princeton University Press, 1987.

————. "Restoration Political Theory and the Debate over the Law of the Double Vote." *Journal of Modern History* 55 (1983): 54–70.

Staël, Mme de. *Considérations sur les principaux événements de la Révolution Française*. Paris: Taillandier, 1983.

————. *Delphine*. 2 vols. Paris: des Femmes, 1981.

Stanton, Elizabeth Cady. *Eighty Years and More (1815–1897): Reminiscences of Elizabeth Cady Stanton*. New York: European Publishing Company, 1898.

Staum, Martin S. *Cabanis: Enlightenment and Medical Philosophy in the French Revolution*. Princeton: Princeton University Press, 1980.

Stoll, Adolf. *Friedrich von Savigny, ein Bild seines Leben mit einer Sammlung seiner Briefe*, 3 vols. Berlin: Ed. C. Heyman, 1917–29.

Sumner, Charles. *The Rebellion: Its Origin and Main-Spring. An Oration Delivered by the Hon. Charles Sumner under the auspices of the Young Men's Republican*

Union of New York, November 27, 1861. New York: Printed for the Young Men's Republican Union, 1861.

Tocqueville, Alexis de. *Oeuvres, papiers et correspondances. Édition définitive, publiée sous la direction de J.-P. Mayer*. Paris: Gallimard, 1951–

Trachtenberg, Marvin. *The Statue of Liberty*. New York: Viking Press, 1976.

Tulard, Jean. *Joseph Fiévée, conseiller secret de Napoléon*. Paris: Fayard, 1985.

Union Franco-Américaine, Discours de Mm. Henri Martin, E.-B. Washburne, Édouard Laboulaye, et J.-W. Forney prononcés au banquet du 6 novembre 1875. Paris: Bibliothèque Charpentier, 1875.

Union Franco-Américaine. Monument commémoratif du centième anniversaire de l'indépendance américaine. Paris: A. La Hure, 1884.

Vinet, Alexander. *Outlines of Philosophy and Literature*. London: 1867.

Voskuil, Louis. "Émile Boutmy: The Political Education of the Third Republic." Ph.D. diss., Loyola University of Chicago, 1977.

Wallon, Henri. "Notice sur la vie et les travaux de M. Édouard-René Lefebvre-Laboulaye, membre ordinaire de l'Académie des Inscriptions et Belles-Lettres." *Mémoires de l'Institut National de France, Académie des Inscriptions et Belles-Lettres* 24 (1887): 286–321.

Welch, Cheryl B. *Liberty and Utility, The French Ideologues and the Transformation of Liberalism*. New York: Columbia University Press, 1984.

White, Andrew D. *Autobiography of Andrew Dickson White*. 2 vols. New York: The Century Company, 1905.

Williams, Roger L. *Henri Rochefort, Prince of the Gutter Press*. New York: Charles Scribner's Sons, 1966.

Winegarten, Renee. *Mme de Staël*. Leamington Spa, Great Britain: Berg, 1985.

Zeldin, Theodore. *Emile Ollivier and the Liberal Empire of Napoleon III*. Oxford: The Clarendon Press, 1963.

———. *France, 1848–1945*. 2 vols. Oxford: The Clarendon Press, 1973–77.

———. *The Political System of Napoleon III*. London: Macmillan, 1958.

Index